THE FABER BOOK OF WRITERS ON WRITERS

The Faber Book of

WRITERS ON WRITERS

edited by Sean French

faber and faber

LONDON · NEW YORK

First published in 1999
by Faber and Faber Limited
3 Queen Square WCIN 3AU

Published in the United States by Faber and Faber, Inc.,
a division of Farrar, Straus and Giroux, Inc., New York

Phototypeset by Intype London Ltd
Printed in England by Clays Ltd, St Ives plc

Sean French is hereby identified as editor
of this work in accordance with the
Copyright, Designs and Patents Act 1988

A CIP record for this book
is available from the British Library

ISBN 0-571-14649-X (U.K.)
ISBN 0-571-20129-6 (U.S.)

2 4 6 8 10 9 7 5 3 1

CONTENTS

INTRODUCTION

How little they live, people with lively minds! Taine
going to bed at nine, getting up at seven, working till
noon, dining at a positively provincial hour, paying
calls, rushing round the libraries, and spending the
evening, after supper, with his mother and his piano.
Flaubert chained to his work like a convict in a mine.
And we ourselves in our cloistered incubations, with
no distractions or family affairs or social life, with the
exception of a fortnightly dinner with the Princess and
a few strolls along the embankments to satisfy the
maniacal curiosity of a pair of bibliographical and
iconographical fanatics.

THE GONCOURT BROTHERS

In general I do not draw well with Literary men – not
that I dislike them but – I never know what to say to
them after I have praised their last publication.

LORD BYRON

Writers have no small talk, said Auden, and so when they run into each
other there is nothing for them to talk about except money. He meant
that there isn't that craftsmanlike relation that painters and musicians
share, the young Claude Monet studying effects of light in the open air
alongside Eugène Boudin at Le Havre or Mozart not only dedicating a
string quartet to Joseph Haydn but playing it with him (the Irish tenor,
Michael Kelly, witnessed the private concert – Haydn on first violin,
Mozart on viola – and pronounced the playing good, but nothing special).

By contrast, the most intense relationship anybody can have with a
writer is by reading their work, alone, in silence. Yet readers seek writers
in search of something additional. It was J. D. Salinger's hero, Holden
Caulfield, who said that what really knocked him out was a book that
'when you're all done reading it, you wish the author that wrote it was
a terrific friend of yours and you could call him up on the phone whenever
you felt like it.' It was also J. D. Salinger who, when *The Catcher in the
Rye* achieved its enormous success, made himself as inaccessible to his
readers as any living author has ever been.

Writers meet writers, out of curiosity or admiration, against their better judgment, out of responsibility or good fellowship or under compulsion. They collaborate, help, refuse help, support, conspire with and against, denounce, borrow money, fight, become friends, become lovers, elope, marry. So far as the records show, they always have.

One of the best-attested facts about William Shakespeare's personal life is that he was a friend and colleague of Ben Jonson. On top of his prodigious rate of composition, Shakespeare also appeared in at least two of Jonson's plays: *Every Man in His Humour* in 1598 and *Sejanus* in 1603. Jonson wrote the famous commendatory poem at the beginning of the First Folio of Shakespeare's plays, describing him as 'Sweet Swan of Avon' and 'not of an age but for all time'. More tellingly, perhaps, he left some brief notes, unpublished at the time of his death, in which he registered his qualified praise but unqualified affection: 'for I loved the man, and do honour his memory (on this side idolatry) as much as any'.

So, William Shakespeare and Ben Jonson were intimate. Jonson lived twenty years after Shakespeare's death, and became the centre of a circle of young writers who styled themselves the 'tribe of Ben'. One of these was Lucius Cary, second Viscount Falkland, who, with many misgivings and regrets, was to fight and die on the Royalist side in the English Civil War. 'So enamoured of peace,' wrote his friend, Edward Hyde, Earl of Clarendon, 'that he would have been glad the King should have bought it at any price.'

Falkland was killed in battle at Newbury in 1643, his body stripped and so badly injured that he could be identified only by the mole on his neck. Clarendon survived to return with Charles II as Lord Chancellor and to write his great *History of the Rebellion*, which included a famous portrait of Falkland. In 1662 a respectful poem was addressed to Clarendon by John Dryden, who, thirty-two years later, addressed a more obviously affectionate poem to his 'Dear Friend Mr Congreve'. He extravagantly praised him, adding:

> All this in blooming youth you have achieved;
> Nor are your foiled contemporaries grieved;
> So much the sweetness of your manners move,
> We cannot envy you because we love.

In the last years of his life, Congreve was visited by the young Voltaire, exiled to England. When Voltaire was in his mid-sixties he received, with vigorously expressed mixed feelings, James Boswell, whose compulsion it was to visit the great men of his age. Boswell is celebrated now, of course, as the greatest of all biographers, but his life and career ended in abject failure, back in Scotland, shut out from London and political preferment, beset by ill-health and money problems. He had lost his great friend Samuel Johnson and was dissatisfied with local men of letters such as Hugh Blair.

Blair was a professor of rhetoric in Edinburgh, a member of a distin-guished literary circle which included David Hume, Thomas Carlyle and Adam Smith, but Boswell considered him a coarse vulgarian and indeed the young poet Samuel Rogers was much offended by his broad Scottish accent. Rogers had an enormously long life. He was already described as 'venerable' by Byron (Hazlitt cruelly said of him in 1818 that in his work 'the decomposition of prose is substituted for the composition of poetry'). In 1849 Elizabeth Gaskell saw him at a soirée at the house of Charles Dickens and thought the 86-year-old poet looked 'very unfit to be in such a large party', though in fact he would live for another six years.

Over the next few years, Gaskell came to know John Ruskin, initially because Ruskin's wife, Effie, had attended the same school she had. But when John Forster (Dickens's closest friend) told her of their separation, laying the blame on the husband, Gaskell strongly disagreed (in a letter dated 17 May 1854):

> I don't believe one word of what you say about Mr Ruskin. It has given me *great* pain to have the idea, the diabolical idea suggested, – but I think I do know enough of them to assure myself it is not true ... Now don't think me hard upon her if I tell you what I have *known* of her. She is very pretty very clever, – and very vain. As a girl ... in Manchester her delight was to add to the list of her offers (27 I think she was *at*, then;) but she never cared for any one of them ... I don't think she has any more serious faults than vanity and cold-heartedness ... She really is very close to a charming character; if she had had the small pox she would have been so.

She conceded 'his bad temper which every body knows', but in the end she trusted her reverence for the author: 'I can not bear to think of the dreadful hypocrisy if the man who wrote those books is a bad one.' The marriage was, in fact, annulled because of non-consummation. The event would remain a strange, embarrassing open secret in Victorian society. Even the 25-year-old Oscar Wilde found it 'odd' when, in 1879, he accompanied Ruskin to a ball given by Mr and Mrs John Everett Millais to celebrate the marriage of their daughter. For Mrs Millais was the ex-Mrs Ruskin.

Wilde himself was to become a figure of rumour and gossip that people took a scandalised delight in meeting. At the end of 1891, when he visited France for two months, *L'Echo de Paris* said that he was *'le "great event" des salons littéraires parisiennes'* of the season. The artist Jacques-Emile Blanche introduced Wilde to a then obscure French writer who was not only knowledgeable about English literature but specifically a translator of Ruskin: Marcel Proust. The meeting, in Proust's apartment at boulevard Haussmann, was disastrous. Proust arrived home late only to be told that Wilde had disappeared into the bathroom and stayed there. 'Monsieur Wilde,' Proust cried through the door. 'Are you ill?' Wilde emerged. 'No,' he said, 'I am not in the least ill. I thought I was to have the pleasure of dining with you alone, but they showed me into the drawing room. I looked at the drawing room and at the end of it were your parents, my courage failed me. Goodbye, dear Monsieur Proust, goodbye . . .'

Did Proust have especially bad luck with Irish writers? On 18 May 1922, Proust, now established as one of the great writers of his time, arrived, late and uninvited, at a supper party for Stravinsky and Diaghilev. James Joyce was already there and already drunk. He had been drinking heavily to cover his embarrassment at not wearing – and, for that matter, not possessing – evening dress. Proust sat down next to Joyce and there are various accounts of what was said. William Carlos Williams said they both complained about their ailments (Proust's were to kill him by the end of the year). Margaret Anderson recalled Proust saying that he had never read Joyce and Joyce replying that he had never read Proust. Joyce himself told a friend:

> Our talk consisted solely of the word 'No.' Proust asked me if I knew
> the duc de so-and-so. I said, 'No.' Our hostess asked Proust if he
> had read such and such a piece of *Ulysses*. Proust said, 'No.' And so
> on. Of course the situation was impossible. Proust's day was just
> beginning. Mine was at an end.

Proust invited the English novelist, Sydney Schiff, and his wife to accompany him back to his apartment in a taxi and Joyce came along. He immediately opened the window but Proust was notoriously sensitive to draughts and Schiff closed it. When they arrived, Proust suggested that Joyce continue on home in the taxi whereas Joyce was now anxious to talk to Proust. But Proust was worried about the cold. He rushed inside while Schiff successfully urged Joyce to leave.

In 1928, Samuel Beckett, a young student of twenty-two, arrived in Paris with a letter of introduction to Joyce from a mutual friend. Beckett became closely involved with the Joyce household. Joyce's daughter, Lucia, fell hopelessly in love with him. When Beckett was stabbed in the street by a madman, Joyce paid for him to be moved to a private room in the hospital. Joyce's wife, Nora, baked him a custard pie.

It has been said that, on occasion, Joyce dictated passages of *Finnegans Wake* to Beckett. Richard Ellmann tells the well-known story in his biography of Joyce:

> In the middle of one such session there was a knock at the door which Beckett didn't hear. Joyce said, 'Come in,' and Beckett wrote it down. Afterwards he read back what he had written and Joyce said, 'What's that "Come in"?' 'Yes, you said that,' said Beckett. Joyce thought for a moment, then said, 'Let it stand.' He was quite willing to accept coincidence.

Sadly, nobody has since been able to locate this incongruous 'come in' in the text of *Finnegans Wake*.

And finally, fifty years later, in June 1979, in a Sloane Square pub near the Royal Court Theatre in London, Samuel Beckett met me. I had become obsessed with Beckett after seeing his own magnificent Schiller Theatre production of *Waiting for Godot* at the Royal Court in 1976. The following year I had directed some friends in a school production of the play. My father, Philip French, then a BBC radio producer, knew the translator, Barbara Bray, who was a close friend of Beckett. I thought Beckett would be fascinated to see the programme I had prepared to accompany the production, which would demonstrate to him my uniquely profound feeling for his work.

The next year Barbara Bray gave me a signed copy of Beckett's play, *Footfalls*, and then in 1979, when he was in London to direct Billie Whitelaw in a revival of *Happy Days*, she rang my father and asked if I would like to meet him. I can remember only fragments. The absurdity of going to the stage door and asking for 'Mr Beckett'. Then an employee took me over the road and the even greater absurdity of him sitting there, in the corner, on his own, with other people having their drinks and paying no attention. I was led across to him and bought a half of Guinness, like the one he had, and sat down opposite him. He was composed, a little wary, largely silent. Twenty years old, and something of a connoisseur of the embarrassed silence in my own right, I realised that if any talking was to be done, it would have to be done by me. I decided to tell him in detail about my production of *Waiting for Godot*.

James Knowlson's biography of Beckett was published in 1996 and I now understand a little more about the background to our meeting. During the long rehearsal period with Billie Whitelaw, Beckett had begun to tinker with details of the text, even after she had learned the supposedly definitive published version. The changes were both trivial ('What now' becoming 'And now', 'speak' becoming 'talk') and numerous, and Beckett became angry when she found it difficult to accommodate them all accurately. The strain became so severe that Whitelaw decided she could no longer work with Beckett. This was managed with great tact, and Whitelaw worked with just the stage manager. Meanwhile, in Knowlson's words, 'Beckett filled his own timetable with innumerable meetings, dinners and drinks. Barbara Bray was in London and doubtless helped him to adopt a sensible attitude towards what had happened.'

I have only met Barbara Bray once. She is a strikingly attractive woman, as well as an intelligent critic and translator. I learned from Knowlson's biography what I had already suspected, which is that she had been having an affair with Beckett for many years. In reality Beckett's famed reclusiveness was really just a refusal to be interviewed. He had many affairs, close friendships, casual acquaintances. It could only have been as a favour to a loved one that he would have agreed to meet a student. On occasion, Beckett could show great interest when encountering someone new. A couple of years later, in the throes of other rehearsals, he was introduced to an American neurosurgeon. Beckett questioned him closely about the details of brain surgery: how much pain did a craniotomy involve? how was the skull removed? where did they put the skull bone while they were at work on the brain tissue? Beckett doubtless had less curiosity about the life of a first-year English Literature student, and when this student began to lecture him at length about his own work, it must have seemed like an episode from one of his bleaker prose works.

Gradually, other people joined us at the table. The film and stage director, Lindsay Anderson. The stage designer, Jocelyn Herbert. An elegant and beautiful foreign woman who kissed Beckett on the cheek. Kissing Beckett. One might as well high-five the Pope, but Beckett didn't seem to be as offended as I was on his behalf. He spoke more now. He had a soft, strange, continental Irish accent. We were all getting on so well together. I knew the bit in *The Catcher in the Rye* about being friends with an author you admired. Maybe Samuel Beckett would want me to be his friend. I also knew about him having been Joyce's secretary. Maybe he would want me to be his secretary.

One of the famous people looked at me quizzically. Who was this person they'd never heard of? 'This is Philip French,' Beckett explained. There had apparently been a mix-up in Barbara Bray's explanation to him of who I was. So, in five minutes' time, when he would forget about my existence for ever, he would actually be forgetting about somebody else's existence. I didn't actually say goodbye. Instead, I just drifted away, as if I was going for another drink and might return.

I could remember nothing specific he had said. I would never meet him again. I realised that for him the meeting had probably been a moderately arduous ordeal. But I was in no way disappointed. I hadn't really wanted to be Beckett's friend. There was nothing I wanted to ask him. I had just wanted to sit in the glow of his presence for a few minutes but that was all I could deal with. Beckett had more fun with people who had less respect for him as a great writer. I was too much like the fan who asked James Joyce if he could kiss the hand that wrote *Ulysses*. 'No,' said Joyce sensibly. 'It did lots of other things as well.'

So, fifteen people and a daisy chain of meetings link me to William Shakespeare. They are, of course, meetings of very different kinds ranging from close working relationships of long standing through dutiful encounters to outright dislike. But the account by a close friend is not always, perhaps not usually, the most revealing. In her book *On Photography* Susan Sontag speculates that if we could choose between Hans Holbein living fifty years later, so that he could have painted Shakespeare, or the Box Brownie camera being miraculously invented 250 years earlier so that he could be photographed, we would choose the photograph. The most incompetent photograph would be preferable to the greatest painting, because he would be *there*, caught.

Ben Jonson's tribute to Shakespeare is touching, but it tells you almost nothing you want to know. One would happily swap it for a few lines of John Aubrey – if Aubrey could have been born thirty years earlier. Jonson tells us that Shakespeare was 'honest, and of an open, and free nature', which is nice, but Aubrey tells us that Thomas Hobbes had difficulty in keeping flies from landing on his bald head.

Aubrey was ahead of his time. He had an antiquarian's interest in collecting anecdotes, details, myths, tall tales about the famous, and he was grievously mocked for it in his lifetime and afterwards. But he was an exception. It was really in the late eighteenth century, in the age of Rousseau, Johnson, Boswell, that the relation between a great writer's life and work starts to be considered significant.

It is sometimes forgotten that when Boswell's *Life of Johnson* was first published, it was considered a cruel betrayal of the intimacy and friendship that the author had enjoyed with his subject. As Lord Macaulay put it:

> No man, surely, ever published such stories respecting persons whom he professed to love and revere. He would infallibly have made his hero as contemptible as he has made himself, had not his hero really possessed some moral and intellectual qualities of a very high order. The best proof that Johnson was really an extraordinary man is that his character, instead of being degraded, has, on the whole, been decidedly raised by a work in which all his vices and weaknesses are exposed more unsparingly than they ever were exposed by Churchill or Kenrick.
>
> Johnson grown old, Johnson in the fullness of his fame and in the enjoyment of a competent fortune, is better known to us than any other man in history. Every thing about him, his coat, his wig, his figure, his face, his scrofula, his St Vitus's dance, his rolling walk, his blinking eye, the outward signs which too clearly marked his approbation of his dinner, his insatiable appetite for fish-sauce and veal-pie with plums, his inextinguishable thirst for tea, his trick of touching the posts as he walked, his mysterious practice of treasuring up scraps of orange-peel, his morning slumbers, his midnight disputations, his contortions, his mutterings, his gruntings, his puffings, his vigorous, acute, and ready eloquence, his sarcastic wit, his vehemence, his insolence, his fits of tempestuous rage, his queer inmates, old Mr Levett and blind Mrs Williams, the cat Hodge and the negro Frank, are as familiar to us as the objects by which we have been surrounded from childhood.

Writers of the Romantic period, like Coleridge and Hazlitt, were not merely interested in Shakespeare's life. They located his greatness in his personality, or the awesomeness of his impersonality. So there is nothing apologetic about the curiosity expressed by Keats in an 1819 letter to his brother, George:

The fire is at its last click – I am sitting with my back to it with one foot rather askew upon the rug and the other with the heel a little elevated from the carpet – I am writing this on the Maid's tragedy which I have read since tea with Great pleasure – Besides this volume of Beaumont & Fletcher – there are on the table two volumes of Chaucer and a new work of Tom Moores call'd 'Tom Cribb's memorial to Congress' – nothing in it – These are trifles – but I require nothing so much of you as that you will give me a like description of yourselves, however it may be when you are writing to me – Could I see the same thing done of any great Man long since dead it would be a great delight: as to know in what position Shakspeare sat when he began 'To be or not to be' – such things become interesting from distance of time or place.

And the added irony is that in evoking what he wanted to know of Shakespeare, he has gratified our interest about Keats. In the work of Keats and his contemporaries, the barriers between published works, manuscripts, early drafts, letters, journals, notebooks, reported conversation, rumour, anecdote, scandal were swept away. From now on, the personality of the writer was, for better or worse, one of the subjects of literature, like love, death, nature. Yes, we respond to Ben Jonson's account of Shakespeare, but what did he *look* like? Turgenev's relationship with Pushkin amounted to a couple of glimpses at parties, but what glimpses:

On entering the hallway of Pletnyov's apartment, I nearly bumped into a man of medium height, who had already put on his hat and coat and who exclaimed in a rich voice as he was taking leave of his host, 'Yes, yes, our Ministers are fine fellows! Yes, indeed!' He laughed and went out. I had just time to notice his white teeth and his bright, quick eyes.

Then once more, at a concert a few days before his death:

He was standing at the door, leaning against the door frame, and, his hands crossed on his broad chest, looking round with a dissatisfied air. I remember his small, dark face, his African lips, the gleam of his large white teeth, his pendent side-whiskers, his dark, jaundiced eyes beneath a high forehead, almost without eyebrows, and his curly hair . . . He threw a cursory glance at me too; the unceremonious way with which I stared at him probably made an unpleasant impression on him: he shrugged his shoulders as though with vexation – he seemed altogether in a bad mood – and walked away. A few days later I saw him lying in his coffin . . .

But might there not be something distasteful, even obscene, about such violations of privacy? As books began to be published revealing the foibles of great writers, doubts were raised. When Thomas Love Peacock reviewed three biographical portraits of his late friend, Shelley, he began by describing Rousseau's aversion to literary visitors because of his suspicion that they would print something about him:

> Rousseau's rule bids fair to become general with all who wish to keep in the *secretum iter et fallentis semita vitae*, and not to become materials for general gossip. For not only is a departed author of any note considered a fair subject to be dissected at the tea-table of the reading public, but all his friends and connexions, however quiet and retiring and unobtrusive may have been the general tenor of their lives, must be served up with him. It is the old village scandal on a larger scale; and as in these days of universal locomotion people know nothing of their neighbours, they prefer tittle-tattle about notorieties to the retailing of whispers about the Jenkinses and Tomkinses of the vicinity.

To put it crudely, it might be said that in the pre-Romantic era, the objection to details of a writer's private life being revealed would have been that they were of no more relevance to the finished work than the personal foibles of a cooper to his barrels. In the post-Romantic era the objection would be that the true artist produces finished works of art that make use of the messy details of his life but transform and transcend them. As Yeats put it, 'Even when the poet seems most himself . . . he is never the bundle of accident and incoherence that sits down to breakfast; he has been reborn as an idea, something intended, complete.' To be obsessed with the circumstances of creation was a way of diminishing the strangeness and beauty of the work of art.

When Henry James reviewed the first published version of Flaubert's letters, he thought a decisive breach had been made:

> . . . we may ask ourselves if the time has not come when it may well cease to be a leading feature of our homage to a distinguished man that we shall sacrifice him with sanguinary rites on the altar of our curiosity. Flaubert's letters, indeed, bring up with singular intensity

the whole question of the rights and duties, the decencies and discretions of the insurmountable desire to *know*. To lay down a general code is perhaps as yet impossible, for there is no doubt that to know is good, or to want to know, at any rate, supremely natural. Some day or other surely we shall all agree that everything is relative, that facts themselves are often falsifying, and that we pay more for some kinds of knowledge than those particular kinds are worth. Then we shall perhaps be sorry to have had it drummed into us that the author of calm, firm masterpieces, of 'Madame Bovary,' of 'Salammbô,' of 'Saint-Julien l'Hospitalier,' was narrow and noisy, and had not personally and morally, as it were, the great dignity of his literary ideal.

Are we in danger of destroying the thing we love when we go behind the work of art to find the Wizard of Oz who has been pulling the wires, sending out the jets of smoke? The novelist Cormac McCarthy is one of the current writers celebrated for being obscure, for not giving interviews, or being photographed, or giving readings. The journalist Mick Brown, who described himself as a passionate admirer of McCarthy's work, wrote an article for the *Sunday Telegraph Magazine* in which he traced the writer to the town in the American west where he lived, found where he ate breakfast, waited for him to arrive and then approached him. An obviously shaken McCarthy said that he didn't want to give an interview and asked if Brown could leave, which he did. It seemed a strange thing to have done, to travel across the world to find your favourite writer and spoil his breakfast.

If some readers sometimes presume too much on their relationship with an author, then many modern authors have made use of the confusion in their work, or found themselves caught up in it. From published journals, letters, biographies – as well as poems – we know that Ted Hughes and Sylvia Plath fell in love with each other as poets and from then on were entangled in each other's work, 'roped together like mountaineers' (as Braque said of his working relationship with Picasso). As great poets, they mythologised themselves and each other. To have read Norman Mailer over the years is to also to have been immersed in the details of his life. The stabbing of his wife may be gossip (though accurate gossip) but his arrest outside the Pentagon is at the heart of one of his finest books, *The Armies of the Night*. Curiously, it may be that the damage to an author's reputation is done not so much by revelations about sexual impropriety but rather by just what Keats wanted to know about Shakespeare, about his work habits.

Claire Bloom's accusation against Philip Roth – that he makes ruthless use of his own life in his work – can't have come as a surprise to many of his readers. More disconcerting is his own description of his way of beginning a new novel, in which he spends week after week writing virtual gibberish: 'I'll go over the first six months of work and underline in red a paragraph, a sentence, sometimes no more than a phrase, that has some life in it, and then I'll type all these out on one page. Usually it doesn't come to more than one page, but if I'm lucky, that's the start of page one.'

Or Vladimir Nabokov, standing at a lectern in a Montreux hotel writing his novels on index cards. Since he had the entire novel in his mind, he could prepare 'this or that passage at any point of the novel and [fill] in the gaps in no special order'.

These are the sort of details you try to forget while you are reading their fiction. Perhaps Philip Larkin was right when he said that talking about the way you write is like talking about the way you make love to your wife.

John Updike has written dubiously about encounters between writers and readers:

> The reader comes equipped with a vivid, fresh, outside impression of works the writer remembers wearily from the inside, as a blur
> of intention, a stretch of doubting drudgery, a tangle of memories and fabrications, a batch of nonsensical reviews, and a disappointed sigh
> from the publisher. The reader knows the writer better than he knows himself; but the writer's physical presence is light from a star that
> has moved on.

Yet this dismissive comment comes from an essay titled 'On Meeting Writers', in which he recalls the encounters with writers that enthralled or disappointed him: James Thurber bored him, repeating stories that Updike already knew, word for word, told better in his books; he was rude to Joyce Cary; he was taunted by Norman Mailer for being handsome: 'I took it to be Maileresque hyperbole, absurd yet nevertheless with something profound in it – perhaps my secret wish to be handsome, which only he, and that by dim streetlight, at a drunken hour, has ever perceived.'

More than this, Updike has always had a flirtatious relationship with his readers. We know – his first wife has complained – that he has made copious use of his life in his stories but his non-fiction too, even his reviews, are sprinkled with shimmering autobiographical fragments. He recalls that he and his first wife had been reading Proust one summer long ago, and clinches his recollection with the detail that a couple of the pages of his edition are still stained with the sun-tan oil that had dripped on to them. And introducing Nabokov's *Lectures on Literature* he mentions that his second wife was one of Nabokov's pupils. His account of her collecting an examination paper from Professor Nabokov becomes a slightly perverse erotic vignette:

> He bent low, eyebrows raised. 'And what is your name?' She told him, and with prestidigitational suddenness he produced her blue book from behind his back. It was marked 97. 'I wanted to see,' he told her, 'what a genius looked like.' And coolly he looked her up and down, while she blushed; that was the extent of their exchange.

Updike has now published three books about the imaginary novelist, Henry Bech, that variously explore, parody and draw on the public life of a successful American author.

He has also become, in his words, 'one who in a small way is himself now and then "met"'. In 'On Meeting Writers', Updike wrote affectionately of a visit to the Soviet Union with John Cheever in which somehow the force of Cheever's personality and imagination turned the grim Soviet bureaucrats into a 'bright scuttle of somewhat suburban characters, invented with marvellous speed and arranged in sudden tableaux expressive, amid wistful neo-Czarist trappings, of the lyric desperation associated with affluence.'

In 1990, after Cheever's death, his letters were collected and published, and Updike was startled to discover that Cheever remembered the experience in different terms: 'Updike, whom I know to be a brilliant man, travelled with me in Russia last autumn and I would go to considerable expense and inconvenience to avoid his company. I think his magnaminity [*sic*] specious and his work seems motivated by covetousness, exhibitionism and a stony heart.' Updike, who has written essays on virtually every imaginable writer and every imaginable topic, duly wrote a sort of meta-memoir of the visit, a reconsideration in the light of Cheever's newly revealed views. With an innocent air of inquiry he considers the reasons why Cheever may have resented him. Jealousy maybe, for, though 'I was twenty years younger than Cheever, a bit more of my work had been translated into Russian'. On another occasion:

At one of our joint appearances, I blush to remember, observing our audience's total ignorance of Cheever's remarkable work, I took it upon myself to stand up and describe it, fulsomely if not accurately, while my topic sat at my side in a dignified silence that retrospectively feels dour.

Yes, how helpful and comforting to the senior writer it must have been for Updike to draw extravagant public attention to this humiliating ignorance, if such it really was. Perhaps writers should be sent on tour alone.

In 1991, Updike became the subject of an entire book on the subject of the intense, and very complicated, personal interest that writers feel for each other: *U and I* by Nicholson Baker. Whatever our English teachers and the New Criticism told us, we don't just read a text, we have some sense of the person who wrote it. There are some writers to whom readers feel particularly close: John Keats and Sylvia Plath are two obvious examples. But Baker is good on the simple difference it makes if we know that the writer is alive:

> The intellectual surface we offer to the dead has undergone a subtle change of texture and chemistry; a thousand particulars of delight and fellow-feeling and forbearance begin reformulating themselves the moment they cross the bar. The living are always potentially thinking about and doing just what we are doing: being pulled through a touchless car wash, watching a pony chew a carrot, noticing that orange scaffolding has gone up around some prominent church. The conclusions they draw we know to be conclusions drawn from how things are now. Indeed, for me, as a beginning novelist, all other living writers form a control group for whom the world is a placebo. The dead can be helpful, needless to say, but we can only guess sloppily about how they would react to this emergent particle of time, which is all the time we have. And when we do guess, we are unfair to them. Even when, as with Barthelme, the dead have died unexpectedly and relatively young, we give them their moment of solemnity and then quickly begin patronizing them biographically, talking about how they 'delighted in' x or 'poked fun' at y – phrases that by their very singsong cuteness betray how alien and childlike the shades now are to us. Posthumously their motives become ludicrously simple, their delights primitive and unvarying: all their emotions wear stage makeup, and we almost never flip their books across the room out of impatience

with something they've said. We can't really understand them anymore.

It might have been thought that the personal, competitive obsession that a younger writer feels for a celebrated older writer could not be taken any further than Baker's *U and I*, but in 1998 Paul Theroux published *Sir Vidia's Shadow*, a book-length account of his 'friendship' with V. S. Naipaul that began when Theroux was an unpublished teacher in central Africa and only ended thirty years later when Theroux, by then an equally famous writer, found the first editions of his books that he had inscribed to Naipaul offered for sale in a bookseller's catalogue. It is almost comical to recall the few thoughtless comments by Edmund Wilson that provoked the fury of his old friend, Vladimir Nabokov. Among much else, Theroux describes Naipaul's racism, his disparagement of almost all other writers including contemporaries, his sexual incapacities, his rudeness and snobbery, his habitual meanness. Theroux also recalls his own sexual attraction to Naipaul's wife and how, serving as a judge for the Booker Prize, he prevented the prize being awarded to Naipaul for *A Bend in the River*. Theroux has defended himself against charges of betrayal, or simple bad manners, by citing the similarly hostile response that Boswell's biography of Dr Johnson received. Of course Johnson was dead when the biography appeared, but that doesn't settle the argument one way or the other. It could be argued that it is more honourable to publish while your subject is alive and able to answer back.

Harold Bloom has famously argued that great writers defined themselves by struggling with, misunderstanding, disowning their major predecessors. *Sir Vidia's Shadow* is an enactment of this Freudian myth, as if a writer can only be born by doing battle with his literary parent.

There is an inherent comedy in the encounters between writers. A reader who is not reading meets a writer who is not writing. There is generally a feeling of bathos, that the writer is not living up to his work, but without examining the notion of what 'living up' to a work of literature would consist of. It is a form of pilgrimage in which nobody is quite sure of the point, and yet the urge to call writers up on the phone persists. Here is an anthology of people who did more than that. They went round in person.

WILLIAM SHAKESPEARE (1564–1616)
by Ben Jonson (1572–1637)

I remember, the Players have often mentioned it as an honour to Shakespeare, that in his writing, (whatsoever he penned) he never blotted out line. My answer hath been, would he had blotted a thousand. Which they thought a malevolent speech. I had not told posterity this, but for their ignorance, who choose that circumstance to commend their friend by, wherein he most faulted. And to justify mine own candor, (for I loved the man, and do honour his memory (on this side Idolatry) as much as any.) He was (indeed) honest, and of an open, and free nature: had an excellent *Phantsie*; brave notions, and gentle expressions: wherein he flow'd with that facility, that sometime it was necessary he should be stopped: *Sufflaminandus erat*; as *Augustus* said of *Haterius*. His wit was in his own power; would the rule of it had been so too. Many times he fell into those things, could not escape laughter: As when he said in the person of *Caesar*, one speaking to him; *Caesar did never wrong, but with just cause*: and such like; which were ridiculous. But he redeemed his vices, with his virtues. There was ever more in him to be praised, than to be pardoned.

'Sufflaminandus erat' means 'He needed the drag chain'. The lines in the printed version of Julius Caesar III i 47–8 *are: 'Know, Caesar doth not wrong, nor without cause/Will he be satisfied.' Did Shakespeare rewrite the lines (for the worse) because of his friend's disapproval?*

JOHN DONNE (1572–1631)
by Izaak Walton (1593–1683)

Before that month ended, he was appointed to preach upon his old constant day, the first Friday in Lent; he had notice of it, and had in his sickness so prepared for that employment, that as he had long thirsted for it: so he resolved his weakness should not hinder his journey; he came therefore to London, some few days before his appointed day of preaching. At his coming thither, many of his friends (who with sorrow saw his sickness had left him but so much flesh as did only cover his bones) doubted his strength to perform that task; and did therefore dissuade him from undertaking it, assuring him however, it was like to shorten his life;

but he passionately denied their requests; saying, he would not doubt that that God who in so many weaknesses had assisted him with an unexpected strength, would now withdraw it in his last employment; professing an holy ambition to perform that sacred work. And, when to the amazement of some beholders he appeared in the pulpit, many of them thought he presented himself not to preach mortification by a living voice: but, mortality by a decayed body and a dying face. And doubtless, many did secretly ask that question in *Ezekiel*: 'Do these bones live? Or, can that soul organize that tongue, to speak so long time as the sand in that glass will move towards its centre, and measure out an hour of this dying man's unspent life?' Doubtless it cannot; and yet, after some faint pauses in his zealous prayer, his strong desires enabled his weak body to discharge his memory of his preconceived meditations, which were of dying: the text being, 'To God the Lord belong the issues from death'. Many that then saw his tears, and heard his faint and hollow voice, professing they thought the Text prophetically chosen, and that Dr Donne had preached his own funeral sermon . . .

It is observed, that a desire of glory or commendation is rooted in the very nature of man; and that those of the severest and most mortified lives, though they may become so humble as to banish self-flattery, and such weeds as naturally grow there: yet they have not been able to kill this desire of glory, but that, like our radical heat, it will both live and die with us; and many think it should do so; and want not sacred examples to justify the desire of having our memory to outlive our lives: which I mention, because Dr Donne, by the persuasion of Dr Fox, easily yielded at this very time to have a monument made for him; but Dr Fox undertook not to persuade him how, or what monument it should be; that was left to Dr Donne himself.

A monument being resolved upon, Dr Donne sent for a carver to make for him in wood the figure of an urn, giving him directions for the compass and height of it; and to bring with it a board of the just height of his body. These being got: then without delay a choice painter was got to be in a readiness to draw his picture, which was taken as followeth. – Several charcoal fires being first made in his large study, he brought with him into that place his winding sheet in his hand, and, having put off all his clothes, had this sheet put on him, and so tied with knots at his head and feet, and his hands so placed, as dead bodies are usually fitted to be shrouded and put into their coffin, or grave. Upon this urn he thus stood with his eyes shut, and with so much of the sheet turned aside as might show his lean, pale, and death-like face, which was purposedly turned toward the east, from whence he expected the second coming of his and our Saviour Jesus. In this posture he was drawn at his just height; and when the picture was fully finished, he caused it to be set by his bed-side, where it continued, and became his hourly object till his death: and, was then given to his dearest friend and executor, Doctor Henry King, then chief Residentiary of St. Pauls, who caused him to be thus carved in one entire piece of white marble, as it now stands in that church ...

He was of stature moderately tall, of a strait and equally proportioned body, to which all his words and actions gave an unexpressible addition of comeliness.

The melancholy and pleasant humour, were in him so contempered, that each gave advantage to the other, and made his company one of the delights of mankind.

His fancy was unimitably high, equalled only by his great wit; both being made useful by a commanding judgement.

His aspect was cheerful, and such as gave a silent testimony of a clear knowing soul, and of a conscience at peace with itself.

His melting eye showed that he had a soft heart, full of noble com-passion; of too brave a soul to offer injuries, and too much a Christian not to pardon them in others.

He did much contemplate (especially after he entered into his sacred calling) the mercies of Almighty God, the immortality of the soul, and the joys of heaven; and would often say, in a kind of sacred ecstasy – Blessed be God that he is God only, and divinely like himself.

He was by nature highly passionate, but more apt to reluct at the excesses of it. A great lover of the offices of humanity, and of so merciful a spirit, that he never beheld the miseries of mankind without pity and relief.

He was earnest and unwearied in the search of knowledge; with which, his vigorous soul is now satisfied, and employed in a continual praise of that God that first breathed it into his active body; that body, which once was a temple of the Holy Ghost, and is now become a small quantity of Christian dust:

But I shall see it reanimated.

THOMAS HOBBES (1588–1679)
by John Aubrey (1626–97)

1634: this summer – I remember 'twas in venison season (July or August) – Mr T. H. came into his native country to visit his friends, and amongst others he came then to see his old schoolmaster, Mr Robert Latimer, at Leigh-de-la-mer, where I was then a little youth at school in the church, newly entered into my grammar by him. Here was the first place and time that ever I had the honour to see this worthy, learned man, who was then pleased to take notice of me, and the next day visited my relations. He was then a proper man, brisk, and in very good habit. His hair was then quite black. He stayed at Malmsbury and in the neighborhood a week or better. His conversation about those times was much about Ben Jonson, Mr Ayton, etc. 'Twas the last time that ever he was in Wiltshire . . .

In his youth he was unhealthy; of an ill complexion (yellowish): he took colds, being wet in his feet (there were no hackney coaches to stand in the streets) and trod both his shoes aside the same way. Notwithstanding he was well beloved: they loved his company for his pleasant facetiousness and good nature.

From forty, or better, he grew healthier, and then he had a fresh, ruddy, complexion. He was *Sanguineo-melancholicus*; which the physiologers say is the most ingenious complexion. He would say that there might be good wits of all complexions; but good-natured, impossible.

In his old age he was very bald (which claimed a veneration) yet within door, he used to study, and sit bare-headed and said he never took cold in his head, but that the greatest trouble was to keep off the flies from pitching on the baldness.

Face not very great; ample forehead; whiskers yellowish-redish, which naturally turned up – which is a sign of a brisk wit. Below he was shaved close, except a little tip under his lip. Not but that nature could have afforded a venerable beard, but being naturally of a cheerful and pleasant humour, he affected not at all austerity and gravity to look severe. He desired not the reputation of his wisdom to be taken from the cut of his beard, but from his reason.

He had a good eye, and that of a hazel colour, which was full of life and spirit, even to the last. When he was earnest in discourse, there shone (as it were) a bright live-coal within it. He had two kinds of looks: when he laughed, was witty and in a merry humour, one could scarce see his

4

eyes; by and by, when he was serious and positive, he opened his eyes round (i.e. his eye-lids.) He had middling eyes, not very big, nor very little.

There was a good painter at the Earl of Devonshire's in Derbyshire not long before Mr Hobbes died, who drew him with the great decays of old age.

Though he left his native country at 14, and lived so long, yet sometimes one might find a little touch of our pronunciation.– Old Sir Thomas Malette, one of the judges of the King's Bench, knew Sir Walter Raleigh, and said that, not withstanding his great travels, conversation, learning, etc., yet he spake broad Devonshire to his dying day.

He had very few books. I never saw (nor Sir William Petty) above half a dozen about him in his chamber. Homer and Virgil were commonly on his table; sometimes Xenophon, or some probable history, and Greek Testament, or so.

He had read much, if one considers his long life; but his contemplation was much more than his reading. He was wont to say that if he had read as much as other men, he should have known no more than other men.

He was wont to say that he had rather have the advice, or take physic from an experienced old woman, that had been at many sick people's bedsides, than from the learnedst but unexperienced physician.

'Tis not consistent with an harmonical soul to be a woman-hater, neither had he an abhorrescence to good wine but he was, even in his youth (generally temperate), both as to wine and women. I have heard him say that he did believe he had been in excess in his life, a hundred times; which, considering his great age, did not amount to above once a year. When he did drink, he would drink to excess to have the benefit of vomiting, which he did easily; by which benefit neither his wit was disturbed longer than he was spewing nor his stomach oppressed; but he never was, nor could not endure to be, habitually a good fellow, i.e. to drink every day wine with company, which, though not to drunkenness, spoils the brain.

For his last 30+ years, his diet, etc., was very moderate and regular. He rose about seven, had his breakfast of bread and butter; and took his walk, meditating till ten; then he did put down the minutes of his thoughts, which he penned in the afternoon. He thought much and with excellent method and steadiness, which made him seldom make a false step.

He had an inch thick board about 16 inches square, whereon paper was pasted. On this board he drew his lines (schemes). When a line came into his head, he would, as he was walking, take a rude memorandum of it, to preserve it in his memory till he came to his chamber. He was never idle; his thoughts were always working.

His dinner was provided for him exactly by eleven, for he could not now stay till his Lord's hour – *scil.* about two: that his stomach could not bear.

After dinner he took a pipe of tobacco, and then threw himself immediately on his bed, with his band off, and slept (took a nap of about half an hour).

In the afternoon he penned his morning thoughts.

Besides his daily walking, he did twice or thrice a year play at tennis (at about 75 he did it) then went to bed there and was well rubbed. This he did believe would make him live two or three years the longer.

In the country, for want of a tennis court, he would walk uphill and downhill in the park, till he was in a great sweat, and then give the servant some money to rub him.

He had always books of prick-song lying on his table: which at night, when he was abed, and the doors made fast, and was sure nobody heard him, he sang aloud, not that he had a very good voice but for his health's sake: he did believe it did his lungs good, and conduced much to prolong his life.

He had the shaking palsy in his hands; which began in France before the year 1650, and has grown upon him by degrees, ever since, so that he has not been able to write very legibly since 1665 or 1666, as I find by some letters he hath honoured me withall. Mr Hobbes was for several years before he died so paralytical that he was scarce able to write his name, and that in the absence of his amanuensis not being able to write anything, he made scrawls on a piece of paper to remind him of the conceptions of his mind he designed to have committed to writing.

Sir Thomas Browne (1605–82)
by John Evelyn (1620–1706)

Next morning [18 October 1671] I went to see Sir Tho: Browne (with whom I had sometime corresponded by letters though never saw before) whose whole house and garden being a paradise and cabinet of rarities, and that of the best collection, especially medals, books, plants, natural things, did exceedingly refresh me after last night's confusion: Sir Thomas had amongst other curiosities, a collection of the eggs of all the fowl and birds he could procure, that country (especially the promontories of Norfolk) being (as he said) frequented with several kinds, which seldom or never, go farther into the land, as cranes, storks, eagles etc: and variety of water fowl: He likewise led me to see all the remarkable places of this ancient city [Norwich], being one of the largest, and certainly (after London) one of the noblest of England, for its venerable cathedral, number of stately churches, cleanness of the streets; and buildings of flint, so exquisitely headed and squared, as I was much astonished at; Sir Tho: told me they had lost the art, of squaring the flint, which once they were so excellent in: and of which the churches, best houses, and walls are built.

JOHN MILTON (1608–74)
by John Aubrey (1626–97)

His sight began to fail him at first upon his writing against Salmasius, and before 'twas full completed one eye absolutely failed. Upon the writing of other books, after that, his other eye decayed. His eyesight was decaying about 20 years before his death. His father read without spectacles at 84. His mother had very weak eyes, and used spectacles presently after she was thirty years old.

His harmonical and ingenious soul did lodge in a beautiful and well proportioned body. He was a spare man. He was scarce so tall as I am (*quaere*, quot feet I am high: *resp*, of middle stature).

He had brown hair. His complexion exceeding fair – he was so fair that they called him the Lady of Christ's College. Oval face. His eye a dark grey.

He was very healthy and free from all diseases: seldom took any physic (only sometimes he took manna): only towards his latter end he was visited with the gout, spring and fall.

He had a delicate tuneable Voice, and had good skill. His father instructed him. He had an organ in his house; he played on that most. Of a very cheerful humour. He would be cheerful even in his gout fits, and sing.

He had a very good memory; but I believe that his excellent method of thinking and disposing did much to help his memory.

His widow has his picture, drawn very well and like, when a Cambridge scholar, which ought to be engraven; for the pictures before his books are not at all like him.

His exercise was chiefly walking. He was an early riser (*scil*. at 4 a clock *manè*) yea, after he lost his sight. He had a man to read to him. The first thing he read was the Hebrew bible, and that was at 4h. *manè*, half h. plus. Then he contemplated. At 7 his man came to him again, and then read to him again, and wrote till dinner; the writing was as much as the reading. His daughter, Deborah, could read to him in Latin, Italian and French, and Greek. Married in Dublin to one Mr Clarke (sells silk, etc.) very like her father. The other sister is Mary, more like her mother.

After dinner he used to walk three or four hours at a time (he always had a garden where he lived) went to bed about nine.

Temperate man, rarely drank between meals. Extreme pleasant in his conversation, and at dinner, supper, etc.; but satirical. (He pronounced the letter R (*littera canina*) very hard– certain sign of a satirical wit – *from John Dryden*.)

Samuel Butler (1613–80)
by John Aubrey (1626–97)

He printed a witty poem called *Hudibras*, which took extremely; so that the King and Lord Chancellor Hyde (who has his picture in his library over the chimney) would have him sent for, and accordingly he was sent for. They both promised him great matters, but to this day he has got no employment, only the King gave him 300 pounds.

After the restoration of His Majesty when the Court at Ludlow was again set up, he was then the King's Steward at the castle there.

He has often said, that way (e.g. Mr Edmund Waller's) of quibbling with sense will hereafter grow as much out of fashion and be as ridicule as quibbling with words.

His verses on the Jesuits, not printed:–

> No Jesuit ever took in hand,
> To plant a church in barren land;
> Or ever thought it worth his while
> A Swede or Russe to reconcile;
> For where there is not store of wealth,

Souls are not worth the charge of health.
Spain on America had two designs
To sell their Gospel for their mines;
For had the Mexicans been poor,
No Spaniard twice had landed on their shore.
'Twas gold the Catholic religion planted,
Which, had they wanted gold, they still had wanted.

Satirical wits disoblige whom they converse with; and consequently make to themselves many enemies and few friends; and this was his manner and case. He was of a leonine-coloured hair, sanguino-choleric, middle sized, strong; a severe and sound judgment, high coloured; a good fellow. He has been much troubled with the gout, and particularly 1679, he stirred not out of his chamber from October till Easter.

He died of a consumption, September 25; and buried 27, according to his appointment, in the churchyard of Convent Garden; *scil.* in the north part next the church at the east end. His feet touch the wall. His grave, two yards distant from the pillaster of the door, (by his desire) six foot deep.

About 25 of his old acquaintance at his funeral. I myself being one of the eldest, helped to carry the pall. His coffin covered with black bays.

ANDREW MARVELL (1621–78)
by John Aubrey (1626–97)

He was of middling stature, pretty strong set, roundish faced, cherry cheeked, hazel eye, brown hair. He was in his conversation very modest, and of very few words: and though he loved wine he would never drink hard in company, and was wont to say that, he would not play the good-fellow in any man's company in whose hands he would not trust his life. He had not a general acquaintance.

In the time of Oliver the Protector he was Latin Secretary. He was a great master of the Latin tongue; an excellent poet in Latin or English: for Latin verses there was no man could come into competition with him.

I remember I have heard him say that the Earl of Rochester was the only man in England that had the true vein of satire.

His native town of Hull loved him so well that they elected him for their representative in Parliament, and gave him an honourable pension to maintain him.

He kept bottles of wine at his lodging, and many times he would drink liberally by himself to refresh his spirits, and exalt his muse. (I remember I have been told that the learned Goclenius (an High German) was wont to keep bottles of good Rhenish wine in his study, and, when his spirits wasted, he would drink a good rummer of it.)

Obiit Londini, Aug. 18 1678; and is buried in St Giles church in-the-fields about the middle of the south aisle. Some suspect that he was poisoned by the Jesuits, but I cannot be positive.

JONATHAN SWIFT (1667–1745)
by Alexander Pope (1688–1744)

LETTER FROM ALEXANDER POPE TO JONATHAN SWIFT, AUGUST 1723

I find a rebuke in a late letter of yours that both stings and pleases me extremely. Your saying that I ought to have writ a postscript to my friend Gay's, makes me not content to write less than a whole letter, and your seeming to receive his kindly gives me hopes you'll look upon this as a sincere effect of friendship. Indeed as I cannot but own, the laziness with which you tax me, and with which I may equally charge you (for both of us I believe have had and one of us has both had and given a surfeit of writing) so I really thought you would know yourself to be so certainly entitled to my friendship, that 'twas a possession, you could not imagine needed any further deeds or writings to assure you of it. It is an honest truth, there's no one living or dead of whom I think oftener, or better than yourself. I look upon you to be, (as to me) in a state between both: you have from me all the passions, and good wishes, that can attend the living; and all that respect and tender sense of loss that we feel for the dead. Whatever you seem to think of your withdrawn and separate state, at this distance, and in this absence, Dr Swift lives still in England, in every place and company where he would choose to live; and I find him in all the conversations I keep, and in all the hearts in which I would have any share. We have never met these many years without mention of you. Besides my old acquaintances I have found that all my friends of a later date, were such as were yours before. Lord Oxford, Lord Harcourt, and Lord Harley, may look upon me as one immediately entailed upon them by you. Lord Bolingbroke is now returned (as I hope) to take me, with all his other hereditary rights; and indeed he seems grown so much a philosopher as to set his heart upon some of 'em as little as upon the poet you gave him. 'Tis sure my particular ill fate, that all those I have most loved and with whom I have most lived, must be banished . . . The top-pleasure of my life is one I learned from you both how to gain, and how to use the freedoms of friendship with men much my superiors. To have pleased great men according to Horace is a praise; but not to have flattered them and yet not to have displeased them is a greater. I have carefully avoided all intercourse with poets and scribblers, unless where by great chance I find a modest one. By these means I have had no quarrels with any personally, and none have been enemies, but who were also strangers to me. And as there is no great need of eclaircissements with such, whatever they writ or said I never retaliated; not only never seeming to know, but often really never knowing anything of the matter. There are very few things that give me the anxiety of a wish: the strongest I have would be to pass my days with you, and a few such as you. But Fate has dispersed them all about the world. And I find to wish it is as vain as to wish to live to see the millennium, and the Kingdom of the Just upon earth.

ALEXANDER POPE (1688–1744) AND LADY MARY WORTLEY MONTAGU (1689–1762)

The reason why the close friendship between Alexander Pope and Lady Mary Wortley Montagu turned into bitter enmity remains a matter of dispute. One possibility is that Pope declared his love for her and was rejected. As is evident from the poems reproduced here, Pope was well known for being hunchbacked, and Lady Mary still bore the traces of smallpox on her face. It was also widely known that the name 'Sappho' in Pope's poetry referred to her.

LETTER FROM ALEXANDER POPE TO LADY MARY WORTLEY MONTAGU, [SEPTEMBER?] 1718

Dear Madam, – 'Tis not possible to express the least part of the joy, your return gives me. Time only, and experience, will convince you how very sincere it is – I excessively long to meet you; to say so much, so very much to you, that I believe I shall say nothing – I have given orders to be sent for the first minute of your arrival, (which I beg you'll let them know at Mr Jervas's.) I am fourscore miles from London, a short journey, compared to that I so often thought at least of undertaking, rather than die without seeing you again. Though the place I am in is such as I would not quit for the town, if I did not value you more than any, nay every, body else, there.

from TO MR GAY, WHO WROTE HIM A CONGRATULATORY LETTER ON THE FINISHING HIS HOUSE [*written by Pope in 1720*]

> Ah, friend, 'tis true – this truth you lovers know –
> In vain my structures rise, my gardens grow,
> In vain fair Thames reflects the double scenes
> Of hanging mountains, and of sloping greens:
> Joy lives not here; to happier seats it flies,
> And only dwells where Wortley casts her eyes.

from THE FIRST SATIRE OF THE SECOND BOOK OF HORACE IMITATED
by Alexander Pope

> Satire's my weapon, but I'm too discreet
> To run amuck, and tilt at all I meet;
> I only wear it in a land of Hectors,
> Thieves, supercargoes, sharpers, and directors.
> Save but our army! and let Jove incrust
> Swords, pikes, and guns, with everlasting rust!
> Peace is my dear delight – not FLEURY's more:
> But touch me, and no minister so sore.
> Who'er offends, at some unlucky time
> Slides into verse, and hitches in a rhyme,
> Sacred to ridicule his whole life long,
> And the sad burden of some merry song.
> Slander or poison, dread from Delia's rage,
> Hard words or hanging, if your judge be Page.
> From furious Sappho scarce a milder fate,
> P-xed by her love, or libelled by her hate.

from VERSES ADDRESSED TO THE IMITATOR OF THE FIRST SATIRE OF
THE SECOND BOOK OF HORACE [*a satire published anonymously on
8 March 1733, by Lady Mary with the assistance of Lord Hervey*]

When God created thee, one would believe
He said the same as to the snake of Eve:
'To human race antipathy declare,
'Twixt them and thee be everlasting war.'
But oh! the sequel of the sentence dread,
And whilst you bruise your heel, beware your head.
   Nor think thy weakness shall be thy defence,
The female scold's protection in offence.
Sure 'tis as fair to beat who cannot fight,
As 'tis to libel those who cannot write.
And if thou draw'st thy pen to aid the law,
Others a cudgel, or rod, may draw.
   If none with vengeance yet thy crimes pursue,
Or give thy manifold affronts their due;
If limbs unbroken, skin without a stain,
Unwhipped, unblanketed, unkicked, unslain,
That wretched little carcase you retain,
The reason is, not that the world wants eyes,
But thou'rt so mean, they see, and they despise:
When fretful porcupine, with rancorous will,
From mounted back shoots forth a harmless quill,
Cool the spectators stand; and all the while
Upon the angry little monster smile.
Thus 'tis with thee:– whilst impotently safe,
You strike unwounding, we unhurt can laugh.
'Who but must laugh, this bully when he sees,
A puny insect shivering at a breeze?'
   Is this the thing to keep mankind in awe,
'To make those tremble who escape the law?'
Is this the ridicule to live so long,
'The deathless satire and immortal song?'
No: like thy self-blown praise, thy scandal flies;
And, as we're told of wasps, it stings and dies.
   If none do yet return th'intended blow,
You all your safety to your dullness owe:

But whilst that armour thy poor corpse defends
'Twill make thy readers few, as are thy friends:
Those, who thy nature loathed, yet loved thy art,
Who liked thy head, and yet abhorred thy heart:
Chose thee to read, but never to converse,
And scorned in prose him whom they prized in verse:
Even they shall now their partial error see,
Shall shun thy writing like thy company;
And to thy books shall ope their eyes no more
Than to thy person they would do their door.
　　Nor thou the justice of the world disown,
That leaves thee thus an outcast and alone;
For though in law to murder be to kill,
In equity the murder's in the will:
Then whilst with coward-hand you stab a name,
And try at least t'assassinate our fame,
Like the first bold assassin's be thy lot,
Ne'er be thy guilt forgiven, or forgot;
But, as thou hat'st, be hated by mankind,
And with the emblem of thy crooked mind
Marked on thy back, like Cain, by God's own hand,
Wander, like him, accursèd through the land.

VOLTAIRE (1694–1778)
by James Boswell (1740–95)

LETTER FROM BOSWELL TO WILLIAM JOHNSON TEMPLE,
28 DECEMBER 1764

I returned yesterday to this enchanted castle. The magician appeared a very little beyond dinner. But in the evening he came into the drawing-room in great spirits. I placed myself by him. I touched the keys in unison with his imagination. I wish you had heard the music. He was all brilliance. He gave me continued flashes of wit. I got him to speak English, which he does in a degree that made me now and then start up and cry, 'Upon my soul this is astonishing!' When he talked our language he was animated with the soul of a Briton. He had bold flights. He had humour. He had an extravagance; he had a forcible oddity of style that the most comical of our *dramatis personae* could not have exceeded. He swore bloodily, as was the fashion when he was in England. He hummed a ballad; he repeated nonsense. Then he talked of our Constitution with a noble enthusiasm. I was proud to hear this from the mouth of an illustrious Frenchman. At last we came upon religion. Then did he rage. The company went to supper. Monsieur de Voltaire and I remained in the drawing-room with a great Bible before us; and if ever two mortal men disputed with vehemence we did. Yes, upon that occasion he was one individual and I another. For a certain portion of time there was a fair opposition between Voltaire and Boswell. The daring bursts of his ridicule confounded my understanding. He stood like an orator of ancient Rome. Tully was never more agitated than he was. He went too far. His aged frame trembled beneath him. He cried, 'Oh, I am very sick; my head turns round,' and he let himself gently fall upon an easy chair. He recovered. I resumed our conversation, but changed the tone. I talked to him serious and earnest. I demanded of him an honest confession of his real senti-ments. He gave it me with candour and with a mild eloquence which touched my heart. I did not believe him capable of thinking in the manner that he declared to me was 'from the bottom of his heart'. He expressed his veneration – his love – of the Supreme Being, and his entire resignation to the will of Him who is All-wise. He expressed his desire to resemble the Author of Goodness by being good himself. His sentiments go no farther. He does not inflame his mind with grand hopes of the immortality of the soul. He says it may be, but he knows nothing of it. And his mind is in perfect tranquillity. I was moved; I was sorry. I doubted his sincerity. I called to him with emotion, 'Are you sincere? are you really sincere?' He answered, 'Before God, I am.' Then with the fire of him whose tragedies have so often shone on the theatre of Paris, he said, 'I suffer much. But I suffer with patience and resignation; not as a Christian – but as a man.'

Temple, was not this an interesting scene? Would a journey from Scot-land to Ferney have been too much to obtain such a remarkable interview? I have given you the great lines. The whole conversation of the evening is fully recorded, and I look upon it as an invaluable treasure. One day the public shall have it. It is a present highly worthy of their attention. I told Monsieur de Voltaire that I had written eight quarto pages of what he had said. He smiled and seemed pleased. Our important scene must not appear till after his death. But I have a great mind to send over to London a little sketch of my reception at Ferney, of the splendid manner in which Monsieur de Voltaire lives, and of the brilliant conversation of this celebrated author at the age of seventy-two. The sketch would be a letter, addressed to you, full of gaiety and full of friendship. I would send it to one of the best public papers or magazines. But this is probably a flight of my over-heated mind. I shall not send the sketch unless you approve of my doing so.

SATURDAY 29 DECEMBER. NOTES ON VOLTAIRE'S ENGLISH CONVERSATION

BOSWELL. 'When I came to see you, I thought to see a very great, but a very bad, man.' VOLTAIRE. 'You are very sincere.' BOSWELL. 'Yes, but the same sincerity makes me own that I find the contrary. Only, your *Dictionnaire philosophique* troubles me. For instance, *Ame*, the Soul –' VOLTAIRE. 'That's a good article.' BOSWELL. 'No. Excuse me. Is it – immortality – not a pleasing imagination? Is it not more noble?' VOLTAIRE. 'Yes. You have a noble desire to be King of Europe. You say, "I wish it, and I ask your protection in continuing to wish it." But it is not probable.' BOSWELL. 'No, but all cannot be the one, and may be the other. Like Cato, we all say, "It must be so," till we possess immortality itself.' VOLTAIRE. 'But before we say that this soul will exist, let us know what it is. I know not the cause. I cannot judge. I cannot be a juryman. Cicero says, *potius optandum quam probandum* [matter of faith rather than of demonstration]. We are ignorant beings. We are the puppets of Providence. I am a poor Punch.' BOSWELL. 'Would you have no public worship?' VOLTAIRE. 'Yes, with all my heart. Let us meet four times a year in a grand temple with music, and thank God for all his gifts. There is one sun. There is one God. Let us have one religion. Then all mankind will be brethren.' BOSWELL. 'May I write in English, and you'll answer?' VOLTAIRE. 'Yes. Farewell.'

RICHARD SAVAGE (*c.*1697–1743)
by Samuel Johnson (1709–84)

The poet Richard Savage is now only remembered as the subject of an extraordinary short biography by Dr Johnson. Johnson describes Savage's belief that he was the illegitimate son of an aristocratic couple, cheated of his inheritance; his conviction for murder and his pardon, his disastrous

literary career and dismal death. It has been described as the first-ever
biography of a literary failure.

Such were the life and death of Richard Savage, a man equally distinguished by his virtues and vices; and at once remarkable for his weaknesses
and abilities.

He was of a middle stature, of a thin habit of body, a long visage,
coarse features, and melancholy aspect; of a grave and manly deportment,
a solemn dignity of mien; but which, upon a nearer acquaintance, softened
into an engaging easiness of manners. His walk was slow, and his voice
tremulous and mournful. He was easily excited to smiles, but very seldom
provoked to laughter.

His mind was in an uncommon degree vigorous and active. His judgment was accurate, his apprehension quick, and his memory so tenacious,
that he was frequently observed to know what he had learned from others
in a short time, better than those by whom he was informed; and could
frequently recollect incidents, with all their combination of circumstances,
which few would have regarded at the present time, but which the quickness of his apprehension impressed upon him. He had the peculiar felicity,
that his attention never deserted him; he was present to every object, and
regardful of the most trifling occurrences. He had the art of escaping from
his own reflections, and accommodating himself to every new scene.

To this quality is to be imputed the extent of his knowledge, compared
with the small time which he spent in visible endeavours to acquire it. He
mingled in cursory conversation with the same steadiness of attention as
others apply to a lecture; and, amidst the appearance of thoughtless gaiety,
lost no new idea that was started, nor any hint that could be improved.
He had therefore made in coffee-houses the same proficiency as others in
their closets: and it is remarkable, that the writings of a man of little
education and little reading have an air of learning scarcely to be found
in any other performances, but which perhaps as often obscures as embellishes them.

His judgment was eminently exact both with regard to writings and to
men. The knowledge of life was indeed his chief attainment; and it is not
without some satisfaction, that I can produce the suffrage of Savage in
favour of human nature, of which he never appeared to entertain such
odious ideas as some, who perhaps had neither his judgment nor experience, have published, either in ostentation of their sagacity, vindication
of their crimes, or gratification of their malice.

His method of life particularly qualified him for conversation, of which he knew how to practise all the graces. He was never vehement or loud, but at once modest and easy, open and respectful; his language was vivacious and elegant, and equally happy upon grave or humourous subjects. He was generally censured for not knowing when to retire; but that was not the defect of his judgment, but of his fortune: when he left his company, he was frequently to spend the remaining part of the night in the street, or at least was abandoned to gloomy reflections, which it is not strange that he delayed as long as he could; and sometimes forgot that he gave others pain to avoid it himself.

It cannot be said, that he made use of his abilities for the direction of his own conduct: an irregular and dissipated manner of life had made him the slave of every passion that happened to be excited by the presence of its object, and that slavery to his passions reciprocally produced a life irregular and dissipated. He was not master of his own motions, nor could promise any thing for the next day.

With regard to his economy, nothing can be added to the relation of his life. He appeared to think himself born to be supported by others, and dispensed from all necessity of providing for himself; he therefore never prosecuted any scheme of advantage, nor endeavoured even to secure the profits which his writings might have afforded him. His temper was, in consequence of the dominion of his passions, uncertain and capricious; he was easily engaged, and easily disgusted; but he is accused of retaining his hatred more tenaciously than his benevolence.

He was compassionate both by nature and principle, and always ready to perform offices of humanity; but when he was provoked (and small offences were sufficient to provoke him), he would prosecute his revenge with the utmost acrimony till his passion had subsided.

His friendship was therefore of little value; for though he was zealous in the support or vindication of those whom he loved, yet it was always dangerous to trust him, because he considered himself as discharged by the first quarrel from all ties of honour or gratitude; and would betray those secrets which, in the warmth of confidence, had been imparted to him. This practice drew upon him an universal accusation of ingratitude: nor can it be denied that he was very ready to set himself free from the load of an obligation; for he could not bear to conceive himself in a state of dependence, his pride being equally powerful with his other passions, and appearing in the form of insolence at one time, and of vanity at another. Vanity, the most innocent species of pride, was most frequently predominant: He could not easily leave off, when he had once begun to mention himself or his works; nor ever read his verses without stealing his eyes from the page, to discover, in the faces of his audience, how they were affected with any favourite passage.

A kinder name than that of vanity ought to be given to the delicacy with which he was always careful to separate his own merit from every other man's, and to reject that praise to which he had no claim. He did not forget, in mentioning his performances, to mark every line that had been suggested or amended; and was so accurate as to relate that he owed three words in *The Wanderer* to the advice of his friends.

His veracity was questioned, but with little reason; his accounts, though not indeed always the same, were generally consistent. When he loved any man, he suppressed all his faults; and, when he had been offended by him, concealed all his virtues: but his characters were generally true, so far as he proceeded; though it cannot be denied, that his partiality might have sometimes the effect of falsehood.

In cases indifferent, he was zealous for virtue, truth, and justice: he knew very well the necessity of goodness to the present and future happiness of mankind; nor is there perhaps any writer who has less endeavoured to please by flattering the appetites, or perverting the judgment.

As an author, therefore, and he now ceases to influence mankind in any other character, if one piece which he had resolved to suppress be excepted, he has very little to fear from the strictest moral or religious censure. And though he may not be altogether secure against the objections of the critic, it must however be acknowledged, that his works are the productions of a genius truly poetical; and, what many writers who have been more lavishly applauded cannot boast, that they have an original air, which has no resemblance of any foregoing work, that the versification and sentiments have a cast peculiar to themselves, which no man can imitate with success, because what was nature in Savage, would in another be affectation. It must be confessed, that his descriptions are striking, his images animated, his fictions justly imagined, and his allegories artfully pursued; that his diction is elevated, though sometimes forced, and his numbers sonorous and majestic, though frequently sluggish and encumbered. Of his style, the general fault is harshness, and its general excellence is dignity; of his sentiments, the prevailing beauty is sublimity, and uniformity the prevailing defect.

For his life, or for his writings, none, who candidly consider his fortune, will think an apology either necessary or difficult. If he was not always sufficiently instructed in his subject, his knowledge was at least greater than could have been attained by others in the same state. If his works were sometimes unfinished, accuracy cannot reasonably be exacted from a man oppressed with want, which he has no hope of relieving but by a speedy publication. The insolence and resentment of which he is accused were not easily to be avoided by a great mind, irritated by perpetual hardships, and constrained hourly to return the spurns of contempt, and repress the insolence of prosperity; and vanity may surely readily be pardoned in him, to whom life afforded no other comforts than barren praises, and the consciousness of deserving them.

Those are no proper judges of his conduct, who have slumbered away their time on the down of plenty; nor will any wise man presume to say, 'Had I been in Savage's condition, I should have lived or written better than Savage.'

This relation will not be wholly without its use, if those, who languish under any part of his sufferings, shall be enabled to fortify their patience, by reflecting that they feel only those afflictions from which the abilities of Savage did not exempt him; or those, who, in confidence of superior capacities or attainment, disregard the common maxims of life, shall be reminded, that nothing will supply the want of prudence; and that negligence and irregularity, long continued, will make knowledge useless, wit ridiculous, and genius contemptible.

HENRY FIELDING (1707–54)
by Lady Mary Wortley Montagu (1689–1762)

LETTER TO LADY BUTE, 22 SEPTEMBER 1755

I am sorry for Henry Fielding's death, not only as I shall read no more of his writings, but I believe he lost more than others, as no man enjoyed life more than he did, though few had less reason to do so, the highest of his preferment being raking in the lowest sinks of vice and misery. I should think it a nobler and less nauseous employment to be one of the staff officers that conduct nocturnal weddings. His happy constitution (even when he had, with great pains, half demolished it) made him forget everything when he was before a venison pasty or over a flask of champagne, and I am persuaded he has known more happy moments than any prince upon earth. His natural spirits gave him rapture with his cookmaid, and cheerfulness when he was fluxing in a garret. There was a great similitude between his character and that of Sir Richard Steele. He had the advantage both in learning and, in my opinion, genius. They both agreed in wanting money in spite of all their friends, and would have wanted it if their hereditary lands had been as extensive as their imagination, yet each of them so formed for happiness, it is a pity they were not immortal.

SAMUEL JOHNSON (1709–84)
by James Boswell (1740–95)

16 MAY 1763

Temple and his brother breakfasted with me. I went to Love's to try to recover some of the money which he owes me. But, alas, a single guinea was all I could get. He was just going to dinner, so I stayed and eat a bit, though I was angry at myself afterwards. I drank tea at Davies's in Russell Street, and about seven came in the great Mr Samuel Johnson, whom I have so long wished to see. Mr Davies introduced me to him. As I knew his mortal antipathy at the Scotch, I cried to Davies, 'Don't tell where I come from.' However, he said, 'From Scotland.' 'Mr Johnson,' said I, 'indeed I come from Scotland, but I cannot help it.' 'Sir,' replied he, 'that, I find, is what a very great many of your countrymen cannot help.' Mr Johnson is a man of a most dreadful appearance. He is a very big man, is troubled with sore eyes, the palsy and the king's evil. He is very slovenly in his dress and speaks with a most uncouth voice. Yet his great knowledge and strength of expression command vast respect and render him very excellent company. He has great humour and is a worthy man. But his dogmatical roughness of manners is disagreeable. I shall mark what I remember of his conversation.

He said that people might be taken in once in imagining that an author is greater than other people in private life. 'Uncommon parts require uncommon opportunities for their exertion.

'In barbarous society superiority of parts is of real consequence. Great strength or wisdom is of value to an individual. But in more polished times you have people to do everything for money. And then there are a number of other superiorities, such as those of birth and fortune and rank, that dissipate men's attention and leave superiority of parts no extraordinary share of respect. And this is wisely ordered by Providence, to preserve a mediocrity.

'Lord Kames's *Elements* is a pretty essay and deserves to be held in some estimation, though it is chimerical.

'Wilkes is safe in the eye of the law. But he is an abusive scoundrel; and instead of sending my Lord Chief Justice to him, I would send a parcel of footmen and have him well ducked.

'The notion of liberty amuses the people of England and helps to keep off the *taedium vitae*. When a butcher says that he is in distress for his country, he has no uneasy feeling.

'Sheridan will not succeed at Bath, for ridicule has gone down before him, and I doubt Derrick is his enemy.'

I was sorry to leave him there at ten, when I had engaged to be at Dr Pringle's, with whom I had a serious conversation much to my mind.

24 MAY 1763

... I went and waited upon Mr Samuel Johnson, who received me very courteously. He has chambers in the Inner Temple, where he lives in literary state, very solemn and very slovenly. He had some people with him, and when they left him, I rose too. But he cried, 'No, don't go away.' 'Sir,' said I, 'I am afraid that I intrude upon you. It is benevolent to allow me to sit and hear you.' He was pleased with this compliment, which I sincerely paid him, and he said he was obliged to any man who visited him. I was proud to sit in such company.

He said that mankind had a great aversion at intellectual employment. But even supposing knowledge easily attained, most people were equally content to be ignorant.

'Moral good depends on the motive from which we act. If I fling half a crown at a beggar with intention to break his head, and he picks it up and buys victuals with it, the physical effect is good; but with respect to me, the action is very wrong. In the same way, religious services, if not performed with an intention to please GOD, avail us nothing. As our Saviour saith of people who perform them from other motives, "Verily they have their own reward." ...

'The Christian religion has very strong evidences. No doubt it appears in some degree strange to reason. But in history we have many undoubted facts against which *a priori* in the way of ratiocination we have more arguments than we have for them; but then testimony has great weight, and casts the balance. I would recommend Grotius, Dr Pearse on Miracles, and Dr Clarke.'

I listened to this great oracle with much satisfaction; and as I feel myself uneasy by reason of scepticism, I had great comfort in hearing so able an advocate for Revelation; and I resolved to read the books he mentioned. He pressed me to stay a second time, which I did. He said he went out at four in the afternoon and did not come home, for most part, till two in the morning. I asked him if he did not think it wrong to live so and not make use of his talents. He said it was a bad habit.

He said Garrick was the first man in the world for sprightly conversation.

I begged that he would favour me with his company at my lodgings some evening. He promised he would. I then left him, and he shook me cordially by the hand. Upon my word, I am very fortunate. I shall cultivate this acquaintance.

14 JULY 1763

I told Mr Johnson what a strange mortal Macpherson was, or affected to be; and how he railed at all established systems. 'So would he tumble in a hog-sty,' said Johnson, 'as long as you look at him and cry to him to come out. But let him alone, never mind him, and he'll soon give it over.'

Mr Johnson and I had formerly drank the health of Sir David Dalrymple, whom he gave as his toast. I this night read part of a letter from Sir David, since my informing him of it, in which he bid me assure him of the veneration which he entertained for the author of *The Rambler* and of *Rasselas*. He paid Mr Johnson some very pretty compliments, which pleased him much.

Mr Johnson considered reading what you have an inclination for as eating what you have an appetite for. But then I consider that a stomach which has fasted very long will have no desire for any kind of food. The longer it wants food, it will be the worse; and therefore we must not wait till an appetite returns, but immediately throw in some wholesome sustenance. The stomach may then recover its tone, and its natural taste may spring up and grow vigorous, and then let it be indulged. So it is with the mind, when by a long course of dissipation it is quite relaxed. We must recover it gradually, and then we can better judge what course of study to pursue. This must now be my endeavour. And when I go to Utrecht, I hope to make proficiency in useful literature.

When we went into the Mitre tonight, Mr Johnson said, 'We will now drink two bottles of port.' When one was drank, he called for another pint; and when we had got to the bottom of that, and I was distributing it equally, 'Come,' said he, 'you need not measure it so exactly.' 'Sir,' said I, 'it is done.' 'Well, Sir,' said he, 'are you not satisfied? or would you choose another?' 'Would you, Sir?' said I. 'Yes,' said he, 'I think I would. I think three bottles would seem to be the quantity for us.' Accordingly we made them out.

I take pleasure in recording every little circumstance about so great a man as Mr Johnson. This little specimen of social pleasantry will serve me to tell as an agreeable story to literary people. He took me cordially by the hand and said, 'My dear Boswell! I do love you very much.' – I *will* be vain, there's enough.

DAVID HUME (1711–76)
by James Boswell (1740–95)

AN ACCOUNT OF MY LAST INTERVIEW WITH DAVID HUME, ESQ.
(PARTLY RECORDED IN MY JOURNAL, PARTLY ENLARGED FROM MY
MEMORY, 3 MARCH 1777)

On Sunday forenoon the 7 of July 1776, being too late for church, I went to Mr David Hume, who was returned from London and Bath, just a-dying. I found him alone, in a reclining posture in his drawing-room. He was lean, ghastly and quite of an earthy appearance. He was dressed in a suit of grey cloth with white metal buttons, and a kind of scratch wig. He was quite different from the plump figure which he used to present. He had before him Dr Campbell's *Philosophy of Rhetoric*. He seemed to be placid and even cheerful. He said he was just approaching to his end. I think these were his words. I know not how I contrived to get the subject of immortality introduced. He said he never had entertained any belief in religion since he began to read Locke and Clarke. I asked him if he was not religious when he was young. He said he was, and he used to read *The Whole Duty of Man*; that he made an abstract from the catalogue of vices at the end of it, and examined himself by this, leaving out murder and theft and such vices as he had no chance of committing, having no inclination to commit them. This, he said, was strange work; for instance, to try if, notwithstanding his excelling his schoolfellows, he had no pride or vanity. He smiled in ridicule of this as absurd and contrary to fixed principles and necessary consequences, not adverting that religious discipline does not mean to extinguish, but to moderate, the passions; and certainly an excess of pride or vanity is dangerous and generally hurtful. He then said flatly that the morality of every religion was bad, and, I really thought, was not jocular when he said that when he heard a man was religious, he concluded he was a rascal, though he had known some instances of very good men being religious. This was just an extravagant reverse of the common remark as to infidels.

I had a strong curiosity to be satisfied if he persisted in disbelieving a future state even when he had death before his eyes. I was persuaded from what he now said, and from his manner of saying it, that he did persist. I asked him if it was not possible that there might be a future state. He answered it was possible that a piece of coal put upon the fire would not burn; and he added that it was a most unreasonable fancy that we should exist for ever. That immortality, if it were all, must be general; that a great proportion of the human race has hardly any intellectual qualities; that a great proportion dies in infancy before being possessed of reason; yet all these must be immortal; that a porter who gets drunk by ten o'clock with gin must be immortal; that the trash of every age must be preserved, and that new universes must be created to contain such infinite numbers. This appeared to me an unphilosophical objection, and I said, 'Mr Hume, you know spirit does not take up space.'. . .

I asked him if the thought of annihilation never gave him any uneasiness. He said not the least; no more than the thought that he had not been, as Lucretius observes. 'Well,' said I, 'Mr Hume, I hope to triumph over you when I meet you in a future state; and remember you are not to pretend that you was joking with all this infidelity.' 'No, no,' said he. 'But I shall have been so long there before you come that it will be nothing new.' In this style of good humour and levity did I conduct the conversation. Perhaps it was wrong on so awful a subject. But as nobody was present, I thought it could have no bad effect. I however felt a degree of horror, mixed with a sort of wild, strange, hurrying recollection of my excellent mother's pious instructions, of Dr Johnson's noble lessons, and of my religious sentiments and affections during the course of my life. I was like a man in sudden danger eagerly seeking his defensive arms; and I could not but be assailed by momentary doubts while I had actually before me a man of such strong abilities and extensive enquiry dying in the persuasion of being annihilated. But I maintained my faith. I told him that I believed the Christian religion as I believed history. Said he: 'You do not believe it as you believe the Revolution.' 'Yes,' said I; 'but the difference is that I am not so much interested in the truth of the Revolution; otherwise I should have anxious doubts concerning it. A man who is in love has doubts of the affection of his mistress, without cause.' I mentioned Soame Jenyn's little book in defence of Christianity, which was just published but which I had not yet read. Mr Hume said, 'I am told there is nothing of his usual spirit in it.'

He had once said to me, on a forenoon while the sun was shining bright, that he did not wish to be immortal. This was a most wonderful thought. The reason he gave was that he was very well in this state of being, and that the chances were very much against his being so well in another state; and he would rather not be more than be worse. I answered that it was reasonable to hope he would be better; that there would be a progressive improvement. I tried him at this interview with that topic, saying that a future state was surely a pleasing idea. He said no, for that it was always seen through a gloomy medium; there was always a Phlegethon or a hell. 'But', said I, 'would it not be agreeable to have hopes of seeing our friends again?' and I mentioned three men lately deceased, for whom I knew he had a high value: Ambassador Keith, Lord Alemoor and Baron Mure. He owned it would be agreeable, but added that none of them entertained such a notion. I believe he said, such a foolish, or such an absurd, notion; for he was indecently and impolitely positive in incredulity. 'Yes,' said I, 'Lord Alemoor was a believer.' David acknowledged that *he* had *some* belief. I somehow or other brought Dr Johnson's name into our conversation. I had often heard him speak of that great man in a very illiberal manner. He said upon this occasion, 'Johnson should be pleased with my *History*.' Nettled by Hume's frequent attacks upon my revered friend in former conversations, I told him now that Dr Johnson did not allow him much credit; for he said, 'Sir, the fellow is a Tory by chance.' I am sorry that I mentioned this at such a time. I was off my guard; for the truth is that Mr Hume's pleasantry was such that there was no solemnity in the scene; and death for the time did not seem dismal. It surprised me to find him talking of different matters with a tranquillity of mind and a clearness of head which few men possess at any time. Two particulars I remember: Smith's *Wealth of Nations*, which he commended much, and Monboddo's *Origin of Language*, which he treated contemptuously. I said, 'If I were you, I should regret annihilation. Had I written such an admirable history, I should be sorry to leave it.'

He said, 'I shall leave that history, of which you are pleased to speak so favourably, as perfect as I can.' He said, too, that all the great abilities with which men had ever been endowed were relative to this world. He said he became a greater friend to the Stuart family as he advanced in studying for his history; and he hoped he had vindicated the two first of them so effectually that they would never again be attacked.

Mr Lauder, his surgeon, came in for a little, and Mr Mure, the Baron's son, for another small interval. He was, as far as I could judge, quite easy with both. He said he had no pain, but was wasting away. I left him with impressions which disturbed me for some time.

JEAN-JACQUES ROUSSEAU (1712–1778)
by James Boswell (1740–1795)

MONDAY, 3 DECEMBER 1764

To prepare myself for the great interview, I walked out alone. I strolled pensive by the side of the River Reuse in a beautiful wild valley surrounded by immense mountains, some covered with frowning rocks, others with clustering pines, and others with glittering snow. The fresh, healthful air and the romantic prospect around me gave me a vigorous and solemn tone. I recalled all my former ideas of J. J. Rousseau, the admiration with which he is regarded over all Europe, his *Héloïse*, his *Emile*: in short, a crowd of great thoughts. This half hour was one of the most remarkable that I ever passed.

I returned to my inn, and the maid delivered to me a card with the following answer from Monsieur Rousseau: 'I am ill, in pain, really in no state to receive visits. Yet I cannot deprive myself of Mr Boswell's company, provided that out of consideration for the state of my health, he is willing to make it short.'

My sensibility dreaded the word 'short'. But I took courage, and went immediately. I found at the street door Mademoiselle Le Vasseur waiting for me. She was a little, lively, neat French girl and did not increase my fear. She conducted me up a darkish stair, then opened a door. I expected, 'Now I shall see him' – but it was not so. I entered a room which serves for vestibule and for kitchen. My fancy formed many, many a portrait of the wild philosopher. At length his door opened and I beheld him, a genteel black man in the dress of an Armenian. I entered saying, 'Many,

many thanks.' After the first looks and bows were over, he said, 'Will you be seated? Or would you rather take a turn with me in the room?' I chose the last, and happy I was to escape being formally placed upon a chair. I asked him how he was. 'Very ill. But I have given up doctors.' 'Yes, yes; you have no love for them.' As it is impossible for me to relate exactly our conversation, I shall not endeavour at order, but give sentences as I recollect them.

BOSWELL. 'The thought of your books, Sir, is a great source of pleasure to you?' ROUSSEAU. 'I am fond of them; but when I think of my books, so many misfortunes which they have brought upon me are revived in my memory that really I cannot answer you. And yet my books have saved my life.' He spoke of the Parlement of Paris: 'If any company could be covered with disgrace, that would be. I could plunge them into deep disgrace simply by printing their edict against me on one side, and the law of nations and equity on the side opposite. But I have reasons against doing so at present.' BOSWELL. 'We shall have it one day, perhaps?' ROUSSEAU. 'Perhaps.' I was dressed in a coat and waistcoat, scarlet with gold lace, buck-skin breeches and boots. Above all I wore a greatcoat of green camlet lined with fox-skin fur, with the collar and cuffs of the same fur. I held under my arm a hat with a solid gold lace, at least with the air of being solid. I had it last winter at The Hague. I had a free air and spoke well, and when Monsieur Rousseau said what touched me more than ordinary, I seized his hand, I thumped him on the shoulder. I was without restraint. When I found that I really pleased him, I said, 'Are you aware, Sir, that I am recommended to you by a man you hold in high regard?'

ROUSSEAU. 'Ah! My Lord Marischal?' BOSWELL. 'Yes, Sir; my Lord furnished me with a note to introduce me to you.' ROUSSEAU. 'And you were unwilling to take advantage of it?' BOSWELL. 'Nay, Sir; I wished to have a proof of my own merits.' ROUSSEAU. 'Sir, there would have been no kind of merit in gaining access to me by a note of Lord Marischal's. Whatever he sends will always find a welcome from me. He is my protector, my father; I would venture to say, my friend.' One circumstance embarrassed me a little: I had forgotten to bring with me from Neuchâtel my Lord's billet. But a generous consciousness of innocence and honesty gives a freedom which cannot be counterfeited. I told Monsieur Rousseau, 'To speak truly, I have forgotten to bring his letter with me; but you accept my word for it?'

ROUSSEAU. 'Why, certainly. Numbers of people have shown themselves ready to serve me in their own fashion; my Lord Marischal has served me in mine. He is the only man on earth to whom I owe an obligation . . .

'Sir, you don't see before you the bear you have heard tell of. Sir, I have no liking for the world. I live here in a world of fantasies, and I cannot tolerate the world as it is.' BOSWELL. 'But when you come across fantastical men, are they not to your liking?' ROUSSEAU. 'Why, Sir, they have not the same fantasies as myself. – Sir, your country is formed for liberty. I like your habits. You and I feel at liberty to stroll here together without talking. That is more than two Frenchmen can do. Mankind disgusts me. And my housekeeper tells me that I am in far better humour on the days when I have been alone than on those when I have been in company.' BOSWELL. 'There has been a great deal written against you, Sir.' ROUSSEAU. 'They have not understood me. As for Monsieur Vernet at Geneva, he is an Arch-Jesuit, that is all I can say of him.'

BOSWELL. 'Tell me, Sir, do you not find that I answer to the description I gave you of myself?

ROUSSEAU. 'Sir, it is too early for me to judge. But all appearances are in your favour.' BOSWELL. 'I fear I have stayed too long. I shall take the honour of returning tomorrow.' ROUSSEAU. 'Oh, as to that, I can't tell.' BOSWELL. 'Sir, I shall stay quietly here in the village. If you are able to see me, I shall be enchanted; if not, I shall make no complaint.' ROUSSEAU. 'My Lord Marischal has a perfect understanding of man's feelings, in solitude no less than in society. I am overwhelmed with visits from idle people.' BOSWELL. 'And how do they spend their time?' ROUSSEAU. 'In paying compliments. Also I get a prodigious quantity of letters. And the writer of each of them believes that he is the only one.' BOSWELL. 'You must be greatly surprised, Sir, that a man who has not the honour of your acquaintance should take the liberty of writing to you?' ROUSSEAU. 'No. I am not at all surprised. For I got a letter like it yesterday, and one the day before yesterday, and others many times before that.' BOSWELL. 'Sir, your very humble servant. – What, you are coming further?' ROUSSEAU. 'I am not coming with you. I am going for a walk in the passage. Goodbye.'

I had great satisfaction after finding that I could support the character which I had given of myself, after finding that I should most certainly be regarded by the illustrious Rousseau. I had a strange kind of feeling after having at last seen the author of whom I had thought so much. I sat down immediately and wrote to Dempster. I sat up too late.

SAMUEL ROGERS (1763–1855)
by George Gordon, Lord Byron (1788–1824)

LETTER TO DOUGLAS KINNAIRD, 26 APRIL 1821

Why should Rogers take the 'Venerable' ill? – He was sixty three years eleven months and fourteen days old when I first knew him ten years ago – come next November. – I meant but a compliment – as for his age I have seen the certificate from Bow Church dated '1747 – October 10th – Baptized Samuel Son of Peter Rogers Scrivener Furnival's Inn'. – He and Dryden – and Chaucer are the oldest upon record who have written so well at that advanced period. His age is a credit to him.

LETTER TO DOUGLAS KINNAIRD, 21 MAY 1821

You are wrong about Rogers – it was not an 'attack' – nor was it 'wanton'. – Would you have me call him *'young?'* – I alluded to 'Human Life' because Bowles had called it a 'more beautiful poem than the Pleasures of Memory' – which is false & foolish. – Now you shall be told something about the said Sam. – Moore told me that Sam hesitated for a *year* or *two* whether he should or should *not* insert a line or two in his 'Human Life' about me – because of the *public run* being then against me on account of Miss Milbanke. – The shabby rascal! – first to think that his petty praise imported a doit to me or to others – and 2dly. not to dare to praise – because a man was persecuted. – It is the moment a brave – or an honest man would say what he *felt –& more readily* than at another time. – You may also say this publicly. – I care not a curse for any or all – or each of them. – As Coriolanus says

> On fair ground –
> I could beat forty of them.

As to Rogers you *know* his amiable way of abusing all the world. – If he wishes for *war* – let him – he shall have it. –
yrs. ever & truly
P.S. – Please to recollect that I never begin *without provocation*. – That once given – they are to be paid off occasionally. – To do as you have *been done by* – is the only way with those Scoundrels the race of Authors and in general – they do not come within the Christian dispensation. –

Nothing can equal my contempt of your *real mere unleavened* author. I never lived with such but with men of the world – and such writers as were like other people. – Your mere writing is nothing but a knack – out of their trade – they are not even clever. –

LETTER TO JOHN MURRAY, 20 SEPTEMBER 1821

I hope that we shall not have Mr Rogers here – there is a mean minuteness in his mind & tittle-tattle that I dislike – ever since I *found him out* (which was but slowly) besides he is not a good man – why don't he go to bed? – what does he do travelling?

MADAME DE STAËL (1766–1817)
by François-René de Chateaubriand (1768–1848)

Returning to Paris after the Hundred Days, the author of *Delphine* had fallen ill on the way; I had seen her since at her house and at Mme la Duchesse de Duras's. As her condition gradually worsened, she was obliged to keep to her bed. One morning I went to see her in the Rue Royale. The shutters of her windows were two-thirds closed; the bed, which had been pushed up towards the wall at the far end of the room, left only a narrow space on the left; the curtains, drawn back on their rods, formed two columns at the head of the bed. Mme de Staël was propped up by pillows in a half-sitting position. I approached and, once my eyes had grown accustomed to the darkness, I was able to make out the patient's features. A feverish flush coloured her cheeks. Her splendid eyes met mine in the shadows, and she said to me, in English:

'Good morning, my dear Francis. I am ailing, but that does not prevent me from loving you.'

She held out her hand, which I pressed and kissed. As I raised my head I saw on the other side of the bed, in the space by the wall, some thing white and thin rising up: it was M. de Rocca [her younger husband], haggard and hollow-cheeked, with bleary eyes and a sallow complexion; he was dying; I had never seen him before and I never saw him again. He did not open his mouth; he bowed as he passed me; the sound of his footsteps was inaudible; he went away like a shadow. Stopping for a moment at the door, he turned round towards the bed to wave goodbye to Mme de Staël. Those two ghosts looking at one another in silence, the one erect and pale, the other seated and flushed with blood that was ready to flow down again and congeal at the heart, made one shudder.

JAMES HOGG (1770–1835)
by George Gordon, Lord Byron (1788–1824)

LETTER TO THOMAS MOORE, 3 AUGUST 1814

... Oh! I have had the most amusing letter from Hogg, the Ettrick minstrel and shepherd. He wants me to recommend him to Murray, and, speaking of his present bookseller, whose 'bills' are never 'lifted,' he adds, *totidem verbis*, 'God d–n him and them both.' The said Hogg is a strange being, but of great, though uncouth, powers. I think very highly of him, as a poet; but he, and half of these Scotch and Lake troubadours, are spoilt by living in little circles and petty societies. London and the world is the only place to take the conceit out of a man – in the milling phrase. [Walter] Scott, he says, is gone to the Orkneys in a gale of wind; – during which wind, he affirms, the said Scott, 'he is sure, is not at his ease, – to say the best of it.' Lord, Lord, if these home-keeping minstrels had crossed your Atlantic or my Mediterranean, and tasted a little open boating in a white squall – or a gale in 'the Gut' – or the 'Bay of Biscay,' with no gale at all – how it would enliven and introduce them to a few of the sensations! – to say nothing of an illicit amour or two upon shore, in the way of essay upon the Passions, beginning with simple adultery, and compounding it as they went along.

WILLIAM WORDSWORTH (1770–1850)
by Dorothy Wordsworth (1771–1855)

Thursday 29th [*April 1802*]. A beautiful morning. The sun shone & all was pleasant. We sent off our parcel to Coleridge by the wagon. Mr Simpson heard the Cuckoo today. Before we went out, after I had written down the Tinker, which William finished this morning, Luff called. He was very lame, limped into the kitchen – he came on a little Pony. We then went to Johns Grove, sat a while at first. Afterwards William lay, &

I lay in the trench under the fence – he with his eyes shut & listening to the waterfalls & the Birds. There was no one waterfall above another – it was a sound of waters in the air – the voice of the air. William heard me breathing & rustling now & then but we both lay still, & unseen by one another – he thought that it would be as sweet thus to lie so in the grave, to hear the peaceful sounds of the earth & just to know that ones dear friends were near. The Lake was still there was a Boat out. Silver how reflected with delicate purple & yellowish hues as I have seen Spar – Lambs on the island & Running races together in the round field near us. The copses greenish, hawthorn green. – Came home to dinner then went to Mr Simpson. We rested a long time under a wall. Sheep & lambs were in the field – cottages smoking. As I lay down on the grass, I observed the glittering silver line on the ridges of the Backs of the sheep, owing to their situation respecting the Sun – which made them look beautiful but with something of a strangeness, like animals of another kind – as if belonging to a more splendid world. Met old Mr S at the door – Mrs S poorly – I got mullens & pansies – I was sick & ill & obliged to come home soon. We went to bed immediately – I slept up stairs. The air coldish where it was felt somewhat frosty.

In 1829 Wordsworth had urged Coleridge to destroy all his letters to him since 'at this day such abominable use is made of every scrap of private anecdote, or transient or permanent sentiment, of every one whose name has ever been at all known by the public.' Ten years later, his worst fears were realised when Thomas De Quincey published an intimate account of the time he had spent in the Wordsworth household in the early years of the century. (See also the entry on Dorothy Wordsworth.)

William Wordsworth
by Thomas De Quincey (1785–1859)

I was ushered up a little flight of stairs, fourteen in all, to a little dining-room, or whatever the reader chooses to call it. Wordsworth himself has described the fire-place of this as his

Half-kitchen and half-parlour fire.

It was not fully seven feet six inches high, and, in other respects, pretty nearly of the same dimensions as the rustic hall below. There was, however, in a small recess, a library of perhaps 300 volumes, which seemed to consecrate the room as the poet's study and composing room; and so occasionally it was. But far oftener he both studied, as I found, and composed on the high road. I had not been two minutes at the fireside, when in came Wordsworth, returning from his friendly attentions to the travellers below, who, it seemed, had been over-persuaded by hospitable solicitations to stay for this night in Grasmere, and to make out the remaining thirteen miles of their road to Keswick on the following day. Wordsworth entered. And 'what-like' – to use a Westmoreland, as well as a Scottish expression – 'what-like' was Wordsworth? A reviewer in *Tait's Magazine*, in noticing some recent collection of literary portraits, gives it as his opinion that Charles Lamb's head was finest amongst them. This remark may have been justified by the engraved portraits; but, certainly, the critic would have cancelled it had he seen the original heads – at least, had he seen them in youth or in maturity; for Charles Lamb bore age with less disadvantage to the intellectual expression of his appearance than Wordsworth, in whom a sanguine or rather coarse complexion, (or rather not complexion, properly speaking, so much as texture of flesh,) has, of late years, usurped upon the original bronze-tint and finer skin; and this change of hue and change in the quality of skin, has been made fourfold more conspicuous, and more unfavourable in its general effect, by the harsh contrast of grizzled hair which has displaced the original brown. No change in personal appearance ever can have been so unfortunate; for, generally speaking, whatever other disadvantages old age may bring along with it, one effect, at least, in male subjects, has a compensating tendency – that it removes any tone of vigour too harsh, and mitigates the expression of power too unsubdued. But, in Wordsworth, the effect of the change has been to substitute an air of animal vigour, or, at least, hardiness, as if derived from constant exposure to the wind and weather, for the fine, sombre complexion which he once had, resembling that of a Venetian senator or a Spanish monk.

Here, however, in describing the personal appearance of Wordsworth, I go back, of course, to the point of time at which I am speaking. To begin with his figure:– Wordsworth was, upon the whole, not a well-made man. His legs were pointedly condemned by all the female connoisseurs in legs that ever I heard lecture upon that topic; not that they were bad in any way which *would* force itself upon your notice – there was no absolute deformity about them; and undoubtedly they had been serviceable legs beyond the average standard of human requisition; for I calculate, upon good data, that with these identical legs Wordsworth must have traversed a distance of 175 to 180,000 English miles – mode of exertion which, to him, stood in the stead of wine, spirits, and all other stimulants whatsoever to the animal spirits; to which he has been indebted for a life of unclouded happiness, and we for much of what is most excellent in his writings. But, useful as they have proved themselves, the Words-worthian legs were certainly not ornamental; and it was really a pity, as I agreed with a lady in thinking, that he had not another pair for evening dress parties – when no boots lend their friendly aid to mask our imperfec-tions from the eyes of female rigorists – the *elegantes formarum spectatrices*. A sculptor would certainly have disapproved of their contour. But the worst part of Wordsworth's person was the bust: there was a narrowness and a droop about the shoulders which became striking, and had an effect of meanness when brought into close juxtaposition with a figure of a most statuesque order . . .

I have gone into so large and circumstantial a review of my recollections in a matter that would have been trifling and tedious in excess, had their recollection related to a less important man; but, with a certain knowledge that the least of them will possess a lasting and a growing interest in connexion with William Wordsworth – a man who is not simply destined to be had in everlasting remembrance by every generation of men, but (which is a modification of the kind worth any multiplication of the degree) to be had in that *sort* of remembrance which has for its shrine the heart of man – that world of fear and grief, of love and trembling hope, which constitutes the essential man; in *that* sort of remembrance, and not in such a remembrance as we grant to the ideas of a great philosopher, a great mathematician, or a great reformer. How different, how peculiar, is the interest which attends the great poets who have made themselves necessary to the human heart; who have first brought into consciousness, and next have clothed in words, those grand catholic feelings that belong to the grand catholic situations of life, through all its stages; who have clothed them in such words that human wit despairs of bettering them! How remote is that burning interest which settles upon men's living memories in our daily thoughts, from that which follows, in a disjoined and limping way, the mere nominal memories of those who have given a direction and movement to the currents of human thought, and who, by some leading impulse, have even quickened into life specu-lations appointed to terminate in positive revolutions of human power over physical agents! Mighty were the powers, solemn and serene is the memory, of Archimedes; and Apollonius shines like 'the starry Galileo,' in the firmament of human genius; yet how frosty is the feeling associated with these names by comparison with that which, upon every sunny brae, by the side of every ancient forest, even in the farthest depths of Canada, many a young innocent girl, perhaps, at this very moment – looking now with fear to the dark recesses of the infinite forest, and now with love to the pages of the infinite poet, until the fear is absorbed and forgotten in the love – cherishes in her heart for the name and person of Shakespeare! The one is abstraction, and a shadow recurring only by distinct efforts of recollection, and even thus to none but the enlightened and the learned; the other is a household image, rising amongst household remembrances, never separated from the spirit of delight, and hallowed by a human love! Such a place in the affections of the young and the ingenuous, no less than of the old and philosophic, who happen to have a depth of feeling, will Wordsworth occupy in every clime and in every land; for the language in which he writes, thanks be to Providence, which as beneficently opened the widest channels for the purest and most elevating literature, is now ineradicably planted in all quarters of the earth; the echoes under every latitude of every longitude now reverberates English words; and all things seem tending to this result – that the English and the Spanish languages will finally share the earth between them. Wordsworth is peculiarly the poet for the solitary and the meditative; and, throughout the countless myriads of future America and future Australia, no less than Polynesia and Southern Africa, there will be situations without end fitted by their loneliness to favour his influence for centuries to come, by the end of which period it may be anticipated that education (of a more enlightened quality and more systematic than yet prevails) may have wrought such changes on the human species, as will uphold the growth of all philosophy, and, therefore, of all poetry which has its foundations laid in the heart of man. Commensurate with the interest in the poetry will be a secondary interest in the poet – in his personal appearance, and his habits of life, *so far as they can be supposed at all dependent upon his intellectual characteristics*; for, with respect to differences that are purely casual, and which illustrate no principle of higher origin than accidents of education or chance position, it is a gossiping taste only that could seek for such information, and a gossiping taste that would choose to consult it. Meantime, it is under no such gossiping taste that volumes have been written upon the mere portraits and upon the possible portraits of Shakespeare;

and how invaluable should we all feel any record to be, which should raise the curtain upon Shakespeare's daily life – his habits, personal and social, his intellectual tastes, and his opinions on contemporary men, books, events, or national prospects! I cannot, therefore, think it necessary to apologize for the most circumstantial notices past or to come of Wordsworth's person and habits of life . . .

One night, as often happened, during the Peninsular war, [Wordsworth] and I had walked up Dunmail Raise, from Grasmere, about midnight, in order to meet the carrier who brought the London newspapers, by a circuitous course from Keswick. The case was this:– Coleridge, for many years, received a copy of the *Courier*, as a mark of esteem, and in acknowledgment of his many contributions to it, from one of the proprietors, Mr Daniel Stewart. This went up in any case, let Coleridge be where be might, to Mrs Coleridge; for a single day, it stayed at Keswick, for the use of Southey; and, on the next, it came on to Wordsworth, by the slow conveyance of a carrier, plying with a long train of carts between Whitehaven and Kendal. Many a time the force of storms or floods would compel the carrier to stop on his route, five miles short of Grasmere, at Wythburn, or even eight miles short, at Legberthwaite. But, as there was always hope until one or two o'clock in the morning, often and often it would happen that, in the deadly impatience for earlier intelligence, Wordsworth and I would walk off to meet him about midnight, to a distance of three or four miles. Upon one of these occasions, when some great crisis in Spain was daily apprehended, we had waited for an hour or more, sitting upon one of the many huge blocks of stone which lie scattered over that narrow field of battle on the desolate frontier of Cumberland and Westmoreland, where King Dun Mail, with all his peerage, fell, more than a thousand years ago. The time had arrived, at length, that all hope for that night had left us: no sound came up through the winding valleys that stretched to the north; and the few cottage lights, gleaming at wide distances, from recesses amidst the rocky hills, had long been extinct. At intervals, Wordsworth had stretched himself at length on the high road, applying his ear to the ground, so as to catch any sound of wheels that might be groaning along at a distance. Once, when he was slowly rising from this effort, his eye caught a bright star that was glittering between the brow of Seat Sandal and of the mighty Hellvellyn. He gazed upon it for a minute or so; and then, upon turning away to descend into Grasmere, he made the following explanation:– 'I have remarked, from my earliest days, that, if under any circumstances, the attention is energetically

37

braced up to an act of steady observation, or of steady expectation, then, if this intense condition of vigilance should suddenly relax, at that moment any beautiful, any impressive visual object, or collection of objects, falling upon the eye, is carried to the heart with a power not known under other circumstances. Just now, my ear was placed upon the stretch, in order to catch any sound of wheels that might come down upon the lake of Wythburn from the Keswick road; at the very instant when I raised my head from the ground, in final abandonment of hope for this night, at the very instant when the organs of attention were all at once relaxing from their tension, the bright star hanging in the air above those outlines of massy blackness suddenly fell upon my eye, and penetrated my capacity of apprehension with a pathos and a sense of the infinite, that would not have arrested me under other circumstances.'

DOROTHY WORDSWORTH (1771–1855)
by Thomas De Quincey (1785–1859)

'Her face was of Egyptian brown'; rarely, in a woman of English birth, had I seen a more determinate gipsy tan. Her eyes were not soft, as Mrs Wordsworth's, nor were they fierce or bold; but they were wild and startling, and hurried in their motion. Her manner was warm and even ardent; her sensibility seemed constitutionally deep; and some subtle fire of impassioned intellect apparently burned within her, which, being alternately pushed forward into a conspicuous expression by the irrepressible instincts of her temperament, and then immediately checked, in obedience to the decorum of her sex and age, and her maidenly condition, (for she rejected all offers of marriage, out of pure sisterly regard to her brother and his children,) gave to her demeanour and to her conversation, an air of embarrassment and even of self-conflict, that was sometimes distressing to witness. Even her very utterance and enunciation often, or rather generally, suffered in point of clearness and steadiness, from the agitation of her excessive organic sensibility, and, perhaps, from some morbid irritability of the nerves. At times, the self-counteraction and self-baffling of her feelings, caused her even to stammer, and so determinately to stammer that a stranger who should have seen her and quitted her in that state of feeling, would have certainly set her down for one plagued with that infirmity of speech, as distressingly as Charles Lamb himself. This was Miss Wordsworth, the only sister of the poet – his 'Dorothy;' who naturally owed so much to the life-long intercourse with her great brother, in his most solitary and sequestered years; but, on the other hand, to whom he has acknowledged obligations of the profoundest nature; and, in particular, this mighty one, through which, we also, the admirers and the worshippers through every age of this great poet, are become equally her debtors – that whereas the intellect of Wordsworth was, by its original tendencies, too stern – too austere – too much enamoured of an ascetic harsh-sublimity, she it was – the lady who paced by his side continually through sylvan and mountain tracks, in Highland glens, and in the dim recesses of German charcoal-burners – that first couched his eye to the sense of beauty – humanized him by the gentler charities, and engrafted, with her delicate female touch, those graces upon the ruder growths of his nature, which have since clothed the forest of his genius with a foliage corresponding in loveliness and beauty to the strength of its boughs and the massiness of its trunks. The greatest deductions from Miss Wordsworth's attractions, and from the exceeding interest which surrounded her in right of her character, her history, and the relation which she fulfilled towards her brother, was the glancing quickness of her motions, and other circumstances in her deportment, (such as her stooping attitude when walking,) which gave an ungraceful, and even an unsexual character to her appearance when out of doors. She did not cultivate the graces which preside over the person and its carriage. But, on the other hand, she was a person of very remarkable endowments intellectually; and, in addition to the other great services which she rendered to her brother, this I may mention, as greater than all the rest, and it was one which equally operated to the benefit of every casual companion in a walk – viz., the exceeding sympathy, always ready and always pro-found, by which she made all that one could tell her, all that one could describe, all that one could quote from a foreign author, reverberate as it were, *à plusieurs reprises*, to one's own feelings, by the manifest impression it made upon her. The pulses of light are not more quick or more inevitable in their flow and undulation, than were the answering and echoing movements of her sympathizing attention. Her knowledge of literature was irregular, and not systematically built up. She was content to be ignorant of many things; but what she knew and had really mastered, lay where it could not be disturbed – in the temple of her own most fervid heart.

SAMUEL TAYLOR COLERIDGE (1772–1834)
by William Hazlitt (1778–1830)

In January 1798, Coleridge came to the house of Hazlitt's father, a Dissenting Minister, in Wem, Shropshire. The young William Hazlitt had already been startled by the experience of hearing Coleridge preach: 'it seemed to me, who was then young, as if the sounds had echoed from the bottom of the human heart, and as if that prayer might have floated in solemn silence through the universe.'

On the Tuesday following, the half-inspired speaker came. I was called down into the room where he was, and went half-hoping, half-afraid. He received me very graciously, and I listened for a long time without uttering a word. I did not suffer in his opinion by my silence. 'For those two hours,' he afterwards was pleased to say, 'he was conversing with William Hazlitt's forehead!' His appearance was different from what I had anticipated from seeing him before. At a distance, and in the dim light of the chapel, there was to me a strange wildness in his aspect, a dusky obscurity, and I thought him pitted with the small-pox. His complexion was at that time clear, and even bright –

As are the children of yon azure sheen.

His forehead was broad and high, light as if built of ivory, with large projecting eyebrows, and his eyes rolling beneath them, like a sea with darkened lustre. 'A certain tender bloom his face o'erspread,' a purple tinge as we see it in the pale thoughtful complexions of the Spanish portrait-painters, Murillo and Velasquez. His mouth was gross, voluptuous, open, eloquent; his chin good-humoured and round; but his nose, the rudder of the face, the index of the will, was small, feeble, nothing – like what he has done. It might seem that the genius of his face as from a height surveyed and projected him (with sufficient capacity and huge aspiration) into the world unknown of thought and imagination, with nothing to support or guide his veering purpose, as if Columbus had launched his adventurous course for the New World in a scallop, without oars or compass. So, at least, I comment on it after the event. Coleridge, in his person, was rather above the common size inclining to the corpulent, or like Lord Hamlet, 'somewhat fat and pursy.' His hair (now, alas! grey) was then black and glossy as the raven's, and fell in smooth masses over his forehead. This long pendulous hair is peculiar to enthusiasts, to those whose minds tend heavenward; and is traditionally inseparable (though of a different colour) from the pictures of Christ. It ought to belong, as a character, to all who preach *Christ crucified*, and Coleridge was at that time one of those! . . .

When I came down to breakfast, I found that he had just received a letter from his friend, T. Wedgwood, making him an offer of 150*l.* a-year if he chose to waive his present pursuit, and devote himself entirely to the study of poetry and philosophy. Coleridge seemed to make up his mind to close with this proposal in the act of tying on one of his shoes. It threw an additional damp on his departure. It took the wayward enthusiast quite from us to cast him into Deva's winding vales, or by the shores of old romance. Instead of living at ten miles' distance, of being the pastor of a Dissenting congregation at Shrewsbury, he was henceforth to inhabit the Hill of Parnassus, to be a Shepherd on the Delectable Mountains. Alas! I knew not the way thither, and felt very little gratitude for Mr Wedgwood's bounty. I was presently relieved from this dilemma; for Mr Coleridge, asking for a pen and ink, and giving me the precious document, said that that was his address, *Mr Coleridge, Nether-Stowey, Somersetshire*; and that he should be glad to see me there in a few weeks' time, and, if I chose, would come halfway to meet me. I was not less surprised than the shepherdboy (this simile is to be found in *Cassandra*), when he sees a thunder-bolt fall close at his feet. I stammered out my acknowledgments and acceptance of this offer (I thought Mr Wedgwood's annuity a trifle to it) as well as I could; and this mighty business being settled, the poet-preacher took leave, and I accompanied him six miles on the road. It was a fine morning in the middle of winter, and he talked the whole way. The scholar in Chaucer is described as going

Sounding on his way.

So Coleridge went on his. In digressing, in dilating, in passing from subject to subject, he appeared to me to float in air, to slide on ice. He told me in confidence (going along) that he should have preached two sermons before he accepted the situation at Shrewsbury, one on Infant Baptism, the other on the Lord's Supper, shewing that he could not administer either, which would have effectually disqualified him for the object in view. I observed that he continually crossed me on the way by shifting from one side of the foot-path to the other. This struck me as an odd movement; but I did not at that time connect it with any instability of purpose or involuntary change of principle, as I have done since. He seemed unable to keep on in a straight line.

Samuel Taylor Coleridge
by Dorothy Wordsworth (1771–1855)

Wednesday 21st [April 1802]. William & I sauntered a little in the garden. Coleridge came to us & repeated the verses he wrote to Sara [*Dejection: An Ode*] – I was affected with them & was on the whole, not being well, in miserable spirits. The sunshine – the green fields & the fair sky made me sadder; even the little happy sporting lambs seemed but sorrowful to me. The pile wort spread out on the grass a thousand shining stars, the primroses were there & the remains of a few Daffodils. The well which we cleaned out last night is still but a little muddy pond, though full of water. I went to bed after dinner, could not sleep, went to bed again. Read Ferguson's life & a poem or two – fell asleep for 5 minutes & awoke better. We got tea. Sate comfortably in the Evening I went to bed early.

Samuel Taylor Coleridge
by John Keats (1795–1821)

LETTER TO GEORGE AND GEORGIANA KEATS, 14 FEBRUARY–3 MAY 1819

Last Sunday I took a Walk towards Highgate and in the lane that winds by the side of Lord Mansfield's park I met Mr Green our Demonstrator at Guy's in conversation with Coleridge – I joined them, after enquiring by a look whether it would be agreeable – I walked with him at his alderman-after dinner pace for near two miles I suppose. In those two Miles he broached a thousand things – let me see if I can give you a list – Nightingales, Poetry – on Poetical sensation – Metaphysics – Different genera and species of Dreams – Nightmare – a dream accompanied by a sense of touch – single and double touch – A dream related – First and second consciousness – the difference explained between will and Volition – so many metaphysicians from a want of smoking the second conscious-ness – Monsters – the Kraken – Mermaids – Southey believes in them –

Southeys belief too much diluted – A Ghost story – Good morning – I heard his voice as he came towards me – I heard it as he moved away – I had heard it all the interval – if it may be called so. He was civil enough to ask me to call on him at Highgate. Good Night!

Samuel Taylor Coleridge
by *Charles Lamb* (1775–1834)

LETTER TO THOMAS MANNING, 17 MARCH 1800

I am living in a continuous feast. Coleridge has been with me now for nigh three weeks, and the more I see of him in the quotidian undress and relaxation of his mind the more cause I see to love him, and believe him a *very good man*, and all those foolish impressions to the contrary fly off like morning slumbers. He is engaged in translations, which I hope will keep him this month to come. He is uncommonly kind and friendly to me. He ferrets me day and night to *do something*. He tends me, amidst all his own worrying and heart-oppressing occupations, as a gardener tends his young *tulip*. Marry come up! what a pretty similitude, and how like your humble servant! He has lugged me to the brink of engaging to a newspaper, and has suggested to me for a first plan the forgery of a supposed manuscript of Burton the anatomist of melancholy. I have even written the introductory letter; and, if I can pick up a few guineas this way, I feel they will be most *refreshing*, bread being so dear. If I go on with it, I will apprise you of it, as you may like to see my things! and the *tulip*, of all flowers, loves to be admired most.

Like Coleridge before him, Lamb was educated at Christ's Hospital school, London.

NOVEMBER 21, 1834

When I heard of the death of Coleridge, it was without grief. It seemed to me that he long had been on the confines of the next world – that he had a hunger for eternity. I grieved then that I could not grieve. But, since, I feel how great a part he was of me. His great and dear spirit haunts me. I cannot think a thought, I cannot make a criticism on men and books, without an ineffectual turning and reference to him. He was the proof and touchstone of all my cogitations. He was a Grecian (or in the first form) at Christ's Hospital, where I was Deputy-Grecian; and the same subordination and deference to him I have preserved through a lifelong acquaintance.

Great in his writings, he was the greatest in his conversation. In him was disproved that old maxim, that we should allow every one his share of talk. He would talk from morn to dewy eve, nor cease till far midnight; yet who ever would interrupt him? who would obstruct that continuous flow of converse, fetched from Helicon or Zion? He had the tact of making the unintelligible seem plain. Many who read the abstruser parts of his 'Friend' would complain that his words did not answer to his spoken wisdom. They were identical. But he had a tone in oral delivery which seemed to convey sense to those who were otherwise imperfect recipients. He was my fifty-years-old friend without a dissension. Never saw I his likeness, nor probably the world can see again. I seem to love the house he died at more passionately than when he lived. I love the faithful Gillmans more than while they exercised their virtues towards him living. What was his mansion is consecrated to me a chapel.

Samuel Taylor Coleridge
by Thomas De Quincey (1785–1859)

... some negotiation was pending between [Coleridge] and the Royal Institution, which ended in their engaging him to deliver a course of lectures on Poetry and the Fine Arts, during the ensuing winter. For this series (twelve or sixteen, I think,) he received a sum of 100 guineas. And considering the slightness of the pains which he bestowed upon them, he was well remunerated. I fear that they did not increase his reputation; for never did any man treat his audience with less respect, or his task with less careful attention. I was in London for part of the time, and can report the circumstances, having made a point of attending duly at the appointed hours. Coleridge was at that time living uncomfortably enough at the *Courier* Office, in the Strand. In such a situation, annoyed by the sound of feet passing his chamber-door continually to the printing rooms of this great establishment, and with no gentle ministrations of female hands to sustain his cheerfulness, naturally enough his spirits flagged; and he took more than ordinary doses of opium. I called upon him daily, and pitied his forlorn condition. There was no bell in the room, which for many months answered the double purpose of bed-room and sitting-room.

Consequently, I often saw him, picturesquely enveloped in night caps, surmounted by handkerchiefs, shouting from the attics of the *Courier* Office, down three or four flights of stairs, to a certain 'Mrs Brainbridge,' his sole attendant, whose dwelling was in the subterranean regions of the house. There did I often see the philosopher, with a most lugubrious face, invoking with all his might this uncouth name of 'Brainbridge,' each syllable of which he intonated with long-drawn emphasis, in order to overpower the hostile hubbub coming downwards from the press, and the roar from the Strand, which entered at all the front windows. 'Mrs Brainbridge! I say, Mrs Brainbridge!' was the perpetual cry, until I expected to hear the Strand, and distant Fleet Street, take up the echo of 'Brainbridge!' Thus unhappily situated, he sank more than ever under the dominion of opium; so that, at two o'clock, when he should have been in attendance at the Royal Institution, he was too often unable to rise from bed. Then came dismissals of audience after audience with pleas of illness; and on many of his lecture days, I have seen all Albemarle Street closed by a 'lock' of carriages filled with women of distinction, until the servants of the Institution or their own footmen advanced to the carriage doors with the intelligence that Mr Coleridge had been suddenly taken ill. This plea, which at first had been received with expressions of concern, began to rouse disgust. Some in anger, and some in real uncertainty whether it would not be trouble thrown away, ceased to attend. And we that were more constant, too often found reason to be disappointed with the quality of his lecture. His appearance was generally that of a person struggling with pain and overmastering illness. His lips were baked with feverish heat, and often black in colour; and in spite of the water which he continued drinking through the whole course of his lecture, he often seemed to labour under an almost paralytic inability to raise the upper jaw from the lower. In such a state it is clear that nothing could save the lecture itself from reflecting his own feebleness and exhaustion, except the advantage of having been precomposed in some happier mood. But that never happened: most unfortunately he relied upon his extempore ability to carry him through. Now, had he been in spirits, or had he gathered animation and kindled by his own motion, no written lecture could have been more effectual than one of his unpremeditated colloquial harangues. But either he was depressed originally below the point from which any re-ascent was possible, or else this re-action was intercepted by continual disgust, from looking back upon his own ill success; for assuredly he never once recovered that free and eloquent movement of thought which he could command at any time in a private company. The passages he read, moreover, in illustrating his doctrines, were generally unhappily chosen at haphazard, from the difficulty of finding, at a moment's summons, those passages which he had in his eye. Nor do I remember any that produced much effect, except two or three, which I myself put ready marked into his hands, among the Metrical Romances edited by Ritson.

Generally speaking, the selections were as injudicious and as inappropriate, as they were ill delivered; for amongst Coleridge's accomplishments good reading was not one; he had neither voice, nor management of voice. This defect is unfortunate in a public lecturer; for it is inconceivable how much weight and effectual pathos can be communicated by sonorous depth, and melodious cadences of the human voice, to sentiments the most trivial; nor, on the other hand, how the grandest are emasculated by a style of reading, which fails in distributing the lights and shadows of a musical intonation. However, this defect chiefly concerned the immediate impression; the most afflicting to a friend of Coleridge's was the entire absence of his own peculiar and majestic intellect; no heart, no soul, was in anything he said; no strength of feeling in recalling universal truths; no power of originality or compass of moral relations in his novelties –all was a poor faint reflection from jewels once scattered in the highway by himself, in the prodigality of his early opulence – a mendicant dependence on the alms dropped from his own overflowing treasury of happier times. Such a collapse, such a quenching of the eagle's talons, never was seen before. And as I returned from one of the most afflicting of these disappointments, I could not but repeat to myself parts of that divine chorus –

> Oh! dark, dark, dark!
> Amid the blaze of noon
> Irrecoverably dark, total eclipse, *&c. &c.*

The next opportunity I had of seeing Coleridge was at the lakes, in the winter of 1809, and up to the autumn of the following year. During this period, it was he that carried on the original publication of '*The Friend*'; and for much the greater part of the time I saw him daily. He lived as a visitor in the house occupied by Mr Wordsworth; this house was in Grasmere; and in another part of the same vale, at a distance of barely one mile, I myself had a cottage and a considerable library. Many of my books being German, Coleridge borrowed them in great numbers. Having a general licence from me to use them as he would, he was in the habit of accumulating them so largely at Allan Bank (the name of Mr Wordsworth's house,) that sometimes as many as five hundred were absent at once; which I mention, in order to notice a practice of Coleridge's, indicating his very scrupulous honour, in what regarded the rights of ownership. Literary people are not always so strict in respecting property of this description; and I know more than one celebrated man, who professes as a maxim, that he holds it no duty of honour to restore a borrowed book; not to speak of many less celebrated persons who, without openly professing such a principle, do however, in fact, exhibit a lax morality in such cases. The more honourable it was to poor Coleridge, who had means so trifling of buying books for himself – that, to prevent my flocks from mixing, and being confounded with the flocks already folded at Allan Bank, (his own and Wordsworth's,) or rather that they *might* mix without danger, he duly inscribed my name in the blank leaves of every volume; a fact which became rather painfully made known to me; for, as he had chosen to dub me *Esquire*, many years after this, it cost myself and a female friend some weeks of labour to hunt out these multitudinous memorials, and to erase this heraldic addition – which else had the appearance to a stranger of having been conferred by myself.

Later in the same book, De Quincey recalled seeing Wordsworth cut the pages of an edition of Burke's writings with a greasy butter knife. This reminded him once more of Coleridge's way with borrowed books:

Meantime, had Wordsworth done as Coleridge did, how cheerfully should I have acquiesced in his destruction (such as it was, in a pecuniary sense) of books, as the very highest obligation he could confer. Coleridge often spoiled a book; but, in the course of doing this, he enriched that book with so many and so valuable notes, tossing about him, with such lavish profusion, from such a cornucopia of discursive reading, and such a fusing intellect, commentaries so many-angled and so many-coloured that I have envied many a man whose luck has placed him in the way of such injuries; and that man must have been a churl (though, God knows! too often this churl has existed) who could have found in his heart to complain. But Wordsworth rarely, indeed, wrote on the margin of books; and, when he did, nothing could less illustrate his intellectual superiority. The comments were such as could have been made by anybody.

Charles Lamb also lent books to Coleridge:

47

Reader, if haply thou art blest with a moderate collection, be shy of showing it; if thy heart overfloweth to lend them, lend thy books; but let it be to such a one as S.T.C. – he will return them (generally anticipating the time appointed) with usury; enriched with annotations tripling their value. I have had experience. Many are these precious MSS. of his – in *matter* oftentimes, and almost in *quantity* not unfrequently, vying with the originals) in no very clerky hand – legible in my Daniel; in old Burton; in Sir Thomas Browne; and those abstruser cogitations of the Greville, now, alas! wandering in Pagan lands. I counsel thee, shut not thy heart, nor thy library against S.T.C.

ROBERT SOUTHEY (1774–1843)
by George Gordon, Lord Byron (1788–1824)

LETTER TO JOHN MURRAY, 24 NOVEMBER 1818

I understand the scoundrel said, on his return from Switzerland two years ago, that 'Shelley and I were in a league of Incest, etc., etc.' He is a burning liar! for the women to whom he alludes are not sisters – one being Godwin's daughter, by Mary Wollstonecraft, and the other daughter of the *present* (second) Mrs G, by a *former* husband; and in the next place, if they had even been so, there was no *promiscuous intercourse* whatever.

You may make what I say here as public as you please – more particularly to Southey, whom I look upon, and will say as publicly, to be a dirty, lying rascal; and will prove it in ink – or in his blood, if I did not believe him to be too much of a poet to risk it. If he had forty reviews at his back – as he has the *Quarterly* – I would have at him in his scribbling capacity, now that he has begun with me; but I will do nothing underhand. Tell him what I say from me, and everyone else you please.

You will see what I have said if the parcel arrives safe. I understand *Coleridge* went about repeating Southey's lie with pleasure. I can believe it, for I had done him what is called a favour. I can understand Coleridge's abusing me, but how or why *Southey* – whom I had never obliged in any sort of way, or done him the remotest service – should go about fibbing and calumniating is more than I readily comprehend.

Does he think to put me down with his *canting* – not being able to do so with his poetry? We will try the question. I have read his review of

Hunt, where he has attacked Shelley in an oblique and shabby manner. Does he know what that review has done? I will tell you. It has *sold* an edition of the *Revolt of Islam*, which, otherwise, nobody would have thought of reading, and few who read can understand – I for one.

Southey would have attacked me, too, there, if he durst, further than by hints about Hunt's friends in general; and some outcry about an 'Epicurean system,' carried on by men of the most opposite habits, tastes, and opinions in life and poetry (I believe), that ever had their names in the same volume – Moore, Byron, Shelley, Hazlitt, Haydon, Leigh Hunt, Lamb – what resemblance do ye find among all or any of these men? and how could any sort of system or plan be carried on, or attempted amongst them? However, let Mr Southey look to himself – since the wine is tapped, let him drink it.

CHARLES LAMB (1775–1834)
by Benjamin Robert Haydon (1786–1846)

In December Wordsworth was in town, and as Keats wished to know him I made up a party to dinner of Charles Lamb, Wordsworth, Keats and Monkhouse, his friend, and a very pleasant party we had.

I wrote to Lamb, and told him the address was '22 Lisson Grove, North, at Rossi's, half way up, right hand corner.' I received his characteristic reply.

My dear Haydon,
I will come with pleasure to 22 Lisson Grove, North, at Rossi's,
half way up, right hand side, if I can find it.
Yours,
C. LAMB.

20. Russel Court,
Covent Garden East,
half way up, next the corner,
left hand side.

On December 28th the immortal dinner came off in my painting-room, with Jerusalem towering up behind us as a background. Wordsworth was a fine cue, and we had a glorious set-to, – on Homer, Shakespeare, Milton and Virgil. Lamb got exceedingly merry and exquisitely witty; and his fun in the midst of Wordsworth's solemn intonations of oratory was like the sarcasm and wit of the fool in the intervals of Lear's passion. He made a speech and voted me absent, and made them drink my health. 'Now,' said Lamb, 'you old lake poet, you rascally poet, why do you call Voltaire dull?' We all defended Wordsworth, and affirmed there was a state of mind when Voltaire would be dull. 'Well,' said Lamb, 'here's Voltaire – the Messiah of the French nation, and a very proper one too.'

He then, in a strain of humour beyond description, abused me for putting Newton's head into my picture, – 'a fellow,' said he, 'who believed nothing unless it was as clear as the three sides of a triangle.' And then he and Keats agreed he had destroyed all the poetry of the rainbow by reducing it to the prismatic colours. It was impossible to resist him, and we all drank 'Newton's health, and confusion to mathematics'. It was delightful to see the good-humour of Wordsworth in giving in to all our frolics without affectation and laughing as heartily as the best of us.

By this time other friends joined, amongst them poor Ritchie who was going to penetrate by Fezzan to Timbuctoo. I introduced him to all as 'a gentleman going to Africa'. Lamb seemed to take no notice; but all of a sudden he roared out, 'Which is the gentleman we are going to lose?' We then drank the victim's health, in which Ritchie joined.

In the morning of this delightful day, a gentleman, a perfect stranger, had called on me. He said he knew my friends, had an enthusiasm for Wordsworth and begged I would procure him the happiness of an introduction. He told me he was a comptroller of stamps, and often had correspondence with the poet. I thought it a liberty; but still, as he seemed a gentleman, I told him he might come.

When we retired to tea we found the comptroller. In introducing him to Wordsworth I forgot to say who he was. After a little time the comptroller looked down, looked up and said to Wordsworth, 'Don't you think, sir, Milton was a great genius?' Keats looked at me, Wordsworth looked at the comptroller. Lamb who was dozing by the fire turned round and said, 'Pray, sir, did you say Milton was a great genius?' 'No sir; I asked Mr Wordsworth if he were not.' 'Oh,' said Lamb, 'then you are a silly fellow.' 'Charles! my dear Charles!' said Wordsworth; but Lamb, perfectly innocent of the confusion he had created, was off again by the fire.

After an awful pause the comptroller said, 'Don't you think Newton a great genius?' I could not stand it any longer. Keats put his head into my books. Ritchie squeezed in a laugh. Wordsworth seemed asking himself,

'Who is this?' Lamb got up, and taking a candle, said, 'Sir, will you allow me to look at your phrenological development?' He then turned his back on the poor man, and at every question of the comptroller he chaunted –

> Diddle diddle dumpling, my son John
> Went to bed with his breeches on.

The man in office, finding Wordsworth did not know who he was, said in a spasmodic and half-chuckling anticipation of assured victory, 'I have had the honour of some correspondence with you, Mr Wordsworth.' 'With me, sir?' said Wordsworth, 'not that I remember.' 'Don't you, sir? I am a comptroller of stamps.' There was a dead silence; – the comptroller evidently thinking that was enough. While we were waiting for Wordsworth's reply, Lamb sung out

> Hey diddle diddle,
> The cat and the fiddle.

'My dear Charles!' said Wordsworth, –

> Diddle diddle dumpling, my son John,

chanted Lamb, and then rising, exclaimed, 'Do let me have another look at that gentleman's organs.' Keats and I hurried Lamb into the painting-room, shut the door and gave way to inextinguishable laughter. Monkhouse followed and tried to get Lamb away. We went back but the comptroller was irreconcilable. We soothed and smiled and asked him to supper. He stayed though his dignity was sorely affected. However, being a good-natured man, we parted all in good-humour, and no ill effects followed.

All the while, until Monkhouse succeeded, we could hear Lamb struggling in the painting-room and calling at intervals, 'Who is that fellow? Allow me to see his organs once more.'

It was indeed an immortal evening. Wordsworth's fine intonation as he quoted Milton and Virgil, Keats' eager inspired look, Lamb's quaint sparkle of lambent humour, so speeded the stream of conversation, that in my life I never passed a more delightful time. All our fun was within bounds. Nor a word passed that an apostle might not have listened to. It was a night worthy of the Elizabethan age, and my solemn Jerusalem flashing up by the flame of the fire, with Christ hanging over us like a vision, all made up a picture which will long glow upon –

> that inward eye
> Which is the bliss of solitude.

Keats made Ritchie promise he would carry his Endymion to the great desert of Sahara and fling it in the midst.

Poor Ritchie went to Africa, and died, as Lamb foresaw, in 1819, Keats died in 1821, at Rome. C. Lamb is gone, joking to the last. Monkhouse is dead, and Wordsworth and I are the only two now living (1841) of that glorious party.

MATTHEW 'MONK' LEWIS (1775–1818)
by George Gordon, Lord Byron (1788–1824)

Lewis was a good man – a clever man but a bore – a damned bore – one may say. – My only revenge or consolation used to be setting him by the ears with some vivacious person who hated Bores especially – Mme. de Stael or Hobhouse for example. – But I liked Lewis – he was a Jewel of a Man had he been better set – I don't mean *personally*, but less *tiresome* – for he was tedious – as well as contradictory to every thing and every body. – Being short-sighted – when we used to ride out together near the Brenta in the twilight in Summer he made me go *before* to pilot him – I am absent at times – especially towards evening – and the consequence of this pilotage was some narrow escapes to the Monk on horseback. – Once I led him *into* a ditch – over which I had passed as usual forgetting to warn my Convoy which *in*commodes passengers – and twice did we both run against the diligence which being heavy and slow did communicate less damage than it received in its leaders who were *terrasé'd* by the charge. – Thrice did I lose him in the gray of the Gloaming and was obliged to bring to to his distant signals of distance and distress. – All the time he went on talking without interruption for he was a man of many words. – Poor fellow – he died a martyr to his new riches – of a second visit to Jamaica –

> I'd give the lands of Deloraine –
> Dark Musgrave were alive again!

that is

> I would give many a Sugar Cane
> Monk Lewis were alive again!

Lewis said to me – 'why do you talk *Venetian* (such as I could talk not very fine to be sure) to the Venetians? & not the usual Italian? I answered – partly from habit – & partly to be understood – if possible, – 'It may be so' – said Lewis – 'but it sounds to me like talking with a *brogue* to an *Irishman.*' –

WILLIAM HAZLITT (1778–1830)
by Charles Lamb (1775–1834)

LETTER TO WILLIAM WORDSWORTH, 26 JUNE 1806

W. Hazlitt is in Town. I took him to see a very pretty girl professedly, where there were two young girls – the very head and sum of the Girlery was two young girls – they neither laughed nor sneered nor giggled nor whispered – but they were young girls – and he sat and frowned blacker and blacker, indignant that there should be such a thing as Youth and Beauty, till he tore me away before supper in perfect misery and owned he could not bear young girls. They drove him mad. So I took him home to my old Nurse, where he recovered perfect tranquillity. Independent of this, and as I am not a young girl myself, he is a great acquisition to us. He is, rather imprudently, I think, printing a political pamphlet on his own account, and will have to pay for the paper, &c. The first duty of an Author, I take it, is never to pay anything.

WRITING IN LONDON MAGAZINE, OCTOBER 1823

What hath soured him, and made him to suspect his friends of infidelity towards him when there was no such matter, I know not. I stood well with him for fifteen years (the proudest of my life), and have ever spoken my full mind of him to some, to whom his panegyric must naturally be least tasteful. I never in thought swerved from him, I never betrayed him, I never slackened in my admiration of him; I was the same to him (neither better nor worse), though he could not see it, as in the days when he thought fit to trust me. At this instant he may be preparing for me some compliment, above my deserts, as he has sprinkled many such among his admirable books, for which I rest his debtor; or, for anything I know, or can guess to the contrary, he may be about to read a lecture on my weaknesses. He is welcome to them (as he was to my humble hearth), if they can divert a spleen, or ventilate a fit of sullenness.

I wish he would not quarrel with the world at the rate he does; but the reconciliation must be effected by himself, and I despair of living to see that day. But protesting against much that he has written, and some things which he chooses to do; judging him by his conversation which I enjoyed so long, and relished so deeply; or by his books, in those places where no clouding passion intervenes – I should belie my own conscience, if I said less, than that I think W.H. to be, in his natural and healthy state, one of the wisest and finest spirits breathing. So far from being ashamed of that intimacy, which was betwixt us, it is my boast that I was able for so many years to have preserved it entire; and I think I shall go to my grave without finding, or expecting to find, such another companion.

THOMAS MOORE (1779–1852)
by George Gordon, Lord Byron (1788–1824)

LETTER TO JOHN MURRAY, 15 SEPTEMBER 1817

I have read 'Lallah Rookh' – but not with sufficient attention yet – for I ride about – & lounge – & ponder & – two or three other things – so that my reading is very desultory & not so attentive as it used to be. – I am very glad to hear of its popularity – for Moore is a very noble fellow in all respects – & will enjoy it without any of the bad feelings which Success – good or evil – sometimes engenders in the men of rhyme. – Of the poem itself I will tell you my opinion when I have mastered it – I say of the poem – for I don't like the prose at all – at all – and in the mean time the 'Fire-worshippers' is the best and the 'Veiled Prophet' the worst, of the volume. – With regard to poetry in general I am convinced the more I think of it – that he and *all* of us – Scott – Southey – Wordsworth – Moore – Campbell – I – are all in the wrong – one as much as another – that we are upon a wrong revolutionary poetical system – or systems – not worth a damn in itself – & from which none but Rogers and Crabbe are free – and that the present & next generations will finally be of this opinion. – I am the more confirmed in this – by having lately gone over some of our Classics – particularly *Pope* – whom I tried in this way – I took Moore's poems & my own & some others – & went over them side by side with Pope's – and I was really astonished (I ought not to have been so) and mortified – at the ineffable distance in point of sense – harmony – effect – and even *Imagination* Passion – & *Invention* – between

the little Queen Anne's Man – & us of the lower Empire – depend upon
it it is all Horace then, and Claudian now among us – and if I had to
begin again – I would model myself accordingly – Crabbe's the man –
but he has got a coarse and impracticable subject – & Rogers the Grandfather of living Poetry – is retired upon half-pay, (I don't mean as a
banker) –

> Since pretty Miss Jaqueline
> With her nose aquiline

and has done enough – unless he were to do as he did formerly.

LEIGH HUNT (1784–1859)
by George Gordon, Lord Byron (1788–1824)

LETTER TO THOMAS MOORE, I JUNE 1818.
The asterisks represent deletions made in Byron's text.

Hunt's letter is probably the exact piece of vulgar coxcombry you might
expect from his situation. He is a good man, with some poetical elements
in his chaos; but spoilt by the Christ Church Hospital and a Sunday
newspaper, – to say nothing of the Surrey Jail, which conceited him into
a martyr. But he is a good man. When I saw 'Rimini' in MSS., I told him
that I deemed it good poetry at bottom, disfigured only by a strange style.
His answer was, that his style was a system, or *upon system*, or some
such cant; and, when a man talks of system, his case is hopeless: so I said
no more to him, and very little to any one else.

He believes his trash of vulgar phrases tortured into compound barbar-
isms to be old English; and we may say of it as Aimwell says of Captain
Gibbet's regiment, when the Captain calls it an 'old corps.' – 'the *oldest*
in Europe, if I may judge by your uniform.' He sent out his 'Foliage' by
Percy Shelley ***, and, of all the ineffable Centaurs that were ever
begotten by Selflove upon a Night-mare, I think this monstrous Sagittary
the most prodigious. *He* (Leigh H.) is an honest Charlatan, who has
persuaded himself into a belief of his own impostures, and talks Punch
in pure simplicity of heart, taking himself (as poor Fitzgerald said of
himself in the Morning Post) for *Vates* in both senses, or nonsenses, of the
word. Did you look at the translations of his own which he prefers to
Pope and Cowper, and says so? – Did you read his skimble-skamble about

Wordsworth being at the head of his own *profession*, in the eyes of *those* who followed it? I thought that Poetry was an *art*, or an *attribute*, and not a *profession*; – but be it one, is that ****** at the head of your profession in your eyes? I'll be curst if he is of mine, or ever shall be. He is the only one of us (but of us he is not) whose coronation I would oppose. Let them take Scott, Campbell, Crabbe, or you, or me, or any of the living, and throne him; – but not this new Jacob Behmen, this **** whose pride might have kept him true, even had his principles turned as perverted as his *soi-disant* poetry.

But Leigh Hunt is a good man, and a good father – see his Odes to all the Masters Hunt; – a good husband – see his Sonnet to Mrs Hunt; – a good friend – see his Epistles to different people; – and a great coxcomb and a very vulgar person in every thing about him. But that's not his fault, but of circumstances.

Leigh Hunt
by Edward John Trelawny (1792–1881)

Towards the end of June, 1822, the long-expected family of the Hunts arrived by sea from England.

Byron observed, 'You will find Leigh Hunt a gentleman in dress and address; at least he was so when I last saw him in England, with a taint of cockneyism.'

I found him a gentleman and something more; and with a quaint fancy and cultivated mind. He was in high spirits, and disposed to be pleased with others. His anticipated literary projects in conjunction with Byron and Shelley were a source of great pleasure to him – so was the land of beauty and song. He had come to it as to a new home, in which, as the immortal Robins the auctioneer would have said: 'You will find no nuisance but the litter of the rose-leaves and the noise of the nightingales.' The pleasure that surpassed all the rest, was the anticipation of seeing speedily his friend Shelley. But alas! all those things which seemed so certain –

> Those juggling fiends
> That keep the word of promise to our ear,
> And break it to our hope.

so kept – and so broke – it with Leigh Hunt.

The first visit I paid to Byron after the Hunts' arrival I found Mrs Hunt was confined to her room, as she generally was, from bad health. Hunt too was in delicate health – a hypochondriac; and the seven children, untamed, the eldest a little more than ten and the youngest a yearling, were scattered about playing on the large marble staircase and in the hall. Hunt's theory and practice were that children should be unrestrained until they were of an age to be reasoned with. If they kept out of his way he was satisfied. On my entering the Poet's study, I said to him, 'The Hunts have effected a lodgement in your palace;' and I was thinking how different must have been his emotion on the arrival of the Hunts from that triumphant morning after the publication of 'Childe Harold,' when he 'awoke and found himself famous.'

Usually meeting him after two or three days' absence his eyes glistened; now they were dull and his brow pale. He said,

'I offered you those rooms. Why did you not take them? have you seen Hunt?'

'Not this morning,' I replied; 'he is in labour for an article in the New Review.'

Byron said, 'It will be an abortion. I shall have nothing to do with it. Gifford and Jeffrey will run him down as you say Shelley's boat was run down. Why did not he stick to the 'Examiner?' He is in Italy, but his mind is in Hampstead, Highgate and Covent Garden.'

When I took my leave he followed me into the passage, and patting the bull-dog on the head he said, 'Don't let any Cockneys pass this way.'

Byron could not realize till the actual experiment was tried the nuisance of having a man with a sick wife and seven disorderly children interrupting his solitude and his ordinary customs, and then Hunt did not conceal that his estimate of Byron's poetry was not exalted. At that time Hunt thought highly of his own poetry and under-estimated all other, as is the wont of the literary guilds. Shelley he thought would have made a great poet if he had written on intelligible subjects. He was smitten with the old rhymesters' quaintness, punning, and playing battledore and shuttle-cock with words. Shelley soared too high for him and Byron flew too near the ground. There was not a single subject on which Byron and Hunt could agree.

GEORGE GORDON, LORD BYRON (1788–1824)
by Stendhal (Henri Beyle) (1788–1842)

Much doubt has been cast on the authenticity of Stendhal's account of Byron. Yet Jonathan Keates writes in his 1994 biography of Stendhal: 'Attempts at picking holes in Stendhal's testimony, of the sort made in 1830 by [Byron's friend, John Cam] Hobhouse and a century later by the doyenne of Byron studies, Doris Langley Moore, merely reinforce the impression that Beyle the romancing romancier has somehow delivered a more authentic portrait in its finished effect than most biographers could have contrived with the accumulation of carefully checked detail.'

LETTER TO ROMAIN COLOMB, 24 AUGUST 1829

One evening in the autumn of 1812, I entered M. de Brême's box [at La Scala opera house] on my return from an excursion on Lake Como. I found that the gathering had a sort of solemn and awkward air: everybody was silent. I was listening to the music, when M. de Brême said to me, indicating my neighbour: 'Monsieur Beyle, this is Lord Byron.' He turned to Lord Byron and repeated the same formula. I beheld a young man with magnificent eyes that had something generous about them: he was quite short. At that time I was mad about *Lara*. From the second glance, I no longer saw Lord Byron as he really was, but as I thought the author of *Lara* should be. Since the conversation had languished, M. de Brême sought to make me speak. This was impossible for me: I was filled with timidity and affection: if I had dared, I would have burst into tears and kissed Lord Byron's hand. Pursued by M. de Brême's questioning, I tried to speak, and uttered only commonplaces, which were of no help against the silence which this evening prevailed amongst the circle. Finally Lord Byron asked me, as the only one who knew English, to tell him the names of the streets that he would have to pass through on the way back to his inn. It was at the other end of the town, near the fortress. I saw that he would go astray: in that part of Milan, at midnight, all the shops were closed. He would wander amidst empty and ill-lit streets, and without knowing a word of the language! In my devoted affection I was so foolish as to advise him to take a carriage. At once a shade of haughtiness passed over his face: he gave me to understand, with all necessary politeness, that what he wanted was the names of the streets, and not advice as to how to use them. He left the box, and I understood why he had reduced it to silence.

George Gordon, Lord Byron
by Edward John Trelawny (1792–1881)

Shelley was drowned in his small schooner, the 'Ariel', in July 1822.

Three white wands had been stuck in the sand to mark the Poet [Shelley]'s grave, but as they were at some distance from each other, we had to cut a trench thirty yards in length, in the line of the sticks, to ascertain the exact spot, and it was nearly an hour before we came upon the grave.

In the meantime Byron and Leigh Hunt arrived in the carriage, attended by soldiers, and the Health Officer, as before. The lonely and grand scenery that surrounded us so exactly harmonized with Shelley's genius, that I could imagine his spirit soaring over us. The sea, with the islands of Gorgona, Capraja, and Elba, was before us; old battlemented watch-towers stretched along the coast, backed by the marble-crested Apennines glistening in the sun, picturesque from their diversified outlines, and not a human dwelling was in sight. As I thought of the delight Shelley felt in such scenes of loneliness and grandeur whilst living, I felt we were no better than a herd of wolves or a pack of wild dogs, in tearing out his battered and naked body from the pure yellow sand that lay so lightly over it, to drag him back to the light of day; but the dead have no voice, nor had I power to check the sacrilege – the work went on silently in the deep and unresisting sand, not a word was spoken, for the Italians have a touch of sentiment, and their feelings are easily excited into sympathy. Byron was silent and thoughtful. We were startled and drawn together by a dull hollow sound that followed the blow of a mattock; the iron had struck a skull, and the body was soon uncovered. Lime had been strewn on it; this, or decomposition, had the effect of staining it of a dark and ghastly indigo colour. Byron asked me to preserve the skull for him; but remembering that he had formerly used one as a drinking-cup, I was determined Shelley's should not be so profaned. The limbs did not separate from the trunk, as in the case of Williams's body, so that the corpse was removed entire into the furnace. I had taken the precaution of having more and larger pieces of timber, in consequence of my experience of the day before of the difficulty of consuming a corpse in the open air with our apparatus. After the fire was well kindled we repeated the ceremony of the previous day; and more wine was poured over Shelley's dead body than he had consumed during his life. This with the oil and salt made the yellow flames glisten and quiver. The heat from the sun and fire was so intense that the atmosphere was tremulous and wavy. The corpse fell open and the heart was laid bare. The frontal bone of the skull, where it had been struck with the mattock, fell off; and, as the back of the head rested on the red-hot bottom bars of the furnace, the brains literally seethed, bubbled and boiled as in a cauldron, for a very long time.

Byron could not face this scene, he withdrew to the beach and swam off to the 'Bolivar.' Leigh Hunt remained in the carriage. The fire was so fierce as to produce a white heat on the iron, and to reduce its contents to grey ashes. The only portions that were not consumed were some fragments of bones, the jaw, and the skull; but what surprised us all was that the heart remained entire. In snatching this relic from the fiery furnace, my hand was severely burnt; and had any one seen me do the act I should have been put in quarantine.

After cooling the iron machine in the sea, I collected the human ashes and placed them in a box, which I took on board the 'Bolivar.' Byron and Hunt retraced their steps to their home, and the officers and soldiers returned to their quarters. I liberally rewarded the men for the admirable manner in which they behaved during the two days they had been with us.

As I undertook and executed this novel ceremony, I have been thus tediously minute in describing it. A sage critic remarks that I performed this cremation in a bungling manner, that I should have used a gas retort. My answer is that neither gas nor retorts were then known in Italy. He further remarks that bodies washed on shore were obliged to be burnt; that is an error. Bodies washed on shore were buried in the sand above the wash of the sea, and as the Inquisition no longer burnt heretics, I followed the practice of the Hindoos in using a funeral pyre.

In all cases of death from suffocation the heart is gorged with blood; consequently it is more difficult to consume, especially in the open air.

Byron's idle talk during the exhumation of Williams's remains did not proceed from want of feeling, but from his anxiety to conceal what he felt from others. When confined to his bed and racked by spasms, which threatened his life, I have heard him talk in a much more unorthodox fashion, the instant he could muster breath to banter. He had been taught during his town-life that any exhibition of sympathy or feeling was maudlin and unmanly, and that the appearance of daring and indifference denoted blood and high breeding.

PERCY BYSSHE SHELLEY (1792–1822)
by Thomas Love Peacock (1785–1866) *and Thomas Jefferson Hogg* (1792–1862)

Peacock, writing in 1858, was discussing books on Shelley by Charles S. Middleton, E. J. Trelawny (see below) and Hogg.

At University College, Oxford, in October, 1810, Mr Hogg first became acquainted with him. In their first conversation Shelley was exalting the physical sciences, especially chemistry. Mr Hogg says:

> As I felt little interest in the subject of his conversation, I had leisure to examine, and I may add to admire, the appearance of my very extraordinary guest. It was a sum of many contradictions. His figure was slight and fragile, and yet his bones and joints were large and strong. He was tall, but he stooped so much that he seemed of a low stature. His clothes were expensive, and made according to the most approved mode of the day; but they were tumbled, rumpled, unbrushed. His gestures were abrupt and sometimes violent, occasionally even awkward, yet more frequently gentle and graceful. His complexion was delicate and almost feminine, of the purest white and red; yet he was tanned and freckled by exposure to the sun . . . His features, his whole face, and particularly his head, were in fact unusually small; yet the last appeared of a remarkable bulk, for his hair was long and bushy . . . he often rubbed it up fiercely with his hands, or passed his fingers through his locks unconsciously, so that it was singularly wild and rough . . . His features were not symmetrical (the mouth perhaps excepted); yet was the effect of the whole extremely powerful. They breathed an animation, a fire, an enthusiasm, a vivid and preternatural intelligence, that I never met with in any other countenance. Nor was the moral expression less beautiful than the intellectual . . . I admired the enthusiasm of my new acquaintance, his ardour in the cause of science, and his thirst for knowledge. But there was one physical blemish that threatened to neutralize all his excellence.

This blemish was his voice.

There is a good deal in these volumes about Shelley's discordant voice. This defect he certainly had; but it was chiefly observable when he spoke under excitement. Then his voice was not only dissonant, like a jarring string, but he spoke in sharp fourths, the most unpleasing sequence of sound that can fall on the human ear: but it was scarcely so when he spoke calmly, and not at all so when he read; on the contrary, he seemed then to have his voice under perfect command: it was good both in tune and in tone; it was low and soft, but clear, distinct and expressive. I have heard him read almost all Shakespeare's tragedies, and some of his more poetical comedies, and it was a pleasure to hear him read them. . . .

The canal in question [the Surrey canal] was a favourite walk with us [when Shelley was staying in London in 1814]. The Croydon Canal branched off from it, and passed very soon into wooded scenery. The Croydon Canal is extinct, and has given place to the, I hope, more useful, but certainly less picturesque, railway. Whether the Surrey exists, I do not know. He had a passion for sailing paper-boats, which he indulged on this canal, and on the Serpentine river. The best spot he had ever found for it was a large pool of transparent water, on a heath above Bracknell, with determined borders free from weeds, which admitted of launching the miniature craft on the windward, and running round to receive it on the leeward, side. On the Serpentine, he would sometimes launch a boat constructed with more than usual care, and freighted with halfpence. He delighted to do this in the presence of boys, who would run round to meet it, and when it landed in safety, and the boys scrambled for their prize, he had difficulty in restraining himself from shouting as loudly as they did. The river was not suitable to this amusement, nor even Virginia Water, on which he sometimes practised it; but the lake was too large to allow of meeting the landing. I sympathized with him in this taste: I had it before I knew him: I am not sure that I did not originate it with him; for which I should scarcely receive the thanks of my friend, Mr Hogg, who never took any pleasure in it, and cordially abominated it, when, as frequently happened, on a cold winter day, in a walk from Bishopgate over Bagshot Heath, we came on a pool of water, which Shelley would not part from till he had rigged out a flotilla from any unfortunate letters he happened to have in his pocket.

Percy Bysshe Shelley
by George Gordon, Lord Byron (1788–1824)

LETTER TO DOUGLAS KINNAIRD, 29 SEPTEMBER 1816

. . . Pray continue to like Shelley – he is a very good – very clever – but a very singular man – he was a great comfort to me here by his intelligence & good nature. –

LETTER TO JOHN MURRAY, 15 MAY 1819

Derived from a suggestion by Byron, The Vampire *was written by his acquaintance, Polidori, and passed off as the work of Byron. Byron once said of Polidori that he was the sort of man to whom 'if he fell overboard one would proffer a straw, to see if the adage be true that drowning men clutch at straws'.*

I have got yr. extract, & the 'Vampire'. I need not say it is *not mine* – there is a rule to go by – you are my publisher (till we quarrel) and what is not published by you is not written by me. – The Story of Shelley's agitation is true – I can't tell what seized him – for he don't want courage. He was once with me in a Gale of Wind in a small boat right under the rocks between Meillerie & St Gingo – we were five in the boat – a servant – two boatmen – & ourselves. The Sail was mismanaged & the boat was filling fast – he can't swim. – I stripped off my coat – made him strip off his – & take hold of an oar – telling him that I thought (being myself an expert swimmer) I could save him if he would not struggle when I took hold of him – unless we got smashed against the rocks which were high & sharp with an awkward Surf on them at that minute; – we were then about a hundred yards from shore – and the boat in peril. – He answered me with the greatest coolness – 'that he had no notion of being saved – & that I would have enough to do to save myself, and begged not to trouble me'. – Luckily the boat righted & baling we got round to a point into St Gingo – where the Inhabitants came down and embraced the boatmen on their escape – the Wind having been high enough to tear up some huge trees from the Alps above us as we saw next day. – And yet the same Shelley who was as cool as it was possible to be in such circumstances – (of which I am no judge myself as the chance of swimming

63

naturally gives self-possession when near shore) certainly had the fit of phantasy which Polidori describes – though not exactly as he describes it.

LETTER TO THOMAS MOORE, 4 MARCH 1822

With respect to 'Religion,' can I never convince you that I have no such opinions as the characters in that drama [*Werner*], which seems to have frightened every body? Yet *they* are nothing to the expressions in Goethe's Faust (which are ten times hardier), and not a whit more bold than those of Milton's Satan. My ideas of a character may run away with me: like all imaginative men, I, of course embody myself with the character while *I draw* it, but not a moment after the pen is from off the paper.

I am no enemy to religion, but the contrary. As a proof, I am educating my natural daughter a strict Catholic in a convent of Romagna; for I think people can never have *enough* of religion, if they are to have any. I incline, myself, very much to the Catholic doctrines; but if I am to write a drama, I must make my characters speak as I conceive them likely to argue.

As to poor Shelley, who is another bugbear to you and the world, he is, to my knowledge, the *least* selfish and the mildest of men – a man who has made more sacrifices of his fortune and feelings for others than any I ever heard of. With his speculative opinions I have nothing in common, nor desire to have.

The truth is, my dear Moore, you live near the *stove* of society, where you are unavoidably influenced by its heat and its vapours.

LETTER TO JOHN MURRAY, 3 AUGUST 1822

I presume you have heard that Mr Shelley & Capt. Williams were lost on the 7th Ulto. in their passage from Leghorn to Spezia in their own open boat. You may imagine the state of their families – I never saw such a scene – nor wish to see such another. – You are all brutally mistaken about Shelley who was without exception – the *best* and least selfish man I ever knew. – I never knew one who was not a beast in comparison.

LETTER TO THOMAS MOORE, 8 AUGUST 1822

You will have heard by this time that Shelley and another gentleman (Captain Williams) were drowned about a month ago (a *month* yesterday), in a squall off the Gulf of Spezia. There is another man gone, about whom the world was ill-naturedly, and ignorantly, and brutally mistaken. It will, perhaps, do him justice *now*, when he can be no better for it.

LETTER TO MARY SHELLEY, [16 NOVEMBER?] 1822

I have always treated him [Leigh Hunt], in our personal intercourse, with such scrupulous delicacy, that I have forborne intruding advice, which I thought might be disagreeable, lest he should impute it to what is called 'taking advantage of a man's situation'.

As to friendship, it is a propensity in which my genius is very limited. I do not know the *male* human being, except Lord Clare, the friend of my infancy, for whom I felt any thing that deserves the name. All my others are men-of-the-world friendships. I did not even feel it for Shelley, however much I admired and esteemed him; so that you see not even vanity could bribe me into it, for, of all men, Shelley thought highest of my talents, – and, perhaps of my disposition.

I will do my duty by my intimates, upon the principle of doing as you would be done by. I have done so, I trust, in most instances. I may be pleased with their conversation – rejoice in their conversation – rejoice in their success – be glad to do them service, or to receive their counsel and assistance in return. But as for friends and friendship, I have (as I already said) named the only remaining male for whom I felt any thing of the kind, excepting, perhaps, Thomas Moore. I have had, and may have still, a thousand friends, as they are called, in *life,* who are like one's partners in the waltz of this world – not much remembered when the ball is over, though very pleasant for the time. Habit, business, and companionship in pleasure or in pain, are links of a similar kind, and the same faith in politics is another.

Percy Bysshe Shelley
by Edward John Trelawny (1792–1881)

To know an author, personally, is too often but to destroy the illusion created by his works; if you withdraw the veil of your idol's sanctuary, and see him in his night-cap, you discover a querulous old crone, a sour pedant, a supercilious coxcomb, a servile tuft-hunter, a saucy snob, or at best, an ordinary mortal. Instead of the high-minded seeker after truth and abstract knowledge, with a nature too refined to bear the vulgarities of life, as we had imagined, we find him full of egotism and vanity, and eternally fretting and fuming about trifles. As a general rule, therefore, it is wise to avoid writers whose works amuse or delight you, for when you see them they will delight you no more. Shelley was a grand exception to this rule. To form a just idea of his poetry, you should have witnessed his daily life; his words and actions best illustrated his writings. If his glorious conception of Gods and men constituted an atheist, I am afraid all that listened were little better. Sometimes he would run through a great work on science, condense the author's laboured exposition, and by substituting simple words for the jargon of the schools, make the most abstruse subject transparent. The cynic Byron acknowledged him to be the best and ablest man he had ever known. The truth was, Shelley loved everything better than himself. Self-preservation is, they say, the first law of nature, with him it was the last; and the only pain he ever gave his friends arose from the utter indifference with which he treated everything concerning himself. I was bathing one day in a deep pool in the Arno, and astonished the Poet by performing a series of aquatic gymnastics, which I had learnt from the natives of the South Seas. On my coming out, whilst dressing, Shelley said, mournfully,

'Why can't I swim? it seems so very easy.'

I answered, 'Because you think you can't. If you determine, you will; take a header off this bank, and when you rise turn on your back, you will float like a duck; but you must reverse the arch in your spine, for it's now bent the wrong way.'

He doffed his jacket and trousers, kicked off his shoes and socks, and plunged in; and there he lay stretched out on the bottom like a conger eel, not making the least effort or struggle to save himself. He would have been drowned if I had not instantly fished him out. When he recovered his breath, he said, 'I always find the bottom of the well, and they say Truth lies there. In another minute I should have found it, and you would have found an empty shell. It is an easy way of getting rid of the body.'

TRE. ' "What is truth?" said jesting Pilate, and would not stay for an answer.' What does Bacon mean by that?

SHELLEY. The truth is a jest; no one has found it.

TRE. That is why the wise men say they know nothing. Bacon might have exposed the great lies.

SHELLEY. If we had known the great truths, they would have laid bare the great lies.

TRE. What do they mean by the great truths?

SHELLEY. They cannot calculate time, measure distance, or say what is above or what is below us. 'What is life? What is death? What are we?'

TRE. The knaves are the cleverest; they profess to know everything; the fools believe them, and so they govern the world.

SHELLEY. Science has done something and will do more; astronomy is working above, and geology below, and chemistry is seeking truth. In another century or two we shall make a beginning; at present we are playing the game of blind man's buff, struggling to clutch truth.

TRE. What would Mrs Shelley have said to me if I had gone back with your empty cage? 'Don't tell Mary – not a word!' he rejoined, and then continued, 'It's a great temptation; in another minute I might have been in another planet, if old women's tales were true.'

'But as you always find the bottom,' I observed, 'you might have sunk "deeper than did ever plummet sound." Do you believe in the immortality of the spirit?'

'Certainly not; how can I? We know nothing; we have no evidence; we cannot express our inmost thoughts. They are incomprehensible even to ourselves.'

'Why,' I asked, 'do you call yourself an atheist? It annihilates you in this world.'

'It is a word of abuse to stop discussion, a painted devil to frighten the foolish, a threat to intimidate the wise and good. I used it to express my abhorrence of superstition; I took up the word as a knight took up a gauntlet, in defiance of injustice. The delusions of Christianity are fatal to genius and originality: they limit thought.'

Shelley's thirst for knowledge was unquenchable. He set to work on a book, or a pyramid of books; his eyes glistening with an energy as fierce as that of the most sordid gold-digger who works at a rock of quartz, crushing his way through all impediments, no grain of the pure ore escaping his eager scrutiny. I called on him one morning at ten, he was in his study with a German folio open, resting on the broad marble mantelpiece, over an old-fashioned fire-place, and with a dictionary in his hand. He always read standing if possible. He had promised over night to go with me, but now begged me to let him off. I then rode to Leghorn, eleven or twelve miles distant, and passed the day there; on returning at six in the evening to dine with Mrs Shelley and the Williamses, as I had engaged to do, I went into the Poet's room and found him exactly in the position in which I had left him in the morning, but looking pale and exhausted.

'Well,' I said, 'have you found it?'

Shutting the book and going to the window, he replied, 'No, I have lost it: with a deep sigh: ' "I have lost a day." '

'Cheer up, my lad, and come to dinner.'

Putting his long fingers through his masses of wild tangled hair, he answered faintly, 'You go, I have dined – late eating won't do for me.'

'What is this?' I asked, as I was going out of the room, pointing to one of his bookshelves with a plate containing bread and cold meat on it.

'That,' – colouring, – 'why that must be my dinner. It's very foolish; I thought I had eaten it.'

Saying I was determined that he should for once have a regular meal, I lugged him into the dining-room, but he brought a book with him and read more than he ate. He seldom ate at stated periods, but only when hungry – and then like the birds, if he saw something edible lying about – but the cupboards of literary ladies are like Mother Hubbard's, bare. His drink was water, or milk if he could get it, bread was literally his staff of life; other things he thought superfluous. An Italian who knew his way of life, not believing it possible that any human being would live as Shelley did, unless compelled by poverty, was astonished when he was told the amount of his income, and thought he was defrauded or grossly ignorant of the value of money. He therefore made a proposition which much amused the Poet, that he, the friendly Italian, would undertake for ten thousand crowns a-year to keep Shelley like a grand Seigneur, to provide his table with luxuries, his house with attendants, a carriage and opera-box for my lady, besides adorning his person after the most approved Parisian style. Mrs Shelley's toilette was not included in the wily Italian's estimates. The fact was, Shelley stinted himself to bare necessaries, and then often lavished the money, saved by unprecedented self-denial, on selfish fellows who denied themselves nothing; such as the great philosopher had in his eye, when he said, 'It is the nature of extreme self-lovers, as they will set a house on fire, an' it were only to roast their own eggs.'

Byron, on our voyage to Greece, talking of England, after commenting on his own wrongs, said, 'And Shelley, too, the best and most benevolent of men; they hooted him out of his country like a mad-dog, for questioning a dogma. Man is the same rancorous beast now that he was from the beginning, and if the Christ they profess to worship reappeared, they would again crucify him.'

THOMAS CARLYLE (1795–1881)
by William Allingham (1824–89)

October. 1877 – To C.'s about 3.30. Mrs Lecky there. To Queen Anne St. and call on Erasmus Darwin. Talk of Mr Martin's Biography. Carlyle wrote to *Athenæum*: 'Mr Frederick Martin has no authority to concern himself with my life – of which he knows nothing.' He remarked that many old things came back clearly which he had not thought of for a great many years.

I asked how far back his memory went. He told of something that happened when he was less than two years old. 'An uncle of mine sent me the gift of a small wooden can – they called it a noggie – to eat my porridge from. The can had two bottoms and some small pebbles between that rattled, – but this was a profound secret to me at the time, the source of the rattling. One day finding myself alone in the kitchen with my noggie, I conceived the scheme of making some porridge for myself, and for the first stage I poured water into my noggie and set this on the kitchen fire to boil. After a little, however, it all suddenly blazed up, and out I rushed shrieking with terror – I was under two, I don't know how much. It must have been some months later, probably in 1798, that we moved from one house to another. A pathway and short-cut led between the two, across a field known to the satirical villagers as Pepper Field, because the owner was said to have made his fortune in the West Indies. I was allowed to suppose myself helping in the flitting, and I recollect very well carrying the stoup or nozzle of a watering pot across Pepper Field and blowing through it like a horn, feeling at the same time a great exultation – some kind of false joy, I suppose, for I don't think I was very happy at the time.'

Going out we found it was a quarter to six. 'Bless me!' said C., 'what an old fool I have been to sit there talking useless stuff when I ought to be at home,' and we hurried to the omnibus as fast as age allowed. He usually takes half an hour's sleep before dinner, and is very methodical in all his ways.

WILLIAM BARNES (1801–86)
by William Allingham (1824–89)

Tuesday, November 1 [1864]. – Rev. Wm. Barnes comes on my invitation to give a lecture at the Literary Institution. He duly arrives by train at 3, and I gladly welcome the good old poet. We walk about the Town and he shows much interest in the Furniture Brokers' shops, old china, pictures, etc. – and bargains for a little oil-painting. Aïdé arrives, whom I have invited to meet Barnes. I take them for a walk to Buckland Rings, supposed ancient British Camp; then dinner at my lodging (which I hope went off tolerably), and we moved to the Lecture Room. Mr Barnes lectured on 'West of England Speech,' and read some of his own poems. What the audience liked best was 'A Bit o' Sly Coortin', which he gave at my particular request. It was evident that on the whole he seemed to them flat, in comparison with the paid Entertainers who occasionally come round.

NIKOLAI GOGOL (1809–52)
by Ivan Turgenev (1818–83)

I was taken to meet Gogol by the late Mikhail Semyonovich Shchepkin. I remember the day of our visit: 20th October 1851. Gogol lived in Moscow at the time, in Nikitsky Street, Talyzin's house, with Count [Alexander] Tolstoy. We arrived at one o'clock in the afternoon: he received us at once. His room was on the right of the entrance hall. We entered and – there was Gogol standing before a tall bureau with a pen in his hand. He was wearing a dark coat, a green velvet waistcoat and brown trousers. A week before I had seen him in the theatre at a performance of *The Government Inspector*; he was in a box in the stalls, near the very door and, craning his neck, looked with nervous anxiety at the stage over the shoulders of two stout ladies, whom he used as a screen from the curiosity of the public. Feokstitov, who was sitting next to me, pointed him out to me. I turned round quickly to have a look at him; he must have noticed my movement, for he shrank back a little into the corner of the box. I was struck by the change that had taken place in his appearance since 1841. I had met him twice then at Avotya Petrovna Yelagin's. At that time he was a stout, thick-set Ukrainian; now he looked a very thin, haggard man who had been through a great deal of trouble in life. A sort of hidden anxiety and pain, a sort of melancholy restlessness hung over the usually shrewd and intelligent expression of his face.

Seeing Shchepkin and myself, he went up to us gaily and, shaking hands with me, said: 'We should have become acquaintances long ago.' We sat down – Shchepkin in an armchair beside him and I next to him on the sofa. I looked at him more closely. His fair hair, which fell straight from the temples, as is usual with Cossacks, still preserved its youthful tint, but had thinned noticeably; his smooth, retreating white forehead conveyed, as before, the impression of great intelligence. His small brown eyes sparkled with gaiety at times – yes, gaiety and not sarcasm; but mostly they looked tired. Gogol's long, pointed nose gave his face a sort of cunning, fox-like expression; his puffy, soft lips under the clipped moustache also produced an unfavourable impression; in their indefinite contours – so at least it seemed to me – the dark side of his character found expression. When he spoke, they opened unpleasantly, showing a row of bad teeth. His small chin disappeared in his wide, black velvet cravat. In Gogol's bearing, in his gestures, there was something not so much professorial as schoolmasterly – something reminiscent of teachers in provincial institutes and secondary schools. 'What an intelligent, queer and sick creature you are!' I could not help thinking as I looked at him. I remember that Shchepkin and I had gone to him as to an extraordinary man, a man of genius, who was a little touched in the head . . . all Moscow was of that opinion of him. Shchepkin had warned me not to talk to him about the continuation of *Dead Souls*, about the second part of his novel, at which he had been working so long and so assiduously and which he burnt before his death. He did not like to talk about it, Shchepkin said. I should not have mentioned his *Selected Passages from the Correspondence with my Friends* myself, for I could not have said anything good about it. As a matter of fact, I was not particularly anxious to discuss anything with him; all I wanted was to see the man whose works I knew almost by heart. It is difficult to explain to our young people of today the fascination his name exerted on us in those days; there is, in fact, no one living today who could become the focus of general attention.

Shchepkin had warned me beforehand that Gogol was anything but talkative; but actually it turned out quite otherwise. Gogol talked a lot and with great animation, enunciating every word clearly and emphasizing it, which not only did not seem unnatural but, on the contrary, lent his speech a sort of agreeable weight and impressiveness. I could not detect any particular Ukrainian accent in his speech, except that he pronounced the letter O without slurring it. Everything he said was absolutely right and to the point. The impression of fatigue and morbid nervous restlessness, which had struck me at first, disappeared. He spoke of the importance of literature, the vocation of the writer, and what one's attitude to one's own works should be; he made a few subtle and true observations about the process of literary work itself, the physiology, if one may put it that way, of authorship; and all that in an imaginative and original language and, as far as I could see, without any preliminary preparation, as is all too often the case with 'famous men'. It was only when he began speaking of the censorship, almost glorifying it, almost approving of it as a means of developing the writer's acumen and skill in protecting his beloved child as well as his patience and a multitude of other Christian and worldly virtues, it was only then that I could not help feeling that he was drawing it all out of a ready-made arsenal. Besides, to prove the need for censorship in this way – is it not tantamount to recommending and almost praising the cunning and craftiness of slavery? I could, I suppose, to some extent accept the verse of the Italian poet: *Si, servi siam; ma servi ognor frementi* [Yes, we are slaves; but slaves who are always mad with rage]; but self-satisfied submission and double-faced hypocrisy of slavery – no; I'd rather not speak of it. In such excogitations and rationalizations of Gogol one could clearly detect the influence of those high-placed personages to whom he had dedicated the greater part of his *Selected Passages*; it was from there that that stale and musty odour came. In fact, I soon felt that there was an impassable gulf between Gogol's outlook on life and mine. It was not the same things we hated and not the same things we loved; but at that moment that did not matter to me. A great poet, a great artist was before me, and I looked at him and listened to him with veneration even when I did not agree with him.

Gogol, I expect, must have known of my relations with Belinsky and Iskander [Herzen]; he never mentioned the first nor Belinsky's letter to him; that name would have scorched his lips. But just at that time there appeared an article by Iskander, an article, published abroad, in which he reproached Gogol with going back on his former opinions in connection with the notorious *Selected Passages*. Gogol began talking of that article himself. From his letters, published after his death (oh, what a great service their editor would have done if he had thrown out two-thirds of them or at least those written to society women – there is a no more hideous mixture of arrogance, servility, sanctimoniousness and vanity, prophetic and cringing tones in all literature!) – from Gogol's letters we know what a festering wound the fiasco of his *Selected Passages* had inflicted on his heart, a fiasco which one cannot help hailing as one of the few salutary manifestations of public opinion in those days. On the day of our visit Shchepkin and I could see how terribly painful that wound was. Gogol began to assure us in a suddenly changed and flurried voice that he could not understand why some people found some sort of opposition in his former works, something that he had betrayed afterwards; that he had always adhered to the same religious and conservative principles and to prove it he was ready to show us certain passages in a book of his he had published ages before. Having said this, Gogol jumped up from the sofa with almost youthful agility and rushed into the next room. Shchepkin just raised his eyebrows and – his forefinger ... 'I've never seen him like that,' he whispered to me.

Gogol returned with the volume *Arabesques* and began reading extracts from one of those childishly bombastic and tiresomely insipid articles with which that book is filled. So far as I can remember it was all about the need for strict order, absolute obedience to the authorities, and so on. 'You see,' said Gogol, 'I was of the same opinion before! I expressed exactly the same convictions as now! Why, then, reproach me with betrayal, apostasy? Me?' And that was said by the author of *The Government Inspector*, one of the most damning comedies that ever appeared on the stage! Shchepkin and I said nothing.

Alfred, Lord Tennyson (1809–92)
by Thomas Carlyle (1795–1881)

LETTER FROM THOMAS CARLYLE TO RALPH WALDO EMERSON, AUGUST 1844

Tennyson is now in Town, and means to come and see me. Of this latter result I shall be very glad: Alfred is one of the few British or foreign figures (a not increasing number, I think!) who are and remain beautiful to me; – a true human soul, or some authentic approximation thereto, to whom your own soul can say, Brother! – However, I doubt he will not come; he often skips me, in these brief visits to Town; skips every-body indeed; being a man solitary and sad, as certain men are, dwelling in an element of gloom, – carrying a bit of Chaos about him, in short, which he is manufacturing into Cosmos!

Alfred is the son of a Lincolnshire gentleman farmer, I think; indeed you see in his verses that he is a native of a 'moated grange', and green fat pastures, not of mountains and their torrents and storms. He had his breeding at Cambridge, as if for the Law, or Church; being master of a small annuity on his father's decease, he preferred clubbing with his mother and some sisters, to live unpromoted and write poems. In this way he lives still, now here now there; the family always within reach of London, never in it; he himself making rare and brief visits, lodging in some old comrade's rooms. I think he must be under forty, not much under it. One of the finest looking men in the world. A great shock of rough dusty-dark hair; bright-laughing hazel eyes; massive aquiline face, most massive yet most delicate, of sallow brown complexion, almost Indian-looking; clothes cynically loose, free-and-easy; – smokes infinite tobacco. His voice is musical metallic, – fit for loud laughter and piercing wail, and all that may lie between; speech and speculation free and plenteous: I do not meet, in these late decades, such company over a pipe! – We shall see what he will grow to. He is often unwell; very chaotic, – his way is thro' Chaos and the Bottomless and Pathless; not handy for making out many miles upon.

Alfred, Lord Tennyson
by William Allingham (1824–89)

In 1853, being in London, from Ireland, for a short holiday, I wrote to Twickenham and had a kind reply under the Poet's hand asking me to come, and adding – 'As my wife is not very well you must "tread softly and speak low." ' So on Thursday the first of November I went from Waterloo Station to Richmond by rail, walked over Richmond Bridge – a fine day, autumnal woodlands mirrored in the river, struck a field path on the left, and passing after a bit under some tall trees emerged through a little gate upon the grass-plot fronting Montpelier Terrace. As I came forward to Chapel House two other men approached the door, one of them something like T., and went in, not without a suspicious glance or two at me.

I was soon in the Poet's much-longed-for presence, who shook hands in the most delightful, simple, friendly way, and asked me to stay and dine; then said he had to go away for a little and handed me a book for my amusement. When he returned he was carrying in his arms his baby son, called 'Hallam'; the child had a ball to amuse him, which he liked to drop on the floor exclaiming, 'Tha!' or 'Da!' as it fell. Then T. took me up to wash my hands in the dressing-room, its window looking across several gardens, and a sunset sky shining through the trees. Returning to the drawing-room I found Mrs Tennyson – sweet, pale, and kind; Mr Frederick Tennyson the eldest of the brothers, and Mr Edward Fitzgerald (*Omar Khayyám*), the two gentlemen whom I had encountered at the front door. Mr Fitzgerald ('Fitz'), an old and intimate friend, told droll stories with a quaint gravity, much amusing Mrs Tennyson in particular. One was about old Miss Edgeworth, whom he knew, and her turban. She used to take it off for coolness and resume it when visitors were announced. One day by some mischance a strange gentleman came into the room and found her writing with her almost bald pate plainly visible. Miss E. started up with the greatest agility seized the turban which lay close by and darted through an opposite door, whence she quickly reappeared with the decoration upon her head, but unluckily turned wrong side foremost. He also told us of Mr Edgeworth's tombs of his three wives in the park at Edgeworthstown.

After dinner, poetry was the subject. Mr Fitzgerald stood up for Pope's 'Homer', and tried in vain to get T.'s approval.

'You think it very wonderful surely?'

T. – 'I don't think I do.'

'O yes you do, Alfred!'

T. – 'No, I do not.'

Frederick T. set Schiller above Goethe, to which I strongly objected. A.T. said: 'If one of you is for Goethe and the other for Schiller, you'll never agree on poetry.' Moore was mentioned; his skilful versification in fitting words to music. T. objected to the line –

She is far from the land where her young hero sleeps.

I did not find much the matter with it, but T. would not allow 'young hero' to pass, the metre requiring a dactyl there: 'I wonder you don't see,' he said. 'Subaltern' I suggested. 'Yes, that would do, as far as sound goes.' We turned to Campbell's 'Soldier's Dream,' and T. objected to 'Our bugles sang truce,' both for the two *ss* and the accentuation. Of the two lines –

> And thousands had sunk on the ground overpowered,
> The weary to sleep and the wounded to die –

he said, 'Those are perfect.' Then we spoke of Shelley's accents, and I quoted –

> Of the snake's adamantine voluminousness

but without effect. I called Browning a *vivid* man, to which T. assented, adding, 'How he did flourish about when he was here!'

Then came on Dickens' cockney *History of England*, Professor Aytoun (not praised), Thackeray's *Book of Snobs*, and Mr Martin Tupper. I spilt some port on the cloth, and T., with his usual imperturbability spread salt on it, remarking as he did so, 'I believe it never comes out!' Then we went upstairs to tea. I praised the view from the windows at the back. He said nothing would grow in his own garden but stones: 'I believe they grow. I pick up all I can see, and the next time I come there are just as many.' Then T., Frederick T., Edward F. and I to the study, where smoking and stories, some of an ammoniacal saltness. When I took my leave, Mr Frederick T. shook hands kindly, in spite of our differences of opinion, and T. came with me to the front garden gate.

When I got to the station the last train was gone, and I walked into London by Kew and Turnham Green, followed all along Kew Garden wall by a possible footpad, whom I outstept.

22 JULY 1867

After dinner we talk of dreams. T. said, 'In my boyhood I had intuitions of immortality – inexpressible! I have never been able to express them. I shall try some day.'

I say that I too have felt something of that kind; whereat T. (being in one of his less amiable moods) growls, 'I don't believe you have. You say it out of rivalry.'

MONDAY, 8 SEPTEMBER 1884

Helen and I to Aldworth. In the drawing-room we find Lady Tennyson – then T. comes in. His two little grandsons run in. Tennyson went to his bedroom and returned with a soap-dish and piece of soap, which he rubbed into a lather, and proceeded to blow bubbles, himself much delighted with the little crystal worlds and their prismatic tints – 'Never was anything seen so beautiful! You artists (to H.) can't get such colours as these.'

The children jumped and laughed, and we fanned the bubbles to the ceiling and watched them burst in various parts of the room. Then T., inverting his pipe, blew up a magic cluster of diamond domes on the saucer, which rolled over and wetted his knees, till we put a newspaper to save him. Next he took his trusty tobacco pipe, lighted it and blew opaque bubbles which burst with a tiny puff of smoke, like shells over a besieged fortress.

Alfred, Lord Tennyson
by C. L. Dodgson ('Lewis Carroll') (1832–98)

LETTER TO WILLIAM WILCOX, 11 MAY 1859

There was a man painting the garden railing when I walked up to the house, of whom I asked if Mr Tennyson were at home, fully expecting the answer 'No', so that it was an agreeable surprise when he said, 'He's there, sir', and pointed him out, and, behold! he was not many yards off, mowing his lawn in a wideawake and spectacles. I had to introduce myself, as he is too short-sighted to recognise people, and when he had finished the bit of mowing he was at, he took me into the house to see Mrs Tennyson, who, I was very sorry to find, had been very ill, and was then suffering from almost total sleeplessness. She was lying on the sofa, looking rather worn and haggard, so that I stayed a very few minutes. She asked me to come to dinner that evening to meet a Mr Warburton (brother of the 'Crescent and the Cross'), but her husband revoked the invitation before I left, as he said he wished her to be as little excited as possible that evening, and begged I would drop in for tea that evening, and dine with them the next day. He took me over the house to see the pictures, etc. (among which my photographs of the family were hung 'on the line', framed in those enamel – what do you call them, cartons?) The view from the garret windows he considers one of the finest in the island, and showed me a picture which his friend Richard Doyle had painted of it for him; also his little smoking-room at the top of the house, where of course he offered me a pipe; also the nursery, where we found the beautiful little Hallam (his son), who remembered me more readily than his father had done.

I went in the evening, and found Mr Warburton an agreeable man, with rather a shy, nervous manner; he is a clergyman, and inspector of schools in that neighbourhood. We got on the subject of clerical duty in the evening, and Tennyson said he thought clergymen as a body didn't do half the good they might if they were less stuck-up and showed a little more sympathy with their people. 'What they want,' he said, 'is force and geniality – geniality without force will of course do no good, but force without geniality will do very little.' All very sound theology, to my thinking. This was up in the little smoking-room, to which we had adjourned after tea, and where we had about two hours' very interesting talk. The proof-sheets of 'The King's Idylls' were lying about, but he would not let me look at them. I looked with some curiosity to see what sort of books occupied the lowest of the swinging bookshelves, most handy to his writing-table; they were all, without exception, Greek or Latin – Homer, Aeschylus, Horace, Lucretius, Virgil, etc. It was a fine moonlight night, and he walked through the garden with me when I left, and pointed out an effect of the moon shining through thin, white cloud, which I had never noticed before – a sort of golden ring, not close round its edge like a halo, but at some distance off. I believe sailors consider it a sign of bad weather. He said he had often noticed it, and had alluded to it in one of his early poems. You will find it in 'Margaret.'

The next day I went to dinner, and met Sir John Simeon, who has an estate some miles off there, an old Ch[rist]. Ch[urch]. man, who has turned Roman Catholic since. He is one of the pleasantest men I ever met, and you may imagine that the evening was a delightful one: I enjoyed it thoroughly, especially the concluding two hours in the smoking-room.

I took over my books of photographs, but Mrs Tennyson was too tired to look at them that evening, and I settled to leave them and come for them next morning, when I could see more of the children, who had only appeared for a few minutes during dinner.

Tennyson told us that often on going to bed after being engaged on composition he had dreamed long passages of poetry ('You, I suppose', turning to me, 'dream photographs?') which he liked very much at the time, but forgot entirely when he woke. One was an enormously long one on fairies, where the lines from being very long at first gradually grew shorter and shorter, till it ended with fifty or sixty lines of two syllables each! The only bit he ever remembered enough to write down was one he dreamed at ten years old, which you may like to possess as a genuine unpublished fragment of the Laureate, though I think you will agree with me that it gives very little indication of his future poetic powers:

> May a cock-sparrow
> Write to a barrow?
> I hope you'll excuse
> My infantine muse.

Up in the smoking-room the conversation turned upon murders, and Tennyson told us several horrible stories from his own experience: he seems rather to revel in such descriptions – one would not guess it from his poetry. Sir John kindly offered me a lift in his carriage back to the hotel, and as we were standing at the door before getting in he said, 'You don't object to a cigar in the carriage, do you?' On which Tennyson growled out, 'He didn't object to *two pipes* in that little den upstairs, and *a feebliori* he's no business to object to one cigar in a carriage.' And so ended one of the most delightful evenings I have spent for many a long day.

Alfred, Lord Tennyson
by Edmund Gosse (1849–1928)

It was the early summer of 1871, and I was palely baking, like a crumpet, in a singularly horrible underground cage, made of steel bars, called the Den. This was a place such as no responsible being is allowed to live in nowadays, where the transcribers on the British Museum staff were immured in a half-light ... I was dolefully engaged here, being then one of the humblest of mankind, a Junior Assistant in the Printed Books Department of the British Museum, on some squalid task, in what was afterwards described by a witness as an atmosphere 'scented with rotten morocco, and an indescribable odour familiar in foreign barracks', when a Senior Assistant, one of the rare just spirits in that academical Dotheboys Hall, W. R. S. Ralston, came dashing down the flights of curling steel staircase, to the danger of his six feet six of height, and of the beard that waved down to his waist. Over me he bent, and in a whisper (we were forbidden to speak out loud in the Den) he said, 'Come upstairs at once and be presented to Mr Tennyson!'

Proud young spirits of the present day, for whom life opens in adulation, will find it scarcely possible to realise what such a summons meant to me. As we climbed those steep and spiral staircases towards light and day, my heart pounded in my chest with agitation. The feeling of excitement was almost overwhelming: it was not peculiar to myself; such ardours were common in those years. Some day a philosopher must analyse it – that enthusiasm of the 1870s, that intoxicating belief in 'the might of poesy'. Tennyson was scarcely a human being to us, he was the God of the Golden Bow; I approached him now like a blank idiot about to be slain, 'or was I a worm, too low-crawling for death, O Delphic Apollo?' It is not merely that no person living now calls forth that kind of devotion, but the sentiment of mystery has disappeared. Not genius itself could survive the Kodak snapshots and the halfpenny newspapers.

It must, I suppose, have been one of those days on which the public was then excluded, since we found Tennyson, with a single companion, alone in what was then the long First Sculpture Gallery. His friend was James Spedding, at whom in other conditions I should have gazed with interest, but in the Delphic presence he was not visible to my dazzled eyes. Mr Thornycroft's statue of the poet, now placed in Trinity College, gives an admirable impression of him at a slightly later date than 1871, if (that is) it is translated out of terms of white into terms of black. Tennyson, at that time, was still one of the darkest of men, as he is familiarly seen in all his earlier portraits. But those portraits do not give, although Mr Thornycroft has suggested, the singular majesty of his figure, standing in repose. Ralston, for all his six feet six, seemed to dwindle before this magnificent presence, while Tennyson stood, bare-headed among the Roman emperors, every inch as imperial-looking as the best of them. He stood there as we approached him, very still, with slightly dropping eyelids, and made no movement, no gesture of approach. When I had been presented, and had shaken his hand, he continued to consider me in a silence which would have been deeply disconcerting if it had not, somehow, seemed kindly, and even, absurd as it sounds, rather shy.

The stillness was broken by Ralston's irrelevantly mentioning that I was presently to start for Norway. The bard then began to talk about that country, which I was surprised to find he had visited some dozen years before. Ralston kindly engaged Spedding in conversation, so that Tennyson might now apply himself to me; with infinite goodness he did so, even 'making conversation', for I was hopelessly tongue-tied, and must, in fact, have cut a very poor figure. Tennyson, it miraculously appeared, had read some of my stammering verses, and was vaguely gracious about them. He seemed to accept me as a sheep in the fold of which he was, so magnificently, the shepherd. This completed my undoing, but he did not demand from me speech. He returned to the subject of Norway, and said it was not the country for him to travel in, since you could only travel in it in funny little round carts, called *karjols*, which you must drive yourself, and that he was far too near-sighted for that. (I had instantly wondered at his double glasses, of a kind I had never seen before.)

Then somebody suggested that we should examine the works of art, which, in that solitude, we could delightfully do. Tennyson led us, and we stopped at any sculpture which attracted his notice. But the only remark which my memory has retained was made before the famous black bust of Antinous. Tennyson bent forward a little, and said, in his deep slow voice, 'Ah! this is the inscrutable Bithynian!' There was a pause, and then he added, gazing into the eyes of the bust: 'If we knew what he knew, we should understand the ancient world.' If I live to be a hundred years old, I shall still hear his rich tones as he said this, without emphasis, without affectation, as though he were speaking to himself. And soon after, the gates of heaven were closed, and I went down three flights of stairs to my hell of rotten morocco.

THÉOPHILE GAUTIER (1811–72)
by Gustave Flaubert (1821–80)

LETTER TO GEORGE SAND, 28–29 OCTOBER 1872

Chère maître,

You guessed aright that there had been a redoubling of my grief, and your letter is sweet and kind. Thank you. And I embrace you even more warmly than usual.

Even though it was expected, poor Théo's death leaves me heart-broken. With him, the last of my intimate friends is gone. The list is now closed. Whom shall I see now, when I go to Paris? Who is there to talk with about what interests me? I know thinkers (or at least people who call themselves such), but an artist – where is there one?

Believe me, he died of disgust with the 'putrefaction of the modern world.' That was his expression, and he repeated it to me several times last winter. 'I'm dying of the Commune,' etc. The fourth of September inaugurated an order of things in which people like him had no place. You can't demand apples from orange trees. Deluxe artisans are useless in a society dominated by the plebs. How I miss him! He and Bouilhet have left a great void in my life, and nothing can replace them. Besides, he was so good, and, whatever they say, so *simple*! He will be recognized later (if anyone ever again cares about literature) as a great poet. Meanwhile he is an absolutely unknown writer. But then, so is Pierre Corneille.

He had two hatreds. In his youth, hatred of Philistines. That gave him his talent. In his maturity, hatred of the rabble. That killed him. He died of repressed rage, of fury at being unable to speak his mind. He was *stifled* by Girardin, by Turgan, Fould, Dalloz. And by the present Republic. I tell you this because I have seen some abominable things, and because I was perhaps the only man in whom he confided fully. He lacked the quality that is most important in life – for oneself as well as for others: *character*. His failure to be elected to the Academy was a real source of grief to him. What weakness! What lack of self-esteem! To seek an honour, no matter what, seems to me an act of incomprehensible humility!

That I missed the funeral was due to Catulle Mendès, who sent me a telegram too late. There was a great crowd. A lot of idiots and rascals came to show off, as usual; and today being Monday, the day for theatre news in the papers, there will certainly be articles. He will make 'good copy.'

To sum up, I don't pity him: I *envy* him. For, frankly, life is not much fun. No, I do not think of happiness as being attainable – tranquillity, yes. That's why I keep away from what irritates me. I am unsociable; therefore I flee Society, and find myself the better for doing so. A trip to Paris is a great undertaking for me, these days. As soon as I shake the bottle, the dregs rise and spoil everything. The slightest discussion with anyone at all exasperates me, because I find everybody idiotic. My sense of justice is continually outraged. All talk is of politics – and *such* talk! Where is there the least sign of an idea? What is there to hold on to? What cause is there to be passionate about?

Still, I don't consider myself a monster of egoism. My *me* is so dispersed in my books that I spend whole days unaware of it. I have had bad moments, it's true. But I pull myself together by reminding myself that at least nobody is bothering me – and soon I'm back on my feet. All in all, it seems to me that I'm following my natural path. Doesn't that mean I'm doing the right thing?

WILLIAM MAKEPEACE THACKERAY (1811–63)
by Charlotte Brontë (1816–55)

Brontë managed a partial anonymity because of the pseudonym, 'Currer Bell', under which Jane Eyre *had been published in 1847. Brontë was embarrassed by publicity, and further embarrassed by a rumour suggesting, quite inaccurately, that the character of Rochester was an at least partial portrait of Thackeray.*

4 DECEMBER 1849

Yesterday I saw Mr Thackeray. He dined here with some other gentlemen. He is a very tall man – above six feet high, with a peculiar face – not handsome, very ugly indeed, generally somewhat stern and satirical in expression, but capable also of a kind look. He was not told who I was, he was not introduced to me, but I soon saw him looking at me through his spectacles; and when we all rose to go down to dinner he just stepped quietly up and said, 'Shake hands'; so I shook hands. He spoke very few words to me, but when he went away he shook hands again in a very kind way. It is better, I should think, to have him for a friend than an enemy, for he is a most formidable-looking personage. I listened to him as he conversed with the other gentlemen. All he says is most simple, but often cynical, harsh, and contradictory. I get on quietly. Most people know me, I think, but they are far too well bred to show that they know me, so that there is none of that bustle or that sense of publicity I dislike . . .

12 JUNE 1850

. . . an interview with Mr Thackeray. He made a morning-call, sat above two hours – Mr [George] Smith [her publisher] only was in the room the whole time. He described it afterwards as a queer scene; and I suppose it was. The giant sat before me – I was moved to speak to him of some of his shortcomings (literary of course). One by one the faults came into my mind and one by one I brought them out and sought some explanation or defence – He did defend himself like a great Turk and heathen – that is to say, the excuses were often worse than the crime itself. The matter ended in decent amity – if all be well I am to dine at his house this evening.

LETTER TO GEORGE SMITH, 7 JANUARY 1851

Thackeray had been late in delivering one of his 'Christmas books', The Kickleburys on the Rhine.

. . . that promise 'really to set about writing' a book of which the publication was announced makes one's hair stand on end. May I ask whether, while the Christmas book, already advertised, was still unwritten, with all this guilt on his head and all this responsibility on his shoulders, Mr Thackeray managed to retain his usual fine appetite, to make good breakfasts, luncheons, and dinners, and to enjoy his natural rest, or whether he did not rather send away choice morsels on his plate untouched, and terrify Mrs Carmichael-Smith, Miss Truelock, and his daughters, by habitually shrieking out in the dead of the night under the visitation of a terrible nightmare, revealing two wrathful forms at his bedside menacing him with drawn swords and demanding his MS. or his life? . . .

I think you did me a kindness in warding off that copy of *Pendennis* intended to be discharged at my head; the necessary note of acknowledgment would have been written by me under difficulties. To have spoken my mind would have been to displease, and I know, if I had written at all, my mind would have insisted on speaking itself.

William Makepeace Thackeray
by Thomas Carlyle (1795–1881)

LETTER TO RALPH WALDO EMERSON, 9 SEPTEMBER 1853

Thackeray has very rarely come athwart me since his return [from America]: he is a big fellow, soul and body; of many gifts and qualities (particularly in the Hogarth line, with a dash of Sterne superadded), of enormous appetite withal, and very uncertain and chaotic in all points, except his outer breeding, which is fixed enough, and perfect according to the modern English style. I rather dread explosions in his history. A *big*, fierce, weeping, hungry man; not a strong one. *Ay de mi!* [Spanish: 'Alas, poor me'].

LETTER TO LADY ASHBURTON, 4 NOVEMBER 1854

Thackeray came over to see us one night; was very gentle and friendly-looking; ingenious too here and there; but extremely difficult to talk with, somehow – his talk lying all in flashes, little detached pools, you nowhere got upon a well or vein.

William Makepeace Thackeray
by *William Allingham* (1824–89)

F. S. Mahony, an ex-Jesuit priest, became famous as a journalist under the pseudonym 'Father Prout'.

AUGUST 1858

Thackeray took me to dine with him in the Palais Royal. He noticed with quiet enjoyment every little incident – beginning with the flourish with which our waiter set down the dishes of Ostend oysters. After tasting his wine Thackeray said, looking at me solemnly through his large spectacles, 'One's first glass of wine in the day is a great event.'

That dinner was delightful. He talked to me with as much ease and familiarity as if I had been a favourite nephew.

After dinner Thackeray proposed that we should go to the Palais Royal Theatre, but on issuing forth he changed his mind, and said we would call up Father Prout. 'His quarters are close by. You know him, don't you?'

'Yes, I know that singing priest a little.'

He was then Paris Correspondent of the *Globe*, and his letters were much admired. It was said that the *Globe* had been obliged to buy a fount of Greek type by reason of Mahony's fondness for classical quotations.

In a narrow street at the back of the Palais Royal, in a large lowish room on the ground floor, we found the learned and witty Padre, loosely arrayed, reclining in front of a book and a bottle of Burgundy. He greeted us well, but in a low voice and said, 'Evening boys, there's a young chap asleep there in the corner.' And in a kind of recess we noted something like bed-clothes. Thackeray was anxious to know who this might be, and Prout explained that it was a young Paddy from Cork or thereabouts, who had been on a lark in Paris and spent his money. Prout found him 'hard up', and knowing something of his friends in Ireland had taken him in to board and lodge, pending the arrival of succour.

This piece of humanity was much to Thackeray's taste, as you may suppose. Thackeray said the Burgundy was 'too strong', and had brandy and water instead.

We talked among other things of Dickens. I said how much a story of Dickens might be improved by a man of good taste with a pencil in his hand, by merely scoring out this and that.

Says Thackeray (with an Irish brogue), 'Young man, you're threadin' on the tail o' me coat!'

I did not understand at first.

'What you've just said applies very much to your humble servant's things.'

I disclaimed this, and Prout said emphatically, 'Not a word too much in them!'

William Makepeace Thackeray
by *Charles Dickens* (1812–70)

This is part of an obituary that Dickens privately confessed to having been very reluctant to write because of the awkwardness of his relations with Thackeray.

I saw him first, nearly twenty-eight years ago, when he proposed to become the first illustrator of my earliest book. I saw him last, shortly before Christmas, at the Athenaeum Club, when he told me that he had been in bed three days – that, after these attacks, he was troubled with cold shiverings, 'which quite took the power of work out of him' – and that he had it in his mind to try a new remedy which he laughingly described. He was very cheerful, and looked very bright. In the night of that day week, he died.

The long interval between those two periods is marked in my remembrance of him by many occasions when he was supremely humorous, when he was irresistibly extravagant, when he was softened and serious, when he was charming with children. But, by none do I recall him more tenderly than by two or three that start out of the crowd, when he unexpectedly presented himself in my room, announcing how that some passage in a certain book had made him cry yesterday, and how that he had come to dinner 'because he couldn't help it', and must talk such passage over. No one can ever have seen him more genial, natural, cordial, fresh, and honestly impulsive, than I have seen him at those times. No one can be surer than I, of the greatness and the goodness of the heart that then disclosed itself.

We had our differences of opinion. I thought that he too much feigned a want of earnestness, and that he made a pretence of undervaluing his art, which was not good for the art that he held in trust. But, when we fell upon these topics, it was never very gravely, and I have a lively image of him in my mind, twisting both his hands in his hair, and stamping about, laughing, to make an end of the discussion . . .

These are slight remembrances, but it is to little familiar things suggestive of the voice, look, manner, never, never more to be encountered on this earth, that the mind first turns in a bereavement.

ROBERT BROWNING (1812–89)
by William Allingham (1824–89)

6 April [1876]: . . . Browning looked at a photograph of himself on my chimney-piece and said, 'There I am – and I don't recollect when or where it was done, or anything about it. I find gaps in my memory. The other day I came by chance on an old letter of my own, telling how I had seen Ristori in Camma – if that was the word, and I could not and cannot recollect in the very least what Camma is, or what I refer to: yet there it was in my own handwriting – a judgment on me for my opinion of my Grandfather, when I asked him if he had seen Garrick in *Richard the Third* and he replied "I suppose I have," and I thought "Bless my soul! shall I ever come to this." People compliment me on my prodigious memory, because I have a knack of remembering rhymes – "hog" and "dog", and so forth; but it's breaking down.'

CHARLES DICKENS (1812–70)
by William Makepeace Thackeray (1811–63)

LETTER TO HIS WIFE, MAY 1843

Did I write to tell you about Mrs Procter's grand ball, and how splendid Mrs Dickens was in pink satin and Mr Dickens in geranium & ringlets?

LETTER TO MRS BROOKFIELD, 24 JULY 1849

I met on the pier (at Ryde, Isle of Wight) as I was running for the dear life, the great Dickens with his wife his children his Miss Hogarth all looking abominably coarse vulgar and happy and bound for Bonchurch where they have taken one of White's houses for the summer.

TO HIS MOTHER, MAY 1858

Here is sad news in the literary world – no less than a separation between Mr & Mrs Dickens – with all sorts of horrible stories buzzing about. The worst is that I'm in a manner dragged in for one – Last week going into the Garrick I heard that D is separated from his wife on account of an intrigue with his sister in law. No says I no such thing – it's with an actress – and the other story has not got to Dickens's ears but this one has – and he fancies that I am going about abusing him! We shall never be allowed to be friends that's clear. I had mine from a man at Epsom the first I ever heard of the matter, and should have said nothing about it but that I heard the other much worse story whereupon I told mine to counteract it. There is some row about an actress in the case, & he denies it with the utmost infuriation any charge against her or himself – but says that it has been known to any one intimate with his family that his and his wife's tempers were horribly incompatible & now that the children are grown up – it is agreed they are to part – the eldest son living with her the daughters &c remaining under the care of Miss Hogarth who has always been mother governess house-keeper everything to the family. I haven't seen the statement but this is what is brought to me on my bed of sickness, and I'd give 100£ (if it weren't true.) To think of the poor matron after 22 years of marriage going away out of her house! O dear me its a fatal story for our trade.

Charles Dickens
by Elizabeth Gaskell (1810–65)

Gaskell went to a party at Dickens's Devonshire Terrace house in May 1849.

We were shown into Mr Dickens' study ... where he writes all his books ... There are books all round, up to the ceiling, and down to the ground, a standing-desk at which he writes and all manner of comfortable easy chairs. There were numbers of people in the room. Mr Rogers (the old poet, who is 86, and looked very unfit to be in such a large party,) Douglas Jerrold, Mr & Mrs Carlyle, Hablot Browne, who illustrated Dickens' works, Mr Forster, Mr and Mrs Tagart, a Mr Kenyon. We waited dinner a long time for Lady Dufferin; (the Hon. Mrs Blackwood who wrote the Irish Emigrant's lament,) but she did not come till after dinner . . . In the evening quantities of other people came in. We were by this time up in the drawing-room, which is not nearly so pretty or so home-like as the study. Frank Stone the artist, Leech & his wife, Benedict the great piano-forte player, Sims Reeves the singer, Thackeray, Lord Dudley Stuart, Lord Headfort, Lady Yonge, Lady Lovelace, Lady Dufferin, and a quantity of others whose names I did not hear. We heard some beautiful music. Mr Tom Taylor was there too, who writes those comical ballads in Punch; and Anne said we had the whole Punch-bowl, which I believe we had. I kept trying to learn people's faces off by heart, that I might remember them; but it was rather confusing there were so very many. There were some nice little Dickens' children in the room, – who were so polite, and well-trained.

Charles Dickens
by George Eliot (1819–80)

Dickens was chairing a meeting on 4 May 1852 held in opposition to the Booksellers' Association's price-fixing policy.

The meeting last night went off triumphantly . . . Dickens in the chair – a position he fills remarkably well, preserving a courteous neutrality of eyebrow, and speaking with clearness and decision. His appearance is certainly disappointing – no benevolence in the face and I think little in the head – the anterior lobe not by any means remarkable. In fact he is not distinguished looking in any way – neither handsome nor ugly, neither fat nor thin, neither tall nor short.

Charles Dickens
by Thomas Carlyle (1795–1881)

LETTER TO JOHN CARLYLE, 29 APRIL 1863

I had to go yesterday to Dickens's Reading, 8 p.m., Hanover Rooms, to the complete upsetting of my evening habitudes and spiritual composure. Dickens does do it capitally, such as it is; acts better than any Macready in the world; a whole tragic, comic, heroic theatre visible, performing under one hat, and keeping us laughing – in a sorry way, some of us thought – the whole night. He is a good creature, too, and makes fifty or sixty pounds by each of these readings.

ANTHONY TROLLOPE (1815–82)
by Thomas Carlyle (1795–1881)

LETTER TO HIS WIFE, 27 JULY 1865

Ruskin's *Sesame and Lilies* must be a pretty thing. Trollope, in reviewing it with considerable insolence, stupidity and vulgarity, produces little specimens far beyond any Trollope sphere of speculation. A distylish little pug, that Trollope; irredeemably embedded in commonplace, and grown fat upon it, and prosperous to an unwholesome degree. Don't you return his love; nasty gritty creature, with no eye for 'the Beautiful', etc., – and awfully 'interesting to himself' he be. Adieu, Dearest; write to me; – sleep oh sleep! . . .

Anthony Trollope
by George Eliot (1819–80)

LETTER TO JOHN BLACKWOOD, 18 OCTOBER 1867

I suppose you have seen in the papers that our friend Mr Trollope has resigned his place in the Post Office. I cannot help being rather sorry, though one is in danger of being rash in such judgements. But it seems to me a thing greatly to be dreaded for a man that he should be in any way led to excessive writing.

Anthony Trollope
by H. Rider Haggard (1856–1925)

Anthony Trollope has been out here [South Africa]. The first I saw of that distinguished author was one morning when I met him in a towering rage (at a roadside inn) because he could not get any breakfast. He stopped in the country about twelve days, and now is going home to write a book about it – in which, no doubt, he will express his opinions with a certainty that an old resident would hesitate to adopt. I talked with him a good deal, he has the most peculiar ideas and is as obstinate as a pig. I call such a proceeding downright dishonesty: making use of a great name to misrepresent a country.

Anthony Trollope
by Henry James (1843–1916)

Abundance, certainly, is in itself a great merit; almost all the greatest writers have been abundant. But Trollope's fertility was gross, importunate; he himself contended, we believe, that he had given to the world a greater number of printed pages of fiction than any of his literary contemporaries. Not only did his novels follow each other without visible intermission, overlapping and treading on each other's heels, but most of these works are of extraordinary length. *Orley Farm, Can You Forgive Her?, He Knew He Was Right*, are exceedingly voluminous tales. *The Way We Live Now* is one of the longest of modern novels. Trollope produced, moreover, in the intervals of larger labour a great number of short stories, many of them charming, as well as various books of travel, and two or three biographies. He was the great *improvvisatore* of these latter years. Two distinguished story-tellers of the other sex – one in France and one in England – have shown an extraordinary facility of composition; but Trollope's pace was brisker even than that of the wonderful Madame Sand and the delightful Mrs Oliphant. He had taught himself to keep this pace, and had reduced his admirable faculty to a system. Every day of his life he wrote a certain number of pages of his current tale, a number sacramental and invariable, independent of mood and place. It was once the fortune of the author of these lines to cross the Atlantic in his company, and he has never forgotten the magnificent example of plain persistence that it was in the power of the eminent novelist to give on that occasion. The season was unpropitious, the vessel overcrowded, the voyage detestable; but Trollope shut himself up in his cabin every morning for a purpose which, on the part of a distinguished writer who was also an invulnerable sailor, could only be communion with the muse. He drove his pen as steadily on the tumbling ocean as in Montague Square; and as his voyages were many, it was his practice before sailing to come down to the ship and confer with the carpenter, who was instructed to rig up a rough writing-table in his small sea-chamber. Trollope has been accused of being deficient in imagination, but in the face of such a fact as that the charge will scarcely seem just. The power to shut one's eyes, one's ears (to say nothing of another sense), upon the scenery of a pitching Cunarder and open them upon the loves and sorrows of Lily Dale or the conjugal embarrassments of Lady Glencora Palliser, is certainly a faculty which could take to itself wings.

CHARLOTTE BRONTË (1816–55)
by Elizabeth Gaskell (1810–65)

Towards the latter end of September I went to Haworth. At the risk of repeating something which I have previously said, I will copy out parts of a letter which I wrote at the time:

'It was a dull, drizzly Indian-inky day, all the way on the railroad to Keighley, which is a rising wool-manufacturing town, lying in a hollow between hills – not a pretty hollow, but more what the Yorkshire people call a "bottom", or "botham". I left Keighley in a car for Haworth, four miles off – four tough, steep, scrambling miles, the road winding between the wave-like hills that rose and fell on every side of the horizon, with a long illimitable sinuous look, as if they were a part of the line of the Great Serpent, which the Norse legend says girdles the world. The day was lead-coloured; the road had stone factories alongside of it, – grey-coloured rows of stone cottages belonging to these factories, and then we came to poor, hungry-looking fields; – stone fences everywhere, and trees nowhere. Haworth is a long, straggling village: one steep narrow street – so steep that the flag-stones with which it is paved are placed end-ways, that the horses' feet may have something to cling to, and not slip down backwards; which if they did, they would soon reach Keighley. But if the horses had cats' feet and claws, they would do all the better. Well, we (the man, horse, car, and I) clambered up this street, and reached the church dedicated to St Autest (who was he?); then we turned off into a lane on the left, past the curate's lodging at the Sexton's, past the school-house, up to the Parsonage yard-door. I went round the house to the front door, looking to the church; – moors everywhere beyond and above. The crowded grave-yard surrounds the house and small grass enclosure for drying clothes.

'I don't know that I ever saw a spot more exquisitely clean; the most dainty place for that I ever saw. To be sure, the life is like clock-work. No one comes to the house; nothing disturbs the deep repose; hardly a voice is heard; you catch the ticking of the clock in the kitchen, or the buzzing of a fly in the parlour, all over the house. Miss Brontë sits alone in her parlour; breakfasting with her father in his study at nine o'clock. She helps in the housework; for one of their servants, Tabby, is nearly ninety, and the other only a girl. Then I accompanied her in her walks on the sweeping moors: the heather-bloom had been blighted by a thunder-storm a day or two before, and was all of a livid brown colour, instead of the blaze of purple glory it ought to have been. Oh! those high, wild, desolate moors, up above the whole world, and the very realms of silence! Home to dinner at two. Mr Brontë has his dinner sent into him. All the small table arrangements had the same dainty simplicity about them. Then we rested, and talked over the clear, bright fire; it is a cold country, and the fires were a pretty warm dancing light all over the house. The parlour has been evidently refurnished within the last few years, since Miss Brontë's success has enabled her to have a little more money to spend. Everything fits into, and is in harmony with, the idea of a country par-sonage, possessed by people of very moderate means. The prevailing colour of the room is crimson, to make a warm setting for the cold grey landscape without. There is her likeness by Richmond, and an engraving from Lawrence's picture of Thackeray; and two recesses, on each side of the high, narrow, old-fashioned mantel-piece, filled with books, – books given to her, books she has bought, and which tell of her individual pursuits and tastes; *not* standard books.

'She cannot see well, and does little beside knitting. The way she weakened her eyesight was this: When she was sixteen or seventeen, she wanted much to draw; and she copied nimini-pimini copper-plate engravings out of annuals, ("stippling", don't the artists call it?) every little point put in, till at the end of six months she had produced an exquisitely faithful copy of the engraving. She wanted to learn to express

her ideas by drawing. After she had tried to *draw* stories, and not succeeded, she took the better mode of writing; but in so small a hand, that
it is almost impossible to decipher what she wrote at this time.

'But now to return to our quiet hour of rest after dinner. I soon observed
that her habits of order were such that she could not go on with the
conversation, if a chair was out of its place; everything was arranged with
delicate regularity. We talked over the old times of her childhood; of her
elder sister's (Maria's) death, – just like that of Helen Burns in "Jane
Eyre;" of those strange starved days at school; of the desire (almost
amounting to illness) of expressing herself in some way, – writing or
drawing; of her weakened eyesight, which prevented her doing anything
for two years, from the age of seventeen to nineteen; of her being a
governess; of her going to Brussels; whereupon I said I disliked Lucy
Snowe, and we discussed M. Paul Emmanuel; and I told her of —'s
admiration of "Shirley", which pleased her, for the character of Shirley
was meant for her sister Emily, about whom she is never tired of talking,
nor I of listening. Emily must have been a remnant of the Titans, – great-
grand-daughter of the giants who used to inhabit earth. One day, Miss
Brontë brought down a rough, common-looking oil-painting, done by her
brother, of herself, – a little rather prim-looking girl of eighteen, – and
the two other sisters, girls of sixteen and fourteen, with cropped hair,
and sad, dreamy-looking eyes ... Emily had a great dog, – half mastiff,
half bull-dog – so savage, &c. ... This dog went to her funeral, walking
side by side with her father; and then, to the day of its death, it slept at
her room door, snuffling under it, and whining every morning.

'We have generally had another walk before tea, which is at six; at
half-past eight, prayers; and by nine, all the household are in bed, except
ourselves. We sit up together till ten, or past; and after I go, I hear Miss
Brontë come down and walk up and down the room for an hour or so.'

Copying this letter has brought the days of that pleasant visit very clear
before me, – very sad in their clearness. We were so happy together; we
were so full of interest in each other's subjects. The day seemed only too
short for what we had to say and to hear. I understood her life the better
for seeing the place where it had been spent – where she had loved and
suffered. Mr Brontë was a most courteous host; and when he was with
us, – at breakfast in his study, or at tea in Charlotte's parlour, – he had a
sort of grand and stately way of describing past times, which tallied well
with his striking appearance. He never seemed quite to have lost the
feeling that Charlotte was a child to be guided and ruled, when she was

present; and she herself submitted to this with a quiet docility that half amused, half astonished me. But when she had to leave the room, then all his pride in her genius and fame came out. He eagerly listened to everything I could tell him of the high admiration I had at any time heard expressed for her works. He would ask for certain speeches over and over again, as if he desired to impress them on his memory.

GEORGE ELIOT (1819–80)
by *William Allingham* (1824–89)

Sunday, October 16 [1881]. – Sandhills. Very fine – cold – Carlyle memoranda. I and the children walk to fir-wood. Buss's Corner, children and nurse return up path. I sit on log and call out good-byes. In passing I call and ask Charles Lewes if he will walk? He has a cold. He lends me my own *Songs, Ballads*, etc., the copy I gave to George Eliot in May 1877.

As I sit on the tree trunk at Buss's Corner I take out the book and turn its leaves. Up this very path, on the edge of which I am sitting, George Eliot, G. H. Lewes and myself walked one fine autumnal afternoon, September 25, 1878. I had come over from Shere, where we had a cottage for the season; called, stayed for luncheon; and they both, when I started to walk home, came with me down their garden, into the little lane, across the railway line, to this corner where I sit, over Hambledon Hill, and up the hollow road; at the end of which we parted, talking at the last moment of Carlyle. Sitting on the log and looking up the path eastwards, I recollect distinctly that just here we talked of death, and George Eliot said, 'I used to try to imagine myself dying – how I should feel when dying, but of course I could not.'

I said that when a child I firmly believed I should in some way escape dying.

George Eliot. – 'You cannot think of yourself as dead.'

G. H. Lewes was deeply silent at all this. I suspected him at the time of thinking the topic frivolous and uninteresting, but now I think he perhaps avoided it as painful. Charles Lewes has told Helen that his father could not bear to think of George Eliot's dying first. That September walk was my last sight of Lewes. Both are gone. And here I sit turning over my own book and looking at her pencil markings.

GUSTAVE FLAUBERT (1821–80)
by George Sand (1804–76)

12 April [1873]: Flaubert arrives during dinner ... We play dominoes. Flaubert plays well, but shows impatience. He prefers to talk, always in an emphatic manner.

1 April: ... [After dinner], dancing. Flaubert puts on a skirt and tries the fandango. He is very funny, but after five minutes he is out of breath. Really, he is older than I! Always mentally exacerbated, to the detriment of his body.

14 April: Flaubert reads us his *Saint Anthony* from three to six and from nine to midnight. It is splendid.

17 April: ... The young people come for dinner. Turkey with truffles ... Afterwards, dancing, singing, shouting – a headache for Flaubert, who keeps wanting everything to stop so that we can talk literature.

18 April: Flaubert talks with animation and humour, but all to do with himself. Turgenev, who is much more interesting, can hardly get a word in. They leave tomorrow.

19 April: One lives with people's characters more than with their intelligence or greatness. I am tired, *worn out,* by my dear Flaubert. I love him very much, however, and he is admirable; but his personality is too obstreperous. He exhausts us ... We miss Turgenev, whom we know less well, for whom we have less affection, but who is graced with real simplicity and charming goodness of heart.

Gustave Flaubert
by Ivan Turgenev (1818–83)

LETTER TO GEORGE SAND, 13 AUGUST 1875

Flaubert faced ruin because his affairs were tied up with the disastrous financial state of his nephew.

Dear Madame Sand,

All goes well here, but there is another friend who finds himself just now in a cruel situation – Flaubert, whose letter I enclose. I reproach myself all the more for not having written you for so long when you see that he never stops thinking of you ... A letter from you would be a great boon to him. And when I think that I have kept his letter for ten days, ah! truly, I am furious with myself for my indolence and selfishness. I well know that in everything Flaubert says there is the involuntary exaggeration of an impressionable and nervous man, accustomed to an easy, unfettered life; still, I feel that he has indeed been stricken, perhaps even more deeply than he realizes. He has tenacity without energy, just as he has self-esteem without vanity. Misfortune enters into his soul as into so much butter. I have twice asked him to let me visit him at Croisset, and he has refused. In a more recent letter to me he speaks again of the mortal wound he has suffered.

Gustave Flaubert
by Henry James (1843–1916)

Flaubert's own voice is clearest to me from the uneffaced sense of a winter week-day afternoon when I found him by exception alone and when something led to his reading me aloud, in support of some judgment he had thrown off, a poem of Théophile Gautier's. He cited it as an example of verse intensely and distinctively French, and French in its melancholy, which neither Goethe nor Heine nor Leopardi, neither Pushkin nor Tennyson nor, as he said, Byron, could at all have matched in *kind*. He converted me at the moment to this perception, alike by the sense of the thing and by his large utterance of it; after which it is dreadful to have to confess not only that the poem was then new to me, but that, hunt as I will in every volume of its author, I am never able to recover it. This is perhaps after all happy, causing Flaubert's own full tone, which was the note of the occasion, to linger the more unquenched. But for the rhyme in fact I could have believed him to be spouting to me something strange and sonorous of his own. The thing really rare would have been to hear him do that – hear him *gueuler*, as he liked to call it. Verse, I felt, we had always with us, and almost any idiot of goodwill could give it a value. The value of so many a passage of 'Salammbô' and of 'L'Education' was on the other hand exactly such as gained when he allowed himself, as had by the legend ever been frequent *dans l'intimité*, to 'bellow' it to its fullest effect.

LEO TOLSTOY (1828–1910)
by Anton Chekhov (1860–1904)

Chekhov did revere Tolstoy: in a letter of 28 January 1900 he wrote: 'To begin with, I have never loved anyone as much as him; I am an unbeliever, but of all the faiths I consider his the nearest to my heart and most suited to me. Then again, as long as there is a Tolstoy in literature it is simple and gratifying to be a literary figure; even the awareness of not having accomplished anything and not expecting to accomplish anything in the future is not so terrible because Tolstoy makes up for all of us.' But . . .

LETTER TO ALEXANDER ERTEL, 17 APRIL 1897

There is nothing new. There is a lull in literature. In the editorial offices people drink tea and cheap wine without relish, all as a result, evidently, of nothing to do. Tolstoy is writing a pamphlet on art. He visited me at the clinic and said he had tossed aside his novel 'Resurrection' because he didn't like it, writes only on art and has read sixty books about it. His ideas on the subject are not new; all the wise old men have repeated them throughout the centuries in various keys. Old men have always been prone to see the end of the world, and assert that morality has fallen to its nec plus ultra, that art has been debased and is out at the elbows, that people have become weak and so on and so forth. Leo Nikolayevich's pamphlet would like to convince the world that art has now entered its final phase and is in a blind alley from which it cannot get out except by going backward.

LETTER TO ALEXEI SUVORIN, 4 JANUARY 1898

Chekhov had now read the pamphlet:

It is all old stuff. Saying of art that it has grown decrepit, drifted into a blind alley, that it isn't what it ought to be, and so forth and so on, is the same as saying that the desire to eat and drink has grown obsolete, seen its day and isn't what it ought to be. Of course hunger is an old story, and in our desire to eat we have entered a blind alley, but still we have to do it and we will keep on eating, whatever the philosophers and angry old men may go to the trouble of saying.

GEORGE DU MAURIER (1834–96)
by Henry James (1843–1916)

In 1894, du Maurier's novel Trilby *was published and achieved an enormous success.*

It was strange enough and sad enough that his vitality began to fail at the very hour at which his situation expanded; and I say this without imputing to him any want of lucidity as to what, as he often said, it all meant. I must not overdo the coincidence of his diminished relish for life and his unprecedented 'boom,' but as I see them together I find small difficulty in seeing them rather painfully related. What I see certainly is that no such violence of publicity can leave untroubled and unadulterated the sources of the production in which it may have found its pretext. The whole phenomenon grew and grew till it became, at any rate for this particular victim, a fountain of gloom and a portent of woe; it darkened all his sky with a hugeness of vulgarity. It became a mere immensity of sound, the senseless hum of a million of newspapers and the irresponsible chatter of ten millions of gossips. The pleasant sense of having done well was deprived of all sweetness, all privacy, all sanctity. The American frenzy was naturally the loudest and seemed to reveal monstrosities of organization: it appeared to present him, to a continent peopled with seventy millions, as an object of such homage as no genius had yet elicited. The demonstrations and revelations encircled him like a *ronde infernale*. He found himself sunk in a landslide of obsessions, of inane, incongruous letters, of interviewers, intruders, invaders, some of them innocent enough, but only the more maddening, others with axes to grind that might have made him call at once, to have it over, for the headsman and the block. Was it only a chance that reverberation had come too late, come, in its perverse way, as if the maleficent fairy of nursery-tales had said, in the far past, at his cradle: 'Oh yes, you shall have it to the full, you shall have it till you stop your ears; but you shall have it long after it may bring you any joy, you shall have it when your spirits have left you and your nerves are exposed, you shall have it in a form from which you will turn for refuge – where?' He appears to me to have turned for refuge to the only quarter where peace is deep, for if the fact, so presented, sounds overstated, the element of the portentous was not less a reality. It consisted not solely of the huge botheration – the word in which he most vented his sense of the preposterous ado. It consisted, in its degree, of an unappeasable alarm at the strange fate of being taken so much more seriously than one had proposed or had dreamed; indeed in a general terror of the temper of the many-headed monster. To have pleased – that came back – would have been a joy, the joy that carries off bravely all usual rewards; but where was the joy of any relation to an attitude unfathomable? To what, great heaven, was one committed by assenting to such a position, and to what, on taking it up *de gaieté de coeur*, did the mighty multitude commit itself? To what did it not, rather, might well have been asked of a public with no mind apparently to reflect on the prodigious keeping up, on one side and the other, that such terms as these implied. A spell recognized on such a scale could only be a spell that would hold its army together and hold it at concert pitch. What might become of the army and what might become of the pitch was a question competent to trouble even the dreams of a wizard: but the anxiety that haunted him most bore upon the possible future of the spell. Was the faculty that produced it not then of a kind to take care of itself? Were not, as mere perception of character and force, such acclamations a fund to draw upon again and again? Unless they meant everything, what did they mean at all? They meant nothing, in short, unless they meant a guarantee. They would therefore always be there; but where, to meet them, would a poor author calculably be? – a poor author into whose account no such assumption of responsibility had for a moment entered.

Du Maurier felt so much, in a word, in the whole business, the want of proportion between effect and cause that he could only shake his head sadly under the obvious suggestion of a friend that he had simply to impose on the public the same charge as the public imposed. Were it not for a fear of making it sound like the spirit of observation gone mad, I should venture to remark that no one of my regrets in the face of the event is greater, perhaps, than for the loss of the spectacle of his chance to watch the success of such an effort. We talked of these things in the first months, talked of them till the conditions quite oppressively changed and the best way to treat them appeared much rather by talking of quite other things. I think of him then as silent about many altogether, and also as, from the beginning of this complication of indifference and pressure, of weariness and fame, more characteristically and humorously mild. He was never so gentle as in all the irritating time. The collapse of his strength seemed, at the last, sudden, and yet there had been signs enough, on looking back, of an ebbing tide. I have no kinder memory of the charming superseded Hampstead than, on the clear, cool nights, the gradual shrinkage, half tacit, half discussed, of his old friendly custom of seeing me down the hill. The hill, for our parting, was long enough to make a series of stages that became a sort of deprecated register of what he could do no more; and it was inveterate enough that I wanted to reascend with him rather than go my way and let him pass alone into the night. Each of us might have, I suppose, at the back of his head, a sense, in all of this, of something symbolic and even vaguely ominous. Rather than let him pass alone into the night I would, assuredly, when the real time came, gladly have taken with him whatever other course might have been the equivalent of remounting the hill into the air of better days. The moment arrived indeed when he came down, as it were, altogether: his death was preceded by the longest stretch of 'real' London that he had attempted for a quarter of a century – a troubled, inconsequent year, in which the clock of his new period kept striking a different hour from the clock of his old spirit. He only wanted to simplify, but there were more forces to reckon with than could be disposed of in the shortening span. He simplified, none the less, to the utmost, and in the way, after all, never really closed to the artist; looking as much as ever, in a kind of resistant placidity, a stoicism of fidelity, at the things he had always loved, turning away more than ever from those he never had, and cultivating, above all, as a refuge from the great botheration, the sight of the London immersions from the summit of the London road-cars. This was the serenest eminence of all, and a source alike of suggestion and of philosophy; yet I reflect that in speaking of it as the last entrenchment I do injustice to the spark, burning still and intense, of his life-long, indefeasible passion for seeing his work through. No conditions, least of all those of its being run away with, could divert him from the nursing attitude. That was always a chamber of peace, and it was the chamber in which, to the utmost, in the multiplication of other obsessions, he shut himself up, at the last, with *The Martian*. The other books had come and gone – so far as execution was concerned – in a flash; on the studio table, with no harm meant and no offence taken, and with friendly music in his ears and friendly confidence all around. To his latest novel, on the other hand, he gave his greatest care; it was a labour of many months, and he went over it again and again. There was nothing indeed that, as the light faded, he did not more intensely go over. Though there are signs of this fading light in those parts of all his concluding illustrative work that were currently reproduced, there is evidence, touching in amount, of his having, in the matter of sketches and studies, during his two or three last years, closed with his idea more ingeniously than ever. He practised, repeated, rehearsed to the very end, and the experiments in question, all preliminary and in pencil, have, to my sense, in comparison with their companions, the charm of being nearer the source. He was happy in that, as in most other things – happy, I mean, in the fact that, throughout, he was justified of every interest, every affection and every trust. It was the completest, securest, most rounded artistic and personal life; and if I hesitate to sum it up by saying that he had achieved what he wished and enjoyed what he wanted, that is only because of an impression which, if it be too whimsical, will, I hope, be forgiven me – the impression that he had both enjoyed and achieved even a good deal more.

THOMAS HARDY (1840–1928)
by G. K. Chesterton (1874–1936)

The first great Victorian I ever met, I met very early, though only for a brief interview: Thomas Hardy. I was then a quite obscure and shabby young writer awaiting an interview with a publisher. And the really remarkable thing about Hardy was this; that he might have been himself an obscure and shabby young writer awaiting a publisher; even a new writer awaiting his first publisher. Yet he was already famous everywhere; he had written his first and finest novels culminating in *Tess*; he had expressed his queer personal pessimism in the famous passage about the President of the Immortals. He had already the wrinkle of worry on his elvish face that might have made a man look old; and yet, in some strange way, he seemed to me very young. If I say as young as I was, I mean as simply pragmatical and even priggish as I was. He did not even avoid the topic of his alleged pessimism; he defended it, but somehow with the innocence of a boys' debating-club. In short, he was in a sort of gentle fuss about his pessimism, just as I was about my optimism. He said something like this: 'I know people say I'm a pessimist; but I don't believe I am naturally; I like a lot of things so much; but I could never get over the idea that it would be better for us to be without both the pleasures and the pains; and that the best experience would be some sort of sleep.' I have always had a weakness for arguing with anybody; and this involved all that contemporary nihilism against which I was then in revolt; and for about five minutes, in a publisher's office, I actually argued with Thomas

Hardy. I argued that non-existence is not an experience; and there can be no question of preferring it or being satisfied with it. Honestly, if I had been quite simply a crude young man, and nothing else, I should have thought his whole argument very superficial and even silly. But I did not think him either superficial or silly.

For this was the rather tremendous truth about Hardy; that he had humility... The whole case for him is that he had the sincerity and simplicity of the village atheist; that is, that he valued atheism as a truth and not a triumph. He was the victim of that decay of our agricultural culture, which gave men bad religion and no philosophy. But he was right in saying, as he said essentially to me all those years ago, that he could enjoy things, including better philosophy or religion.

Thomas Hardy
by W. Somerset Maugham (1874–1965)

I met Thomas Hardy but once. This was at a dinner-party at Lady St Helier's, better known in the social history of the day as Lady Jeune, who liked to ask to her house (in a much more exclusive world than the world of today) every one that in some way or another had caught the public eye. I was then a popular and fashionable playwright. It was one of those great dinner-parties that people gave before the war, with a vast number of courses, thick and clear soup, fish, a couple of entrées, sorbet (to give you a chance to get your second wind), joint, game, sweet, ice, and savoury; and there were twenty-four people all of whom by rank, political eminence or artistic achievement, were distinguished. When the ladies retired to the drawing-room, I found myself sitting next to Thomas Hardy. I remember a little man with an earthy face. In his evening clothes, with his boiled shirt and high collar, he had still a strange look of the soil. He was amiable and mild. It struck me at the time that there was in him a curious mixture of shyness and self-assurance. I do not remember what we talked about, but I know that we talked for three-quarters of an hour. At the end of it he paid me a great compliment: he asked me (not having heard my name) what was my profession.

Thomas Hardy
by Robert Graves (1895–1985)

We found ourselves near Dorchester, so we turned in there to visit Thomas Hardy, whom we had met not long before when he came up to Oxford to get his honorary doctor's degree. We found him active and gay, with none of the aphasia and wandering of attention that we had noticed in him at Oxford . . .

We had tea in the drawing-room, which, like the rest of the house, was crowded with furniture and ornaments. Hardy had an affection for old possessions, and Mrs Hardy was too fond to suggest that anything at all should be removed. Hardy, his cup of tea in hand, began making jokes about bishops at the Athenaeum Club and imitating their episcopal tones when they ordered: 'China tea and a little bread and butter (Yes, my lord!).' Apparently he considered bishops were fair game. He was soon censuring Sir Edmund Gosse, who had recently stayed with them, for a breach of good taste in imitating his old friend, Henry James, eating soup. Loyalty to his friends was always a passion with Hardy.

After tea we went into the garden, and Hardy asked to see some of my recent poems. I showed him one, and he asked if he might make some suggestions. He objected to the phrase the 'scent of thyme', which he said was one of the clichés which the poets of his generation studied to avoid. I replied that they had avoided it so well that it could be used again now without offence, and he withdrew the objection. He asked whether I wrote easily, and I said that this poem was in its sixth draft and would probably be finished in two more. 'Why!' he said, 'I have never in my life taken more than three, or perhaps four, drafts for a poem. I am afraid of it losing its freshness.' He said that he had been able to sit down and write novels by timetable, but that poetry was always accidental, and perhaps it was for that reason that he prized it more highly.

He spoke disparagingly of his novels, though admitting that there were chapters in them that he had enjoyed writing. We were walking round the garden, and Hardy paused at a spot near the greenhouse. He said that he had once been pruning a tree here when an idea suddenly had come into his head for a story, the best story that he had ever thought of. It came complete with characters, setting, and even some of the dialogue. By the time he sat down to recall it, all was utterly gone. 'Always carry a pencil and paper,' he said. He added: 'Of course, even if I could remember that story now, I couldn't write it. I am past novel-writing. I often wonder what it was.'

ÉMILE ZOLA (1840–1902)
by Henry James (1843–1916)

Several men of letters of a group in which almost every member either had arrived at renown or was well on his way to it, were assembled under the roof of the most distinguished of their number [Flaubert], where they exchanged free confidences on current work, on plans and ambitions, in a manner full of interest for one never previously privileged to see artistic conviction, artistic passion (at least on the literary ground) so systematic and so articulate. 'Well, I on my side,' I remember Zola's saying, 'am engaged on a book, a study of the *moeurs* of the people, for which I am making a collection of all the "bad words," the *gros mots*, of the language, those with which the vocabulary of the people, those with which their familiar talk, bristles.' I was struck with the tone in which he made the announcement – without bravado and without apology, as an interesting idea that had come to him and that he was working, really to arrive at character and particular truth, with all his conscience; just as I was struck with the unqualified interest that his plan excited. It was *on* a plan that he was working – formidably, almost grimly, as his fatigued face showed; and the whole consideration of this interesting element partook of the general seriousness.

Émile Zola
by Edmond de Goncourt (1822–1896)

4 AUGUST 1893

Every six months Zola feels the need to feel our pulses, Daudet's and mine, to find out how we are, physically and mentally. Today then, he was to dine here. And we waited for him with a certain apprehension, in view of the nervous condition we were both in. Mme Daudet advised us not to be so tense and urged me to take a really restful siesta before Zola spoke of the theatre, saying that he was tired of it but that it was a field in which he thought he might be able to break new ground, and that he was tempted to write a play between his novels *Lourdes* and *Rome*. Then, jumping from one subject to another, he admitted to a passion for cakes, confessing that he ate a whole plateful with his four o'clock tea; and then he launched into a eulogy of insomnia, saying that it was while he was lying awake in bed that he made his decisions, which he started executing as soon as he had put on his boots, an action which he performed while thinking aloud: 'Here I am on my feet again!'

Then came the sweetly hypocritical compliments, the questions which are traps, the declarations which, if you follow him, he will suddenly interrupt with an: 'Oh, my dear fellow, I wouldn't go as far as you!' followed by a virtual recantation of his previous arguments. In fact that art of talking without saying anything of which the man of Médan is the unrivalled master.

Meanwhile Mme Zola, aged, wrinkled, influenza-ridden, and in Mme Daudet's words looking like an old doll in the window of a bankrupt toy shop, was sitting in a corner with Mme Daudet, describing her sad life at Médan, and saying of her husband: 'I only see him at lunch ... After lunch he takes a few turns round the garden, waiting for the papers to arrive and until then throwing me a few words ... telling me to look after the cow. But I don't know anything about that sort of thing, and it seems to me that it's more a job for the gardener. . . . Then he goes back upstairs to read the papers and take his siesta. . . . I had a cousin of mine to stay the last few years; this year I miss her; she's at the seaside.' And I could see Zola anxiously following the conversation from a distance.

We sat down to dinner, and a black cloud which seemed to foreshadow a storm led Mme Zola to tell us once more of Zola's fear of thunder, both as a child, when he had to be taken down to the cellar, wrapped in blankets, and now, when in the billiard-room at Médan, with the windows shut and all the lamps lit, he still covered his eyes with a handkerchief.

HENRY JAMES (1843–1916)
by G. K. Chesterton (1874–1936)

Henry James inhabited the house with all the gravity and loyalty of the family ghosts; not without something of the oppressive delicacy of a highly cultured family butler. He was in point of fact a very stately and courteous old gentleman; and, in some social aspects especially, rather uniquely gracious. He proved in one point that there was a truth in his cult of tact. He was serious with children. I saw a little boy gravely present him with a crushed and dirty dandelion, he bowed; but he did not smile. That restraint was a better proof of the understanding of children than the writing of *What Maisie Knew*. But in all relations of life he erred, on the side of solemnity and slowness; ... here we are halted at the moment when Mr Henry James heard of our arrival in Rye and proceeded (after exactly the correct interval) to pay his call in state.

Needless to say, it was a very stately call of state; and James seemed to fill worthily the formal frock-coat of those far-off days. As no man is so dreadfully well-dressed as a well-dressed American, so no man is so terribly well-mannered as a well-mannered American. He brought his brother William with him, the famous American philosopher; and though William James was breezier than his brother when you knew him, there was something finally ceremonial about this idea of the whole family on the march. We talked about the best literature of the day; James a little tactfully, myself a little nervously. I found he was more strict than I had imagined about the rules of artistic arrangement; he deplored rather than depreciated Bernard Shaw, because plays like *Getting Married* were practically formless. He said something complimentary about something of mine; but represented himself as respectfully wondering how I wrote all I did. I suspected him of meaning why rather than how. We then proceeded to consider gravely the work of Hugh Walpole, with many delicate degrees of appreciation and doubt; when I heard from the front-garden a loud bellowing noise resembling that of an impatient fog-horn. I knew, however, that it was not a fog-horn; because it was roaring out, 'Gilbert! Gilbert!' and was like only one voice in the world; as rousing as that recalled in one of its former phrases, of those who

> Heard Ney shouting to the guns to unlimber
> And hold the Bersina Bridge at night.

I knew it was [Hilaire] Belloc, probably shouting for bacon and beer; but even I had no notion of the form or guise under which he would present himself.

I had every reason to believe that he was a hundred miles away in France. And so, apparently, he had been; walking with a friend of his in the Foreign Office, a co-religionist of one of the old Catholic families; and by some miscalculation they had found themselves in the middle of their travels entirely without money ...

They started to get home practically without money. Their clothes collapsed and they managed to get into some workmen's slops. They had no razors and could not afford a shave. They must have saved their last penny to recross the sea; and then they started walking from Dover to Rye; where they knew their nearest friend for the moment resided. They arrived, roaring for food and drink and derisively accusing each other of having secretly washed, in violation of an implied contract between tramps. In this fashion they burst in upon the balanced tea-cup and tentative sentence of Mr Henry James.

Henry James had a name for being subtle; but I think that situation was too subtle for him. I doubt to this day whether he, of all men, did not miss the irony of the best comedy in which he ever played a part. He left America because he loved Europe, and all that was meant by England or France; the gentry, the gallantry, the traditions of lineage and locality, the life that had been lived beneath old portraits in oak-panelled rooms. And there, on the other side of the tea-table, was Europe, was the old thing that made France and England, the posterity of the English squires and the French soldiers; ragged, unshaven, shouting for beer, shameless above all shades of poverty and wealth; sprawling, indifferent, secure. And what looked across at it was still the Puritan refinement of Boston; and the space it looked across was wider than the Atlantic.

Henry James
by Edith Wharton (1862–1937)

Not infrequently, on my annual visit to Qu'acre, I 'took off' from Lamb House, where I also went annually for a visit to Henry James. The motor run between Rye and Windsor being an easy one, I was often accompanied by Henry James, who generally arranged to have his visit to Qu'acre coincide with mine. James, who was a frequent companion on our English motor-trips, was firmly convinced that, because he lived in England, and our chauffeur (an American) did not, it was necessary that the latter should be guided by him through the intricacies of the English countryside. Signposts were rare in England in those days, and for many years afterward, and a truly British reserve seemed to make the local authorities reluctant to communicate with the invading stranger. Indeed, considerable difficulty existed as to the formulating of advice and instructions, and I remember in one village the agitated warning: 'Motorists! Beware of the children!' – while in general there was a marked absence of indications as to the whereabouts of the next village.

It chanced, however, that Charles Cook, our faithful and skilful driver, was a born path-finder, while James's sense of direction was non-existent, or rather actively but always erroneously alert; and the consequences of his intervention were always bewildering, and sometimes extremely fatiguing. The first time that my husband and I went to Lamb House by motor (coming from France) James, who had travelled to Folkestone by train to meet us, insisted on seating himself next to Cook, on the plea that the roads across Romney marsh formed such a tangle that only an old inhabitant could guide us to Rye. The suggestion resulted in our turning around and around in our tracks till long after dark, though Rye, conspicuous on its conical hill, was just ahead of us, and Cook could easily have landed us there in time for tea.

Another year we had been motoring in the west country, and on the way back were to spend a night at Malvern. As we approached (at the close of a dark rainy afternoon) I saw James growing restless, and was not surprised to hear him say: 'My dear, I once spent a summer at Malvern, and know it very well; and as it is rather difficult to find the way to the hotel, it might be well if Edward were to change places with me, and let me sit beside Cook.' My husband of course acceded (though with doubt in his heart), and James having taken his place, we awaited the result. Malvern, if I am not mistaken, is encircled by a sort of upper boulevard, of the kind called in Italy a *strada di circonvallazione*, and for an hour we circled about above the outspread city, while James vainly tried to remember which particular street led down most directly to our hotel. At each corner (literally) he stopped the motor, and we heard a muttering, first confident and then anguished. 'This – this, my dear Cook, yes ... this certainly is the right corner. But no; stay! A moment longer, please – in this light it's so difficult ... appearances are so misleading ... It may be ... yes! I think it is the next turn ... "a little farther lend thy guiding hand" ... that is, drive on; but slowly, please, my dear Cook; *very* slowly!' And at the next corner the same agitated monologue would be repeated; till at length Cook, the mildest of men, interrupted gently: 'I guess any turn'll get us down into the town, Mr James, and after that I can ask. –' and late, hungry and exhausted we arrived at length at our destination, James still convinced that the next turn would have been the right one, if only we had been more patient.

The most absurd of these episodes occurred on another rainy evening, when James and I chanced to arrive at Windsor long after dark. We must have been driven by a strange chauffeur – perhaps Cook was on holiday; at any rate, having fallen into the lazy habit of trusting to him to know the way, I found myself at a loss to direct his substitute to the King's Road. While I was hesitating, and peering out into the darkness, James spied an ancient doddering man who had stopped in the rain to gaze at us. 'Wait a moment, my dear – I'll ask him where we are'; and leaning out he signalled to the spectator.

'My good man, if you'll be good enough to come here, please; a little nearer – so', and as the old man came up: 'My friend, to put it to you in two words, this lady and I have just arrived here from *Slough*; that is to say, to be more strictly accurate, we have recently *passed through* Slough on our way here, having actually motored to Windsor from Rye, which was our point of departure; and the darkness having overtaken us, we should be much obliged if you would tell us where we now are in relation, say, to the High Street, which, as you of course know, leads to the Castle, after leaving on the left hand the turn down to the railway station.'

I was not surprised to have this extraordinary appeal met by silence, and a dazed expression on the old wrinkled face at the window; nor to have James go on: 'In short' (his invariable prelude to a fresh series of explanatory ramifications), 'in short, my good man, what I want to put to you in a word is this: supposing we have already (as I have reason to think we have) driven past the turn down to the railway station (which, in that case, by the way, would probably not have been on our left hand, but on our right), where are we now in relation to . . .'

'Oh, please,' I interrupted, feeling myself utterly unable to sit through another parenthesis, 'do ask him where the King's Road is.'

'Ah – ? The King's Road? Just so! Quite right! Can you, as a matter of fact, my good man, tell us where, in relation to our present position, the King's Road exactly *is*?' 'Ye're in it', said the aged face at the window.

Henry James
by Virginia Woolf (1882–1941)

LETTER TO VIOLET DICKINSON, 25 AUGUST 1907

. . . we went and had tea with Henry James today, and Mr and Mrs Prothero, at the golf club; and Henry James fixed me with his staring blank eye – it is like a child's marble – and said 'My dear Virginia, they tell me – they tell me – they tell me – that you – as indeed being your father's daughter nay your grandfather's grandchild – the descendant I may say of a century – of a century – of quill pens and ink – ink – inkpots, yes, yes, yes, they tell me – ahm m m – that you, that you, that you *write* in short.' This went on in the public street, while we all waited, as farmers wait for the hen to lay an egg – do they? – nervous, polite, and now on this foot now on that. I felt like a condemned person, who sees the knife drop and stick and drop again. Never did any woman hate 'writing' as much as I do. But when I am old and famous I shall discourse like Henry James. We had to stop periodically to let him shake himself free of the thing; he made phrases over the bread and butter 'rude and rapid' it was, and told us all the scandal of Rye. 'Mr Jones has eloped, I regret to say, to Tasmania; leaving 12 little Jones, and a possible 13th to Mrs Jones; most regrettable, most unfortunate, and yet not wholly an action to which one has no private key of one's own so to speak.'

W. E. HENLEY (1849–1903)
by Robert Louis Stevenson (1850–1894)

Yesterday, Leslie Stephen, who was down here to lecture, called on me and took me up to see a poor fellow, a bit of a poet who writes for him, and who has been eighteen months in our Infirmary and may be, for all I know, eighteen months more. It was very sad to see him there, in a little room with two beds, and a couple of sick children in the other bed; a girl came in to visit the children and played dominoes on the counterpane with them; the gas flared and crackled, the fire burned in a dull economical way; Stephen and I sat on a couple of chairs and the poor fellow sat up in his bed, with his hair and beard all tangled, and talked as cheerfully as if he had been in a King's Palace, or the great King's Palace of the blue air. He has taught himself two languages since he has been lying there. I shall try to be of use to him.

LETTER TO CHARLES BAXTER, 22 MARCH 1888

In a letter to Stevenson, Henley had accused Stevenson's wife of plagiarising a short story. It was a complicated affair, and in the words of the leading Stevenson expert, Ernest Mehew, 'the rights and wrongs cannot now be determined'.

My dear Charles, I am going to write what I should not, and shall probably not send; but in the melancholy that falls upon me, I must break out at least upon paper. I fear I have come to an end with Henley; the Lord knows if I have not tried hard to be a friend to him, the Lord knows even that I have not altogether failed. There is not one of that crew that I have not helped in every kind of strait, with money, with service, and that I was not willing to have risked my life for; and yet the years come, and every year there is a fresh outburst against me and mine. If the troubles that have been brewed for me in Shepherd's Bush had been taken out of my last years, they would have been a different season. And I have forgiven, and forgiven, and forgotten and forgotten; and still they get their heads together and there springs up a fresh enmity or a fresh accusation. Why, I leave to them – and above all to Henley – to explain: I never failed one of them. But when they get together round the bowl, they brew for themselves hot heads and ugly feelings.

But this, as I say, I have known and suffered under long; I knew long ago, how Henley tried to make trouble for me, and I not only held my peace, when I had the evidence; I willingly forgave also; for I understood all his nature, and much of it I love. And I would have gone on forgiving, too, or so I think *ad libitum*; but unless this business comes to a termination I dare scarcely hope, it is what I cannot pass over; even as it is, the best reconciliation to be hoped will be largely formal. If this letter go, which I much question, and I am sure it had better not – I shall put you in no false position by calling it private; I shall only ask you to judge, and to be wiser in what you do with it than I am in writing it. It is hard for me to recognize my old friends falling away from me; whatever my defects, I do not think they have changed; but I daresay I deceive myself and I have indeed altered for the worse; if I have not, some singular feeling springs spontaneously in the bosom of those whom I love. For God's sake, don't let us . . . But hush upon that.

LETTER TO CHARLES BAXTER, *c.*15 JULY 1894

I have had a letter from Henley, which I thought to be in very good taste and rather touching. My wife, with that appalling instinct of the injured female to see mischief, thought it was a letter preparatory to the asking of money; and truly, when I read it again, it will bear this construction. This leads us direct to the consideration of what is to be done if H. does ask for money. I may say at once that I give it with a great deal of distaste. He has had bad luck of course; but he has had good luck too and has never known how to behave under it. On the other hand I feel as if I were near the end of my production. If it were nothing else, the growing effort and time that it takes me to produce anything forms a very broad hint. Now I want all the money that I can make for my family, and alas, for my possible old age, which is on the cards and will never be a lively affair for me, money or no money; but which would be a hideous humiliation to me if I had squandered all this money in the meanwhile and had to come forward as a beggar at the last. All which premised, I hereby authorise you to pay (when necessary) five pounds a month to Henley. He can't starve at that; it's enough – more than he had when I first knew him; and if I gave him more, it would only lead to his starting a gig and a Pomeranian dog.

Henley learned of this last phrase, and in 1901 wrote a savage posthumous attack on Stevenson.

GUY DE MAUPASSANT (1850–93)
by Gustave Flaubert (1821–80)

LETTER TO GUY DE MAUPASSANT, AUGUST 1878

Now let's talk about you. You complain about fucking being 'monotonous.' There's a very simple remedy: stop doing it. 'The news in the papers is always the same,' you say. That is a Realist's complaint, and besides, what do you know about it? You should scrutinize things more closely. Have you ever believed in the existence of things? Isn't everything an illusion? Only so-called relations – that is, our ways of perceiving objects – are true. 'The vices are trivial,' you say; but everything is trivial! 'There are not enough different ways to compose a sentence.' Seek and ye shall find.

Come now, my dear friend: you seem badly troubled, and that distresses me, for you could spend your time more agreeably. You *must* – do you hear me, young man? – you *must* work more than you do. I've come to suspect you of being something of a loafer. Too many whores! Too much rowing! Too much exercise! Yes, sir: civilized man doesn't need as much locomotion as doctors pretend. You were born to write poetry: write it! *All the rest is futile* – beginning with your fun and your health: get that into your head. Besides, your health will be the better for your following your calling. That remark is philosophically, or, rather, hygienically, profound.

You are living in an inferno of shit, I know, and I pity you from the bottom of my heart. But from five in the evening to ten in the morning all your time can be devoted to the muse, who is still the best bitch of all. Come, my dear fellow, chin up. What's the use of constantly probing your melancholy? You must set yourself up as a strong man in your own eyes: that's the way to become one. A little more pride, damn it! . . . What you lack are 'principles.' Say what you will, one has to have them; it remains to find out which ones. For an artist there is only one: sacrifice everything to Art. Life must be considered by the artist as a means, nothing more, and the first person he shouldn't give a hang about is himself.

. . . Let me sum up, my dear Guy: beware of melancholy. It's a vice. You take pleasure in affliction, and then, when affliction has passed, you find yourself dazed and deadened, for you have used up precious strength. And then you have regrets, but it's too late. Have faith in the experience of a sheikh to whom no folly is unknown!

ROBERT LOUIS STEVENSON (1850–94)
by Henry James (1843–1916)

If there be a writer of our language at the present moment who has the effect of making us regret the extinction of the pleasant fashion of the literary portrait, it is certainly the bright particular genius whose name I have written at the head of these remarks. Mr Stevenson fairly challenges portraiture, as we pass him on the highway of literature (if that be the road, rather than some wandering, sun-chequered by-lane, that he may be said to follow), just as the possible model, in local attire, challenges the painter who wanders through the streets of a foreign town looking for subjects. He gives us new ground to wonder why the effort to fix a face and figure, to seize a literary character and transfer it to the canvas of the critic, should have fallen into such discredit among us, and have given way, to the mere multiplication of little private judgment-seats, where the scales and the judicial wig, both of them considerably awry, and not rendered more august by the company of a vicious-looking switch, have taken the place, as the symbols of office, of the kindly, disinterested palette and brush. It has become the fashion to be effective at the expense of the sitter, to make some little point, or inflict some little dig, with a heated party air, rather than to catch a talent in the fact, follow its line, and put a finger on its essence: so that the exquisite art of criticism, smothered in grossness, finds itself turned into a question of 'sides.' The critic industriously keeps his score, but it is seldom to be hoped that the author, criminal though he may be, will be apprehended by justice through the handbills given out in the case; for it is of the essence of a happy description that it shall have been preceded by a happy observation and a free curiosity; and desuetude, as we may say, has overtaken these amiable, uninvidious faculties, which have not the glory of organs and chairs.

We hasten to add that it is not the purpose of these few pages to restore their lustre or to bring back the more penetrating vision of which we lament the disappearance. No individual can bring it back, for the light that we look at things by is, after all, made by all of us. It is sufficient to note, in passing, that if Mr Stevenson had presented himself in an age, or in a country, of portraiture, the painters would certainly each have had a turn at him. The easels and benches would have bristled, the circle would have been close, and quick, from the canvas to the sitter, the rising and falling of heads. It has happened to all of us to have gone into a studio, a studio of pupils, and seen the thick cluster of bent backs and the conscious model in the midst. It has happened to us to be struck, or not to be struck, with the beauty or the symmetry of this personage, and to have made some remark which, whether expressing admiration or disappointment, has elicited from one of the attentive workers the exclamation, 'Character, character is what he has!' These words may be applied to Mr Robert Louis Stevenson; in the language of that art which depends most on direct observation, character, character is what he has. He is essentially a model, in the sense of a sitter; I do not mean, of course, in the sense of a pattern or a guiding light. And if the figures who have a life in literature may also be divided into two great classes, we may add that he is conspicuously one of the draped: he would never, if I may be allowed the expression, pose for the nude. There are writers who present themselves before the critic with just the amount of drapery that is necessary for decency; but Mr Stevenson is not one of these – he makes his appearance in an amplitude of costume. His costume is part of the character of which I just now spoke; it never occurs to us to ask how he would look without it. Before all things he is a writer with a style – a model with a complexity of curious and picturesque garments. It is by the cut and the colour of this rich and becoming frippery – I use the term endearingly, as a painter might – that he arrests the eye and solicits the brush.

RUDYARD KIPLING (1865–1936)
by Mark Twain (1835–1910)

11 Aug 1906. This morning's cables contain a verse or two from Kipling, voicing his protest against a liberalising new policy of the British Government which he fears will deliver the balance of power in South Africa into the hands of the conquered Boers. Kipling's name, and Kipling's words always stir me now, stir me more than do any other living man's. But I remember a time, seventeen or eighteen years back, when the name did not suggest anything to me and only the words moved me. At that time Kipling's name was beginning to be known here and there, in spots, in India, but had not travelled outside of that empire. He came over and travelled about America, maintaining himself by correspondence with Indian journals. He wrote dashing, free-handed, brilliant letters but no one outside of India knew about it.

On his way through the State of New York he stopped off at Elmira and made a tedious and blistering journey up to Quarry Farm in quest of me. He ought to have telephoned the farm first; then he could have learned that I was at the Langdon homestead, hardly a quarter of a mile from his hotel. But he was only a lad of twenty-four and properly impulsive and he set out without inquiring on that dusty and roasting journey up the hill. He found Susy Crane and my little Susy there, and they came as near making him comfortable as the weather and the circumstances would permit.

13 Aug 1906. The group sat on the verandah and while Kipling rested and refreshed himself he refreshed the others with his talk, talk of a quality which was well above what they were accustomed to, talk which might be likened to footprints, so strong and definite was the impression which it left behind. They often spoke wonderingly of Kipling's talk afterward, and they recognised that they had been in contact with an extraordinary man, but it is more than likely that they were not the only persons who had perceived that he was extraordinary. It is not likely that they perceived his full magnitude, it is most likely that they were Eric

Ericsons, who had discovered a continent but did not suspect the horizon-less extent of it. His was an unknown name and was to remain unknown for a year yet, but Susy kept his card and treasured it as an interesting possession. Its address was Allalabad.

No doubt India had been to her an imaginary land up to this time, a fairyland, a dreamland, a land made out of poetry and moonlight for the Arabian Nights to do their gorgeous miracles in; and doubtless Kipling's flesh and blood and modern clothes realised it to her for the first time and solidified it. I think so because she more than once remarked upon its incredible remoteness from the world that we were living in, and computed that remoteness and pronounced the result with a sort of awe, 14,000 miles, or 16,000, whichever it was. Kipling had written upon the card a compliment to me. This gave the card an additional value in Susy's eyes, since as a distinction it was the next thing to being recognised by a denizen of the moon.

Kipling came down that afternoon and spent a couple of hours with me, and at the end of that time I had surprised him as much as he had surprised me, and the honours were easy. I believe that he knew more than any person I had met before, and I knew that he knew I knew less than any person he had met before – though he did not say it and I was not expecting that he would. When he was gone, Mr Langdon wanted to know about my visitor. I said, 'He is a stranger to me but is a most remarkable man – and I am the other one. Between us, we cover all knowledge; he knows all that can be known, and I know the rest.'

He was a stranger to me and to all the world, and remained so for twelve months, then he became suddenly known and universally known. From that day to this he has held this unique distinction: that of being the only living person, not head of a nation, whose voice is heard around the world the moment it drops a remark, the only such voice in existence that does not go by slow ship and rail but always travels first-class by cable.

About a year after Kipling's visit to Elmira, George Warner came into our library one morning in Hartford, with a small book in his hand, and asked me if I had ever heard of Rudyard Kipling. I said, 'No.'

He said I would hear of him very soon, and that the noise he was going to make would be loud and continuous. The little book was the *Plain Tales* and he left it for me to read, saying it was charged with a new and inspiriting fragrance and would blow a refreshing breath around the world that would revive the nations. A day or two later he brought a copy of the *London World* which had a sketch of Kipling in it, and a mention of the fact that he had travelled in the United States. According to the sketch he had passed through Elmira. This remark, added to the additional fact that he hailed from India, attracted my attention – also Susy's. She went to her room and brought the card from its place in the frame of her mirror, and the Quarry Farm visitor stood identified.

I am not acquainted with my own books but I know Kipling's – at any rate I know them better than I know anybody else's books. They never grow pale to me; they keep their colour; they are always fresh. Certain of the ballads have a peculiar and satisfying charm for me. To my mind, the incomparable Jungle Books must remain unfellowed permanently. I think it was worth the journey to India to qualify myself to read *Kim* understandingly and to realise how great a book it is. The deep and subtle and fascinating charm of India pervades no other book as it pervades *Kim. Kim* is pervaded by it as by an atmosphere. I read the book every year and in this way I go back to India without fatigue – the only foreign land I ever daydream about or deeply long to see again.

W. B. YEATS (1865–1939)
by John Berryman (1914–72)

Berryman is here 'speaking' in an interview for the Paris Review.

All I can say is that my mouth was dry and my heart was in my mouth. [Dylan] Thomas had very nearly succeeded in getting me drunk earlier in the day. He was full of scorn for Yeats, as he was for Eliot, Pound, Auden. He thought my admiration for Yeats was the funniest thing in that part of London. It wasn't until about three o'clock that I realized that he and I were drinking more than usual. I didn't drink much at that time; Thomas drank much more than I did. I had the sense to leave. I went back to my chambers, Cartwright Gardens, took a cold bath, and just made it for the appointment. I remember the taxi ride over. The taxi was left over from the First World War, and when we arrived in Pall Mall – we could see the Athenaeum – the driver said he didn't feel he could get in. Finally I decided to abandon ship and take off on my own. So I went in and asked for Mr Yeats. Very much like asking, 'Is Mr Ben Jonson here?' And he came down. He was much taller than I expected, and haggard. Big, though, big head, rather wonderful looking in a sort of a blunt, patrician kind of way, but there was something shrunken also. He told me he was just recovering from an illness. He was very courteous, and we went in to tea. At a certain point, I had a cigarette, and I asked him if he would like one. To my great surprise he said yes. So I gave him a Craven-A and then lit it for him, and I thought, Immortality is mine! From now on it's just a question of reaping the fruits of my effort. At one point he said, 'I have reached the age when my daughter can beat me at croquet,' and I thought, Hurrah, he's human! I made notes on the interview afterwards, which I have probably lost. One comment in particular I remember. He said, 'I never revise now' – you know how much he revised his stuff – 'but in the interests of a more passionate syntax.' Now that struck me as a very good remark. I have no idea what it meant and still don't know, but the longer I think about it, the better I like it. He recommended various books to me by his friend, the liar, Gogarty, and I forget who else. The main thing was just the presence and existence of my hero.

W. B. Yeats
by Louis MacNeice (1907–63)

[E. R.] Dodds and I went to tea with W. B. Yeats in Rathfarnham. Yeats in spite of his paunch was elegant in a smooth light suit and a just sufficiently crooked bow tie. His manner was hierophantic, even when he said: 'This afternoon I have been playing croquet with my daughter.' We were hoping he would talk poetry and gossip, but knowing that Dodds was a professor of Greek he confined the conversation to spiritualism and the phases of the moon, retailing much that he had already printed. Burnet, Yeats said, was all wrong; the Ionian physicists had of course not been physicists at all. The Ionian physicists were spiritualists.

He talked a great deal about the spirits to whom his wife, being a medium, had introduced him. 'Have you ever seen them?' Dodds asked (Dodds could never keep back such questions). Yeats was a little piqued. No, he said grudgingly, he had never actually seen them . . . but – with a flash of triumph – he had often *smelt* them.

Arnold Bennett (1867–1931)
by Virginia Woolf (1882–1941)

LETTER TO LADY CECIL, 28 DECEMBER 1927

I dined with Arnold Bennett the other night. Do you know him? He is a kind old walrus, who suddenly shuts his eyes like a dead fish and waits three minutes before he can finish his sentence. He makes enormous sums of money; but has horrible dinners; slabs of fish; huge potatoes; everything half cold; and then he took me to look at his bed. I should say that I had led to this by talking about comfort. All his furniture is very solid, but not comfortable; and uglier than you can even begin to imagine. So was his bed. He says that great artists need all the comfort they can get. But is he a great artist? I detest all novels, so I can't say.

SATURDAY 28 MARCH 1931

Arnold Bennett died last night; which leaves me sadder than I should have supposed. A lovable genuine man; impeded, somehow a little awkward in life; well meaning; ponderous; kindly; coarse; knowing he was coarse; dimly floundering & feeling for something else. Glutted with success; wounded in his feeling; avid; thick lipped; prosaic intolerably; rather dignified; set upon writing; yet always taken in; deluded by splendour & success; but naîve; an old bore; an egotist; much at the mercy of life for all his competence; a shop keeper's view of literature; yet with the rudiments, covered over with fat & prosperity & the desire for hideous Empire furniture, of sensibility. Some real understanding power, as well as a gigantic absorbing power. – These are the sort of things that I think by fits & starts this morning, as I sit journalising; I remember his determination to write, 1000 words daily; & how he trotted off to do it at night; & feel sorrow that now he will never sit down & begin methodically covering his regulation number of pages in his workmanlike beautiful but dull hand. Queer how one regrets the dispersal of any body who seemed – as I say – genuine; who had direct contact with life – for he abused me; & yet I rather wished him to go on abusing me; & me abusing him. An element in life – even in mine that was so remote – taken away. This is what one minds.

Bennett is dead, and I had the pleasure of being almost the last to talk to him before he drank a glass of water swarming with typhoid germs. 'Then' he said as he got up to go, 'men will say one morning "He's dead".' I, thinking this referred to his works, said 'Oh you mean your books?' 'No no no – myself.' So we parted, and though his books are dead as mutton, he had a relish for life – wore waistcoats of incredible beauty – so I'm sorry because I myself don't want to drink typhoid from a tumbler yet.

LÉON DAUDET (1867–1942)
by Marcel Proust (1871–1922)

Daudet is now remembered chiefly as the founder, with Charles Maurras, of the notorious ultra-nationalistic paper, L'Action Française.

LETTER TO REYNALDO HAHN, 15 NOVEMBER 1895

Dinner yesterday at the Daudets with my little dear one [Hahn], M. de Goncourt, Coppée, M. Philipe, M. Vacquès. Noted with sadness the frightful materialism, so surprising in 'intellectuals'. They account for character and genius by physical habits or race. Differences between Musset, Baudelaire and Verlaine explained by the properties of the spirits they drank, the characters of certain persons by their race (anti-Semitism). Even more astounding in Daudet, a pure and brilliant intellect shining through the mists and storms of his nerves, a small star on the sea. All that is most intelligent. The narrowest view of the mind (for everything is a view of the mind) is one in which it has not yet gained sufficient self-awareness and believes itself to be derived from the body . . .

Daudet is delightful, the son of a Moorish king who might have married a princess of Avignon, but simplistic in his intelligence. He thinks Mallarmé is fooling the public. One must always assume that a pact has been made between the poet's intelligence and his sensibility of which he himself is unaware, that he is its plaything. It's more interesting and more profound. Laziness or narrow-mindedness to be explained by a physical pact (with charlatanesque intention) with his disciples. If it were that, it would cease to interest us. And it cannot be that.

JOHN GALSWORTHY (1867–1933)
by Anthony Powell (1905–)

One hot summer afternoon [in the offices of the publishers, Duckworths], I was reading a manuscript, when the door opened quietly. A tall man, dressed in the deepest black, stood there in silence, clothes and bearing suggesting a clergyman. He smiled – to use an epithet he might well have employed in his own writing – 'quizzically'. I withdrew my feet from the desk, but he seemed to expect more than that; indeed instant acknowledgment of something in himself. A further survey convinced me that here was John Galsworthy. He gave off the redolence of boundless vanity, a condition not at all uncommon among authors, in this case more noticeable than usual.

I was about to alert Lewis, bent double at his desk over a sheaf of estimates, which, according to habit, he was examining at a range of about two inches off the paper, but Galsworthy, making the conventional gesture of finger to lips, indicated silence. He was just within sight of Lewis round the corner of the desk, the implication being that by sheer personality Galsworthy would send out rays which would compel Lewis to look up.

We both awaited a respectful burst of recognition. For some reason the magnetism did not work. Galsworthy stood there smiling with benevolent condescension; the smile becoming increasingly fixed, as Lewis continued to ponder the estimates. Finally Galsworthy gave it up as a bad job. He announced his presence abruptly by word of mouth. He was evidently disappointed in Lewis's lack of antennae, where famous writers were concerned. Lewis raised his head to see who had spoken, then, taking in at a glance one of the firm's most lucrative properties, jumped up full of apologies, and hurried the Great Man into the Senior Partner's room.

HILAIRE BELLOC (1870–1953)
by Evelyn Waugh (1903–66)

SUNDAY 28 SEPTEMBER 1952

Drove to visit Belloc, prearranged with letters and telephones, with Jebbs. Kingland, Shipley. Farm house, brick at corner of lane; dilapidated windmill near it. Some milk churns suggestive of dairy farming. Greeted by two Jebb boys, one handsome in sailor's sweater, other small, natty, cherubic, paralysed hand. Very welcoming, decanter of sherry. Fair-sized hall, book-lined and prints of sentimental interest; photographs. Clean and comfortable. Younger boy went to fetch 'Granda'. Sounds of shuffling. Enter old man, shaggy white beard, black clothes garnished with food and tobacco. Thinner than I last saw him, with benevolent gleam. Like an old peasant or fisherman in French film. We went to greet him at door. Smell like fox. He kissed Laura's hand, bowed to me saying, 'I am pleased to make your acquaintance, sir.' Shuffled to chair by fire. During whole visit he was occupied with unsuccessful attempts to light an empty pipe.

'Old age is an extraordinary thing. It makes a man into a shuffling beast, but his mind remains clear as a youth's.'

He noticed my stick near the door and told the boys to put it away. Also a leaf that had blown in, which he had expelled. He looked hard at Laura and said: 'You are very like your mother, are you not?'

'She is taller.'

'English women are enormous. So are the men – giants.'

'I am short.'

'Are you, sir? I am no judge.' He could not follow anything said to him, but enjoyed pronouncing the great truths which presumably he ponders. Great zeal over wine – a rarity. 'Wine. What next? A man should drink a bottle a meal, etc.' 'It is a good thing to write poetry. That is the thing to be remembered.' 'Very few poets nowadays.' 'I write poetry constantly, great poetry. Not much at a time.' 'These things are not come by easily.' He lapsed into French, telling a story for whose indelicacy he apologised. He spotted that I didn't understand it. 'Would you rather have two languages, sir, or one?' Conversation trailed off. Complained that Nancy Astor did not ask his wife to dinner. Told Lord Astor dying; couldn't take that in. Still talking of arrogance of the rich. Nothing about religion. 'Sunday? What next?' 'How long have all men dressed alike?' (We were a singularly heterogeneous lot.) 'Is it since the French Revolution?' Attempts to remark on extreme fashions of the Directoire not understood. 'What do they say about Napoleon now? Do they say he was a rascal?' But like jesting Pilate would not stay for an answer. Physical – pleasure in wine, annoyance with pipe. Authentic pleasures few. Showed terrible etching of Beauvais Cathedral with great pride; 'the largest ever made.'

STEPHEN CRANE (1871–1900)
by Ford Madox Ford (1873–1939)

Crane was the most beautiful spirit I have ever known. He was small, frail, energetic, at times virulent. He was full of fantasies and fantasticisms. He would fly at and deny every statement before it was out of your mouth. He wore breeches, riding leggings, spurs, a cowboy's shirt, and there was always a gun near him in the medieval building that he inhabited seven miles from Winchelsea. In that ancient edifice he would swat flies with precision and satisfaction with the bead-sight of his gun. He proclaimed all day long that he had no use for corner lots nor battlefields, but he got his death in a corner, on the most momentous of all battlefields for Anglo-Saxons. Brede Manor saw the encampment of Harold before Hastings.

He was an American, pure-blooded, and of ostentatious manners when he wanted to be. He used to declare at one time that he was the son of an uptown New York Bishop; at another, that he had been born in the Bowery and there dragged up. At one moment his voice would be harsh, like a raven's, uttering phrases like: 'I'm a fly-guy that's wise to the all-night push,' if he wanted to be taken for a Bowery tough; or 'He was a mangy, sheep-stealing coyote,' if he desired to be thought of cowboy ancestry. At other times, he would talk rather low in very selected English. That was all boyishness.

But he was honourable, physically brave, infinitely hopeful, generous, charitable to excess, observant beyond belief, morally courageous, of unswerving loyalty, a beautiful poet – and of untiring industry. With his physical frailty, his idealism, his love of freedom and of truth he seemed to me to be like Shelley. His eyes with their long fringes of lashes were almost incredibly beautiful – and as if vengeful. Of his infinite industry he had need. . . .

The effect on [Henry] James of poor Steevie was devastating. Crane rode about the countryside on one of two immense coach-horses that he possessed. On their raw-boned carcases his frail figure looked infinitely tiny and forlorn. At times he would rein up before the Old Man's door and going in would tell the master's titled guests that he was a fly-guy that was wise to all the all-night pushes of the world. The master's titled guests liked it. It was, they thought, characteristic of Americans. If the movies had then existed they would have thought themselves confronted with someone from Hollywood. James winced and found it unbearable.

From Steevie he had stood and would have stood a great deal more. The boy for him was always: 'My young compatriot of genius.' But he would explain his wincings to English people by: 'It's as if . . . oh dear lady . . . it's as if you should find in a staid drawing room on Beacon Hill or Washington Square or at an intimate reception at an Embassy at Washington a Cockney – oh, I admit of the greatest genius – but a Cockney, still, a costermonger from Whitechapel. And, oh heavens, received, surrounded and adulated . . . by, ah, the choicest, the loveliest, the most sympathetic and, ah, the most ornamented . . .'

And the joke – or, for the Old Man the tragedy – was that Crane assumed his Bowery cloak for the sole purpose of teasing the Master. In much the same way, taking me for a Pre-Raphaelite poet, at the beginning of our friendship, he would be for ever harshly denouncing those who paid special prices for antiquities. To [Joseph] Conrad or to [W. H.] Hudson, on the other hand, he spoke and behaved as a reasoning and perceptive human being.

THEODORE DREISER (1871–1945)
by John Dos Passos (1896–1970)

From my youth I'd had great admiration for Dreiser. It was the ponderous battering ram of his novels that opened the way through the genteel reticences of American nineteenth-century fiction for what seemed to me to be a truthful description of people's lives. Without Dreiser's treading out a path for naturalism none of us would have had a chance to publish even.

The first time I met him he made me think of an elephant. It was something about his nose and the way the skin wrinkled about his eyes. He was pachydermic yet sensitive, standoffish, opinionated; but slyly alert and subject to a sudden flush of understanding when you least expected it. He was curious about what I was up to. I occasionally ate an uncomfortable lunch at his invitation at his hotel at Broadway and 72nd Street in New York.

He had no smalltalk and neither did I. Since he didn't eat lunch he would sit there, in the rather mustyseedy hotel sitting room, watching me while I ate. He was obviously happier talking to women than to men. I would sit there abashedly munching the tasteless food and go away with the feeling of having performed a reverential duty.

Max Beerbohm (1872–1956)
by Virginia Woolf (1882–1941)

18 DECEMBER 1928

. . . I met him at Ethel [Smyth]'s the other night. As I came in a thick set old man (such was my impression) rose, & I was introduced. No freakishness, no fancy about him. His face is solidified; has a thick moustache; a red veined skin, heavy lines; but then his eyes are perfectly round, very large, & sky blue. His eyes become dreamy & merry when the rest of him is well groomed & decorous in the extreme. He is brushed, neat, urbane. Halfway through dinner he turned to me & we began a 'nice', interesting flattering, charming kind of talk; he told me how he had read an article on Addison at Bognor during the war; when literature seemed extinct; & there was his own name. I daresay V.W. catches your eye as M.B. does mine. And nothing has encouraged me more. So I said, as I think, that he is immortal. In a small way, he said; but with complacency. Like a jewel which is hard & flawless, yet always changing. A charming image he said, very kind, approving, & what half flattered half saddened me, equal. Am I on that level? Virginia Woolf says – V.W. thinks – how do you write? & so on: I was one of his colleagues & fellows in the art of writing; but not I hoped quite so old. Anyhow he asked me how I wrote. For he hacks every step with his pen, & therefore never alters. He thought I wrote like this. I told him I had to cut out great chunks. I wish you could send them to me, he said; simply; Indeed, he was nothing if not kind; but looked long and steadily. Looked at Lord David [Cecil] – that queer painters look, so matching, so considering apart from human intent; yet with him not entirely. After dinner, he leant on the mantelpiece & Maurice Baring & I flittered round him like a pair of butterflies, praising, laughing, extravagant. And he said he was so pleased by the praise of intelligent people like ourselves. But always he had to be led off to talk politely to this person & that; finally disappeared, very dignified, very discreet in his white waistcoat, pressing my hand in his plump firm one long; & saying what a pleasure &c. I own that I dont find much difference between the great & ourselves – indeed they are like us: I mean they dont have the frills & furbelows of the small; come to terms quickly & simply.

But we got, of course, very little way. He talked of Hardy, & said that he couldnt bear Jude the Obscure: thought it falsified life, for there is really more happiness than sorrow in life, & Hardy tries to prove the opposite. And his writing is so bad. Then I ran down – but he reads my essays and knows this – Belloc. M.B. said that Belloc, one must remember, poured out ten books a year on history poetry &c. He was one of those full unequal people who were never perfect, as he, M.B., might be called perfect in a small way. But he was glad I didnt like him. Charles Lamb had the most beautiful things in him & then he spoilt them. He had never read a book except Pendennis & Tess of the d'Urbervilles till he left Oxford. And now at last, at Rapallo, he reads. He is taking Elizabeth & Orlando (pronounced in the French way) to read; treats he looks forward to.

1 NOVEMBER 1938

Max like a Cheshire cat. Orbicular. Jowled. Blue eyed. Eyes grow vague. Something like Bruce Richmond [editor of the *Times Literary Supplement*] – all curves. What he said was, Ive never been in a group. No, not even as a young man. It was a serious fault. When you're a young man you ought to think Theres only one right way. And I thought – this is very profound, but you maynt realise it – 'It takes all sorts to make a world.' I was outside all the groups. Now dear Roger Fry who, like me, was a born leader. No one so 'illuminated'. He looked it. Never saw anyone look it so much. I heard him lecture, on the Aesthetics of Art. I was disappointed. He kept on turning the page – turning the page. . . . Hampstead hasnt yet been spoilt. I stayed at Jack Straw's Castle some years ago. My wife had been having influenza. And the barmaid, looking over her shoulder said – my wife had had influenza twice – 'Quite a greedy one arent you?' Now thats immortal. There's all the race of barmaids in that. I suppose I've been ten times into public houses. George Moore never used his eyes. He never knew what men & women think. He got it all out of books. Ah I was afraid you would remind me of *Ave Atque Vale* [Moore's three volumes of memoirs]. Yes. That's beautiful. Yes, its true he used his eyes then. Otherwise its like a lovely lake, with no fish in it . . .

About his own writing: dear Lytton Strachey said to me: first I write one sentence; then I write another. Thats how I write. And so I go on. But I have a feeling writing ought to be like running through a field. Thats your way. Now how do you go down to your room, after breakfast – what do you feel? I used to look at the clock, & say Oh dear me its time I began my article . . . No, I'll read the paper first. I never wanted to write. But I used to come home from a dinner party & take my brush & draw caricature after caricature. They seemed to bubble up from here . . . he pressed his stomach. That was a kind of inspiration I suppose. What you said in your beautiful essay about me & Charles Lamb was quite true. He was crazy, he had the gift . . . genius. I'm too like Jack Horner. I pull out my plum. Its too rounded, too perfect . . . I have a public of about 1500 – Oh I'm famous, largely thanks to you, & people of importance at the top like you. I often read over my own work. And I have a habit of reading it through the eyes of people I respect. I often read it as Virginia Woolf would read it – picking out the kind of things you would like. You never do that? Oh you should try it.

FORD MADOX FORD (1873–1939)
by Ernest Hemingway (1899–1961)

Hemingway was first introduced to Ford by Ezra Pound in Paris in 1924. Though Ford encouraged and helped the young writer, Hemingway quickly grew to despise Ford. One of Hemingway's biographers, Jeffrey Meyers, has written of this relationship: 'Hemingway could not bear to be helped, and fiercely judged his own faults – sexual adventures and telling lies – when he saw them manifested in others.' This unreliable account of the twenties was written in the late fifties and published after Hemingway's death.

On this evening I was sitting at a table outside of the Lilas watching the light change on the trees and the outer boulevards. The door of the café opened behind me and to my right and a man came out and walked to my table.

'Oh here you are,' he said.

It was Ford Madox Ford, as he called himself then, and he was breathing heavily through a heavy, stained moustache and holding himself as upright as an ambulatory, well-clothed, up-ended hogshead.

'May I sit with you?' he asked, sitting down, and his eyes, which were a washed-out blue under colourless lids and eyebrows, looked out at the boulevard.

'I spent good years of my life that those beasts should be slaughtered humanely,' he said.

'You told me,' I said.

'I don't think so.'

'I'm quite sure.'

'Very odd. I've never told anyone in my life.'

'Will you have a drink?'

The waiter stood there and Ford told him he would have a Chambéry cassis. The waiter, who was tall and thin and bald on the top of his head with hair slicked over and who wore a heavy old-style dragoon moustache repeated the order.

'No. Make it a *fine à l'eau*,' Ford said. 'A *fine à l'eau* for Monsieur,' the waiter confirmed the order. I had always avoided looking at Ford when I could and I always held my breath when I was near him in a closed room, but this was the open air and the fallen leaves blew along the sidewalks from my side of the table past his, so I took a good look at him, repented, and looked across the boulevard. The light was changed again and I had missed the change. I took a drink to see if his coming had fouled it, but it still tasted good.

'You're very glum,' he said.

'No.'

'Yes, you are. You need to get out more. I stopped by to ask you to the little evenings we're giving in that amusing Bal Musette near the place Contrescarpe on the rue du Cardinal Lemoine.'

'I lived above it for two years before you came to Paris this last time.'

'How odd. Are you sure?'

'Yes,' I said. 'I'm sure. The man who owned it had a taxi and when I had to get a plane he'd take me out to the field, and we'd stop at the zinc bar of the Bal and drink a glass of white wine in the dark before we'd start for the airfield.'

'I've never cared for flying,' Ford said. 'You and your wife plan to come to the Bal Musette Saturday night. It's quite gay. I'll draw you a map so you can find it. I stumbled on it quite by chance.'

'It's under seventy-four rue du Cardinal Lemoine,' I said. 'I lived on the third floor.'

'There's no number,' Ford said. 'But you'll be able to find it if you can find the place Contrescarpe.'

I took another long drink. The waiter had brought Ford's drink and Ford was correcting him. 'It wasn't a brandy and soda,' he said helpfully but severely. 'I ordered a Chambéry vermouth and cassis.'

'It's all right, Jean,' I said. 'I'll take the *fine*. Bring monsieur what he orders now.' 'What I ordered,' corrected Ford.

At that moment a rather gaunt man wearing a cape passed on the sidewalk. He was with a tall woman and he glanced at our table and then away and went on his way down the boulevard.

'Did you see me cut him?' Ford said. '*Did* you see me cut him?' 'No. Who did you cut?'

'Belloc,' Ford said. '*Did* I cut him?' 'I didn't see it,' I said. 'Why did you cut him?'

'For every good reason in the world,' Ford said. '*Did* I cut him though!' He was thoroughly and completely happy. I had never seen Belloc and I did not believe that he had seen us. He looked like a man who had been thinking of something and had glanced at the table almost automatically. I felt badly that Ford had been rude to him, as, being a young man who was commencing his education, I had a high regard for him as an older writer. This is not understandable now but in those days it was a common occurrence.

I thought it would have been pleasant if Belloc had stopped at the table and I might have met him. The afternoon had been spoiled by seeing Ford but I thought Belloc might have made it better.

'What are you drinking brandy for?' Ford asked me. 'Don't you know it's fatal for a young writer to start drinking brandy?'

'Can't an American be a gentleman?'

'Perhaps John Quinn,' Ford explained. 'Certain of your ambassadors.'

'Myron T. Herrick?'

'Possible.'

'Was Henry James a gentleman?'

'Very nearly.'

'Are you a gentleman?'

'Naturally. I have held His Majesty's commission.'

'It's very complicated,' I said. 'Am I a gentleman?'

'Absolutely not,' Ford said.

'Then why are you drinking with me?'

'I'm drinking with you as a promising young writer. As a fellow writer, in fact.'

'Good of you,' I said.

'You might be considered a gentleman in Italy,' Ford said magnanimously.

'But I'm not a cad.'

'Of course not, dear boy. Who ever said such a thing?'

'I might become one,' I said sadly. 'Drinking brandy and all. That was what did for Lord Harry Hotspur in Trollope. Tell me, was Trollope a gentleman?'

'Of course not.'

'You're sure?'

'There might be two opinions. But not in mine.'

'Was Fielding? He was a judge.'

'Technically, perhaps.'

'Marlowe?'

'Of course not.'

'John Donne?'

'He was a parson.'

'It's fascinating,' I said.

'I'm glad you're interested,' Ford said. 'I'll have a brandy and water with you before you go.'

After Ford left it was dark and I walked over to the kiosk and bought a *Paris-Sport Complet*, the final edition of the afternoon racing paper with the results at Auteuil, and the line on the next day's meeting at Enghien. The waiter Emile, who had replaced Jean on duty, came to the table to see the results of the last race at Auteuil. A great friend of mine who rarely came to the Lilas came over to the table and sat down, and just then as my friend was ordering a drink from Emile the gaunt man in the cape with the tall woman passed us on the sidewalk. His glance drifted towards the table and then away.

'That's Hilaire Belloc,' I said to my friend. 'Ford was here this afternoon and cut him dead.'

'Don't be a silly ass,' my friend said. 'That's Aleister Crowley, the diabolist. He's supposed to be the wickedest man in the world.'

'Sorry,' I said.

Ford Madox Ford
by Robert Lowell (1917–77)

Taking in longhand Ford's dictation in Provence,
the great Prosateur swallowing his Yorkshire British,
I fishing for what he said each second sentence –
'You have no ear,' he said, 'for the Lord's prose,

Shakespeare's medium: *No king, be his cause never so spotless,
will try it out with all unspotted soldiers.'*
I brought him my loaded and overloaded lines.
He said, 'You have your butterfly existence:
half hour of work, two minutes to love, the rest boredom.
Conrad spent a day finding the *mot juste*; then killed it.'
In time, he thought, I might live to be an artist.
'Most of them are born to fill the graveyards.'
'If he fails as a writer,' Ford wrote my father, 'at least
he'll be Ambassador to England, or President of Harvard.'

W. SOMERSET MAUGHAM (1874–1965)
by Virginia Woolf (1882–1941)

LETTER TO VANESSA BELL, 2 NOVEMBER 1938

Then there was Somerset Maugham, a grim figure; rat eyed; dead man
cheeked, unshaven; a criminal I should have said had I met him in a bus.
Very suspicious and tortured.

W. Somerset Maugham
by Evelyn Waugh (1903–63)

LETTER TO HAROLD ACTON, 14 APRIL 1952

I spent two nights at Cap Ferat with Mr Maugham (who has lost his fine
cook) & made a great gaffe. The first evening he asked me what someone
was like and I said 'A pansy with a stammer'. All the Picassos on the
walls blanched.

WALLACE STEVENS (1878–1955)
by Marianne Moore (1887–1972)

Quoting 'order is mastery' from the poem, 'The Idea of Order at Key
West,' I have a picture in my mind of the office and desk of Wallace
Stevens at the Hartford Accident and Indemnity Company. On my way
home from New England one time, I had an errand at Trinity College –

to save an English Department student the trouble of coming to Brooklyn to ask questions about a paper involving a degree. My brother that day was to take me to meet relatives, and finding me with half an hour, said, 'If you have shopping to do, there is a good store nearby; or is there anything else you might like to do?' I hesitated, then said, 'I'd like to call on Wallace Stevens, but have no appointment.' My brother said, 'Here's a nickel; call him up.' I said, 'With Wallace Stevens, you aren't haphazard . . .' and deliberated. 'He is formal.' My brother stepped into a telephone-booth, saying, 'I'll call him up.' The door of the booth was open and I heard him say, 'Have you had lunch, Mr Stevens?' He came out. 'What did he say?' I asked. 'Said "Come right over."' The building where we were expected stood on a grassy eminence and has eleven or twelve white marble columns along the facade. (Mr Stevens' offices previously had been at 125 Trumbull Avenue; he occupied the office where we saw him after 1921, the year in which the building was finished.) We were escorted down a wide corridor to his door which was open. His desk, of mahogany or other dark polished wood, had nothing on it – no pen stabbed into a marble slab at an angle. It was summer. Opening a drawer presently, Mr Stevens brought out a post-card, a Paul Klee reproduction from Laura Sweeney (Mrs James Sweeney) explaining that she was in Paris, said, 'Such a pleasure she always is, don't you think?' and after other comment, when we said we must go, Mr Stevens said, 'Since this is your first visit, let me show you the building.' We crossed the corridor and through a short connecting one, entering a large room with many windows, its desks not too near together and not too small. As we passed the many desks, each of the persons working on papers or at a typewriter looked up at Mr Stevens with a pleased smile, reminding me of a visitor to a writing-conference I had attended who said when Hartford insurance was mentioned, 'They aren't bothered with strikes there; the girls at the Hartford have it nice,' and explained that she had a friend, a clerk in the Hartford Indemnity and Accident Company. We left by a door opposite the one by which we had entered, descended a few stone steps to a row of tall green arbor vitae at right angles to a drive. I said we had not wished to interrupt at a bad moment – that I owed the visit to my brother's initiative. Mr Stevens said to him, 'If you let me know when you are going to be here again, I'd like to take you for lunch to the Canoe Club, and to the house.' . . .

One other recollection, permissible because not induced – as descriptive of Mr Stevens' diction. When I was leaving a reception given by Mrs

Church, Mr Stevens detained me for a moment to inquire for my brother, adding, 'Your brother is an ornament to civilization.' Why? Perhaps because my brother had suspected that it might be time to go, after having only recently come? Or had Mr Stevens found visitors too self-determined to preface a visit by considerately inquiring, 'Have you had lunch?'

Wallace Stevens
by Delmore Schwartz (1913–66)

In 1936 Stevens read his poems for the first time at Harvard – it was probably the first time he had ever read his poetry in public – and the occasion was at once an indescribable ordeal and a precious event: precious because he had been an undergraduate and a poet at Harvard some thirty-seven years before and had not returned since then, in his own person, although he had often gone to the Yale-Harvard games incognito. Before and after reading each poem, Stevens spoke of the nature of poetry, a subject which naturally obsessed him: the least sound counts, he said, the least sound and the least syllable. His illustration of this observation was wholly characteristic: he told of how he had wakened that week after midnight and heard the sounds made by a cat walking delicately and carefully on the crusted snow outside his house. He was listening, as in his lifelong vigil of awareness, for such phrases as this one, describing autumn leaves: 'The skreak and skritter of evening gone'; no single one of thousands of such inventions is enough to suggest his genius for experience and language.

After his comment, Stevens returned to his typescript, prepared and bound for the occasion with a fabulous elegance which also was characteristic: but an old Cambridge lady, holding an ear trumpet aloft, and dressed in a style which must have been chic at Rutherford Hayes' inauguration, shouted out, hoarse and peremptory as crows, that she must ask Mr Stevens to speak loudly and clearly, loudly and clearly, if you please. She might just as well have been shouting at President Hayes. Stevens continued in a very low voice, reading poems which were written in that bravura style, that extravagant, luxurious, misunderstood rhetoric which is as passionate as the most excited Elizabethan blank verse. And throughout the reading, although Stevens was extremely nervous and constrained, this showed only as a rigid impassivity which, since it might have expressed a very different state of mind, made his feelings invisible;

nevertheless, as such readings became more frequent in recent years, it was impossible to persuade Stevens that no one save himself perceived his overwhelming nervousness, just as, when the first reading ended, Stevens said to the teacher who had introduced him: 'I wonder what the boys at the office would think of this?' The office was the Hartford Accident and Indemnity Co., the boys were those who knew him as a vice-president, lawyer, and the most solid of citizens.

No one who thought a poet looked pale, distracted, unkempt and unbarbered was likely to recognize Stevens: he was a physical giant, robust, red-faced, and his large round head suggested not only a banker and judge, but Jupiter. He said then and after that the boys would hardly be more shocked to discover him the secret head of an opium ring – and although I could guess that in this instance he may have mistaken tact for ignorance – the important point is that he felt sure that this was how others regarded a poet. He had written poetry for many years as a kind of 'secret vice,' and he told many stories about himself of the same kind, resorting to that self-irony which often marks his poetic style.

E. M. FORSTER (1879–1970)
by D. H. Lawrence (1885–1930)

LETTER TO BERTRAND RUSSELL, 12 FEBRUARY 1915

We have had E. M. Forster here for three days. There is more in him than ever comes out. But he is not dead yet. I hope to see him pregnant with his own soul. We were on the edge of a fierce quarrel all the time. He went to bed muttering that he was not sure we – my wife and I – weren't just playing round his knees: he seized a candle and went to bed, neither would he say good night. Which is rather nice. He sucks his dummy – you know, those child's comforters – long after his age. But there is something very real in him, if he will not cause it to die. He is *much* more than his dummy-sucking, clever little habits allow him to be.

LETTER TO MARY CANNAN, 24 FEBRUARY 1915

We had E. M. Forster here for a day or two. I liked him, but his life is so ridiculously inane, the man is dying of inanition. He was very angry with me for telling him about himself.

JAMES JOYCE (1882–1941)
by T. S. Eliot (1888–1965)

LETTER TO SYDNEY SCHIFF, 22 AUGUST 1920

We dined with Joyce in Paris, as you will I am sure be interested to know. Fritz Vanderpyl, a friend of Pound and myself, was also present, and I enclose a sketch (by me) of the party. Joyce is a quiet but rather dogmatic man, and has (as I am convinced most superior persons have) a sense of his own importance. He has a sort of gravity which seems more Protestant than Catholic. He is obviously the man who wrote his books – that is, he impresses you as an important enough personage for that. We will talk about him later.

LETTER TO ROBERT MCALMON, 2 MAY 1921

Joyce I admire as a person who seems to be independent of outside stimulus, and therefore is likely to go on producing first-rate work until he dies.

VIRGINIA WOOLF (1882–1941)
by Rebecca West (1892–1983)

I have heard people say that they gathered the two sisters were madonna-like. The Madonna is always represented as extremely tidy, even in the disadvantageous circumstance, such as the flight into Egypt. But Virginia and Vanessa were extremely untidy. They always looked as if they had been drawn through a hedge backwards before they went out. At the time I used to meet her I was untidy myself, being overworked and rather ill, but I always used to gain confidence from the sight of Virginia. There was a beautiful phrase, late Victorian and Edwardian, 'a well-turned-out woman'. Virginia was not well turned out. But she was certainly very beautiful in a Leonardo way. Both her face and her body could not have belonged to a person not of rare gifts. In the Crush Bar at Covent Garden I once heard a man say to his wife, 'Look at that funny-looking woman.' His wife peered through her glasses and objected, 'Ssh, you shouldn't say that about her, she's . . .' and her voice died away in vague respect, almost awe. It was an authentic compliment.

Virginia Woolf
by Christopher Isherwood (1904–86)

*Years after this obituary first appeared, Isherwood admitted that 'Jeremy'
was actually the novelist, Hugh Walpole.*

It is usually easy to describe strangers. Yet, although I didn't meet Virginia
more than half a dozen times, I find it nearly impossible to write anything
about her which will carry the breath of life. Which century did she belong
to? Which generation? You could not tell: she simply defied analysis. At
the time of our first meeting, she was, I now realize, an elderly lady, yet
she seemed, in some mysterious way, to be very much older and very
much younger than her age. I could never decide whether she reminded
me of my grandmother – if she had taken some rejuvenating drug and
lived a hundred and twenty years, to become the brilliant leader of an
intensely modern Georgian salon.

One remembers, first of all, those wonderful, forlorn eyes; the slim,
erect, high-shouldered figure, strangely tense, as if always on the alert for
some distant sound; the hair folded back from the eggshell fragility of the
temples; the small, beautifully cut face, like a Tennysonian cameo –
Mariana, or The Lady of Shalott. Yes, that is the impression one would
like to convey – an unhappy, high-born lady in a ballad, a fairy-story
princess under a spell; slightly remote from the rest of us, a profile seen
against the dying light, hands dropped helplessly in the lap, a shocking,
momentary glimpse of intense grief.

What rubbish! We are at the tea table. Virginia is sparkling with gaiety,
delicate malice and gossip – the gossip which is the style of her books
and which made her the best hostess in London; listening to her, we
missed appointments, forgot love-affairs, stayed on and on into the small
hours, when we had to be hinted, gently, but firmly, out of the house.
This time the guest of honour is a famous novelist, whose substantial
income proves that Art, after all, can really pay. He is modest enough –
but Virginia, with sadistic curiosity, which is like the teasing of an elder
sister, drags it all out of him: how much time New York publishers gave,
how much the movie people, and what the King said, and the Crown
Prince of Sweden – she has no mercy. And then, when it is all over, 'You
know, Jeremy,' she tells him, smiling almost tenderly, 'you remind me of
a very beautiful prize-winning cow . . .' 'A cow, Virginia . . .?' The novelist

gulps but grins bravely at me; determined to show he can take it. 'Yes . . .
a very, very fine cow. You go out into the world, and win all sorts of
prizes, but gradually your coat gets covered with burrs, and so you have
to come back again into your field. And in the middle of the field is a
rough old stone post, and you rub yourself against it to get the burrs off.
Don't you think, Leonard . . .' she looks across at her husband, 'that that's
our real mission in life? We're Jeremy's old stone scratching-post.'

D. H. LAWRENCE (1885–1930)
by John Galsworthy (1867–1933)

Lunched with Pinker to meet D. H. Lawrence, that provincial genius.
Interesting, but a type I could not get on with. Obsessed with self. Dead
eyes, and a red beard, long narrow pale face. A strange bird.

*Of the same – evidently unsuccessful – lunch, in a letter to Lady Cynthia
Asquith, Lawrence wrote: 'I lunched with John Galsworthy yesterday –
sawdust bore.'*

D. H. Lawrence
by Virginia Woolf (1882–1941)

LETTER TO VANESSA BELL, 9 APRIL 1927

Looking out of the carriage window at Civita Vecchia, whom should we
see, sitting side by side on a bench, but D. H. Lawrence and Norman
Douglas – unmistakable: Lawrence pierced and penetrated; Douglas hog-
like and brindled – They were swept off by train one way and we went
on to Rome.

LETTER TO ETHEL SMYTH, 20 APRIL 1931

I'm reading Lawrence, Sons and Lovers, for the first time; and so ponder
your question about contemporaries. [Middleton] Murry, that bald necked
blood dripping vulture, kept me off Lawrence with his obscene objur-
gations. Now I realise with regret that a man of genius wrote in my time
and I never read him. Yes but genius obscured and distorted I think: the
fact about contemporaries (I write hand to mouth) is that they're doing

the same thing on another railway line: one resents their distracting one, flashing past, the wrong way – something like that: from timidity, partly, one keeps one's eyes on one's own road.

EZRA POUND (1885–1972)
by Robert Lowell (1917–77)

Horizontal in a deckchair on the bleak ward,
some feeble-minded felon in pajamas, clawing
a Social Credit broadside from your table, you saying,
'. . . here with a black suit and black briefcase; in the briefcase,
an abomination, Possum's *hommage* to Milton.'
Then sprung; Rapallo, and then the decade gone;
then three years, then Eliot dead, you saying,
'And who is left to understand my jokes?
My old Brother in the arts . . . and besides, he was a smash of a poet.'
He showed us his blotched, bent hands, saying, 'Worms.
When I talked that nonsense about Jews on the Rome
wireless, she knew it was shit, and still loved me.'
And I, 'Who else has been in Purgatory?'
And he, 'To begin with a swelled head and end with swelled feet.'

SIEGFRIED SASSOON (1886–1967)
by Wilfred Owen (1893–1918)

LETTER TO LESLIE GUNSTON, 22 AUGUST 1917

At last I have an event worth a letter. I have beknown myself to Siegfried Sassoon. Went in to him last night (my second call). The first visit was one morning last week. The sun blazed into his room making his purple dressing suit of a brilliance – almost matching my sonnet! He is very tall and stately, with a fine firm chisel'd (how's that?) head, ordinary short brown hair. The general expression of his face is one of boredom. Last night when I went in he was struggling to read a letter from Wells; whose handwriting is not only a slurred *suggestion* of words, but in a dim pale pink ink! . . .

So the last thing he said was 'Sweat your guts out writing poetry!' 'Eh?'

says I. 'Sweat your guts out, I say!' He also warned me against early publishing: but recommended Martin Secker for a small volume of 10 or 20 poems.

He himself is 30! Looks under 25!

LETTER TO SUSAN OWEN (HIS MOTHER), 10 SEPTEMBER 1917

Sassoon I like equally in all the ways you mention, as a man, as a friend, as a poet.

The *man* is tall and noble-looking. Before I knew him I was told this and by this much only I spotted him! . . .

He is thirty-one. Let it be thoroughly understood that I nourish no admiration for his nose or any other feature whatever.

The *Friend* is intensely sympathetic*, with me about ever vital question on the planet or off it. He keeps all effusiveness strictly within his pages. In this he is eminently *English*. It is so restful after the French absurdities, and after Mrs Gray who gushes all over me. But there is no denying to myself that he is already a *closer* friend than, say, Leslie. Just as this assertion is not the result of having been with him so much lately, neither is it derogated by the shortness of our acquaintance-time. We have followed parallel trenches all our lives, and have more friends in common, authors I mean, than most people can boast of in a lifetime.

As for the *Poet* you know my judgement.

* sympathy = feeling with (Greek) [Owen's note]

RUPERT BROOKE (1887–1915)
by Henry James (1843–1916)

The following is a preface to Rupert Brooke's Letters from America *but really a lament for the poet who had died the previous year. According to Desmond MacCarthy, who was present when James first met Brooke, in Cambridge in 1909, James asked: 'Who was the long quiet youth with fair hair who sometimes smiled?' MacCarthy said it was Brooke and that he wrote bad poetry, to which James replied: 'Well, I must say I am relieved, for with that appearance if he also had talent it would be too unfair.'*

The fact was that if one liked him – and I may as well say at once that few young men, in our time, can have gone through life under a greater burden, more easily carried and kept in its place, of being liked – one liked absolutely everything about him, without the smallest exception; so that he appeared to convert before one's eyes all that happened to him, or that had or that ever might, not only to his advantage as a source of life and experience, but to the enjoyment on its own side of a sort of illustrational virtue or glory. This appearance of universal assimilation – often indeed by incalculable ironic reactions which were of the very essence of the restless young intelligence rejoicing in its gaiety – made each part of his rich consciousness, so rapidly acquired, cling, as it were, to the company of all the other parts, so as at once neither to miss any touch of the luck (one keeps coming back to that), incurred by them, or to let them suffer any want of its own rightness. It was as right, through the spell he cast altogether, that he should have come into the world and have passed his boyhood in that Rugby home, as that he should have been able later on to wander as irrepressibly as the spirit moved him, or as that he should have found himself fitting as intimately as he was very soon to do into any number of the incalculabilities, the intellectual at least, of the poetic temperament. He had them all, he gave himself in his short career up to them all – and I confess that, partly for reasons to be further developed, I am unable even to guess what they might eventually have made of him; which is of course what brings us round again to that view of him as the young poet with absolutely nothing but his generic spontaneity to trouble about, the young poet profiting for happiness by a general condition unprecedented for young poets, that I began by indulging in.

He went from Rugby to Cambridge, where, after a while, he carried off a Fellowship at King's, and where, during a short visit there in 'May week,' or otherwise early in June 1909, I first, and as I was to find, very unforgettingly, met him. He reappears to me as with his felicities all most promptly divinable, in that splendid setting of the river at the 'backs'; as to which indeed I remember vaguely wondering what it was left to such a place to do with the added, the verily wasted, grace of such a person, or how even such a person could hold his own, as who should say, at such a pitch of simple scenic perfection. Any difficulty dropped, however, to the reconciling vision; for that the young man was publicly and responsibly a poet seemed the fact a little over-officiously involved – to the promotion of a certain surprise (on one's own part) at his having to 'be' anything. It was to come over me still more afterwards that nothing of that or of any other sort need really have rested on him with a weight or obligation, and in fact I cannot but think that life might have been seen and felt to suggest to him, in an exposed unanimous conspiracy, that his status should be left to the general sense of others, ever so many others, who would sufficiently take care of it, and that such a fine rare case was accordingly as arguable as it possibly *could* be – with the pure, undischarged poetry of him and the latent presumption of his dying for his country the only things to gainsay it. The question was to a certain extent crude, 'Why *need* he be a poet, why need he so specialise?' but if this was so it was only, it was already, symptomatic of the interesting final truth that he was going to testify to his function in the unparalleled way. He was going to have the life (the unanimous conspiracy so far achieved *that*), was going to have it under no more formal guarantee than that of his appetite and genius for it; and this was to help us all to the complete appreciation of him. No single scrap of the English fortune at its easiest and truest – which means of course with every vulgarity dropped out – but was to brush him as by the readiest instinctive wing, never overstraining a point or achieving a miracle to do so; only trusting his exquisite imagination and temper to respond to the succession of his opportunities. It is in the light of what this succession could in the most natural and most familiar way in the world amount to for him that we find this idea of a beautiful crowning modernness above all to meet his case. The promptitude, the perception, the understanding, the quality of humour and sociability, the happy lapses in the logic of inward reactions (save for all their infallibly being poetic), of which he availed himself consented to be as illustrational as any fondest friend could wish, whether the subject of the exhibition was aware of the degree or not, and made his vivacity of vision, his exercise of fancy and irony, of observation at its freest, inevitable – while at the same time setting in motion no machinery of experience in which his curiosity, or in other words, the quickness of his familiarity, didn't move faster than anything else.

Rupert, who had joined the Naval Brigade, took part in the rather distractedly improvised – as it at least at the moment appeared – movement for the relief of the doomed Antwerp, but was, later on, after the return of the force so engaged, for a few days in London, whither he had come up from camp in Dorsetshire, briefly invalided; thanks to which accident I had on a couple of occasions my last sight of him. It was all auspiciously, well-nigh extravagantly, congruous; nothing certainly could have been called more modern than all the elements and suggestions of his situation for the hour, the very spot in London that could best serve as a centre for vibrations the keenest and most various; a challenge to the appreciation of life, to that of the whole range of the possible English future, at its most uplifting. He had not yet so much struck me as an admirable nature *en disponibilité* and such as any cause, however high, might swallow up with a sense of being the sounder and sweeter for. More definitely perhaps the young poet, with all the wind alive in his sails, was as evident there in the guise of the young soldier and the thrice welcome young friend, who yet, I all recognisably remember, insisted on himself as little as ever in either character, and seemed even more disposed than usual not to let his intelligibility interfere with his modesty. He promptly recovered and returned to camp, whence it was testified that his specific practical aptitude, under the lively call, left nothing to be desired – a fact that expressed again, to the perception of his circle, with what truth the spring of inspiration worked in him, in the sense, I mean, that his imagination itself shouldered and made light of the material load. It had not yet, at the same time, been more associatedly active in a finer sense; my own next apprehension of it at least was in reading the five admirable sonnets that had been published in 'New Numbers' after the departure of his contingent for the campaign at the Dardanelles. To read these in the light of one's personal knowledge of him was to draw from them, inevitably, a meaning still deeper seated than their noble beauty, an authority, of the purest, attended with which his name inscribes itself in its own character on the great English scroll.

MARIANNE MOORE (1887–1972)
by *Wallace Stevens* (1878–1955)

LETTER TO BARBARA CHURCH, 9 APRIL 1951

Your letter about Marianne Moore came this morning. She is, as you say, fond of people, which is her salvation. When you* think of what her life might be and of what it is – the way she talks, the things she does, you* feel as if you* and she were a pair of sailors just off the boat, determined to see things through. She is a moral force 'in light blue' at a time when moral forces of any kind are few and far between.

* impersonal [Stevens's note]

LETTER TO NORMAN HOLMES PEARSON, 24 JANUARY 1952

It made me happy too to hear of the award [of the Bollingen Prize for poetry] to Marianne Moore. She belongs to an older and much more personal world: the world of closer, human intimacies which existed when you and I were young – from which she and her brother have been extruded like lost sheep. As a matter of nature they stick together. What she has she has tried to make perfect. The truth is that I am much moved by what she is going through. It is easy to say that Marianne, the human being, does not concern us. *Mais, mon Dieu,* it is what concerns us most.

KATHERINE MANSFIELD (1888–1923)
by Virginia Woolf (1882–1941)

LETTER TO LYTTON STRACHEY, 25 JULY 1916

Katherine Mansfield has dogged my steps for three years – I'm always on the point of meeting her, or of reading her stories, and I have never managed to do either. But once Sydney Waterlow produced Middleton Murry instead of her – a moon calf looking youth – her husband? Do arrange a meeting – We go to Cornwall in September, and if I see anyone answering to your account on a rock or in the sea I shall accost her.

11 OCTOBER 1917

The dinner last night went off: the delicate things were discussed. We could both wish that ones first impression of K.M. was not that she stinks like a – well civet cat that had taken to street walking. In truth, I'm a little shocked by her commonness at first sight; lines so hard & cheap. However, when this diminishes, she is so intelligent & inscrutable that she repays friendship.

22 MARCH 1919

... And again, as usual, I find with Katherine what I don't find with the other clever women a sense of ease & interest, which is, I suppose, due to her caring so genuinely if so differently from the way I care, about our precious art. Though Katherine is now in the very heart of the professional world – 4 books on her table to review – she is, & will always be I fancy, not the least of a hack. I don't feel as I feel with Molly Hamilton that is to say, ashamed of the inkpot.

25 AUGUST 1920

For the third time this summer, though no other summer, I went to London Monday, paid 5/- for a plate of ham, & said good bye to Katherine. I had my euphemism at parting; about coming again before she goes; but it is useless to extend these farewell visits. They have something crowded & unnaturally calm too about them, & after all, visits can't do away with the fact that she goes for two years, is ill, & heaven knows when we shall meet again. These partings make one pinch oneself as if to make sure of feeling. Do I feel this as much as I ought? Am I heartless? Will she mind my going either? And then, after noting my own callousness, of a sudden comes the blankness of not having her to talk to. So on my side the feeling is genuine. A woman caring as I care for writing is rare enough I suppose to give me the queerest sense of echo coming back to me from her mind the second after I've spoken. Then, too, there's something in what she says of our being the only women, at this moment (I must modestly limit this to in our circle) with gift enough to make talk of writing interesting. How much I dictate to other people! How often too I'm silent, judging it useless to speak. I said how my own character seemed to cut out a shape like a shadow in front of me. This she understood (I give it as an example of her understanding) & proved it by telling me that she thought this bad: one ought to merge into things. Her senses are amazingly acute – a long description she gave of hosing plants – putting the hose over the high trees, then over the shrubs, then over the mignonette. And Murry said slowly, 'You've got it wrong, Katherine. Youth wasn't like that. At least I'm sure mine wasn't.' Murry playing tennis all day; an oddly detached couple. It suddenly strikes me as I write that I should like to ask her what certainty she has of her work's merit. – But we propose to write to each other – She will send me her diary. Shall we? Will she? If I were left to myself I should; being the simpler, the more direct of the two. I can't follow people who don't do the obvious things in these ways. I've recanted about her book; I shall review it; but whether she really wanted me to, God knows. Strange how little we know our friends.

16 JANUARY 1923

Katherine has been dead a week, & how far am I obeying her 'do not quite forget Katherine' which I read in one of her old letters? Am I already forgetting her? It is strange to trace the progress of one's feelings. Nelly said in her sensational way at breakfast on Friday 'Mrs Murry's dead! It says so in the paper!' At that one feels what? A shock of relief? – A rival the less? Then confusion at feeling so little – then, gradually, blankness & disappointment; then a depression which I could not rouse myself from all that day. When I began to write, it seemed to me there was no point in writing. Katherine won't read it. Katherine's my rival no longer. More generously I felt, But though I can do this better than she could, where is she, who could do what I can't! Then, as usual with me, visual impressions kept coming & coming before me – always of Katherine putting on a white wreath, & leaving us, called away; made dignified, chosen. And then one pitied her. And one felt her reluctant to wear that wreath, which was an ice cold one. And she was only 33. And I could see her before me so exactly, & the room at Portland Villas. I go up. She gets up, very slowly, from her writing table. A glass of milk & a medicine bottle stood there. There were also piles of novels. Everything was very tidy, bright, & somehow like a dolls house. At once, or almost, we got out of shyness. She (it was summer) half lay on the sofa by the window. She had her look of a Japanese doll, with the fringe combed quite straight across her forehead. Sometimes we looked very steadfastly at each other, as though we had reached some durable relationship, independent of the changes of the body, through the eyes. Hers were beautiful eyes – rather doglike, brown, very wide apart, with a steady slow rather faithful & sad expression. Her nose was sharp, & a little vulgar. Her lips thin & hard. She wore short skirts & liked 'to have a line round her' she said. She looked very ill – very drawn, & moved languidly, drawing herself across the room, like some suffering animal. I suppose I have written down some of the things we said. Most days I think we reached that kind of certainty, in talk about books, or rather about our writings, which I thought had something durable about it. And then she was inscrutable. Did she care for me? Sometimes she would say so – would kiss me – would look at me as if (is this sentiment?) her eyes would like always to be faithful. She would promise never never to forget. That was what we said at the end of our last talk. She said she would send me her diary to read, & would write always. For our friendship was a real thing we said, looking at each other quite straight. It would always go on whatever happened. What happened was, I suppose, faultfindings & perhaps gossip. She never answered my letter. Yet I still feel, somehow, that friendship persists. Still there are things about writing I think of & want to tell Katherine. If I had been in Paris & gone to her, she would have got up & in three minutes, we should have been talking again. Only I could not take the step. The surroundings – Murry & so on – & the small lies & treacheries, the perpetual playing and teasing, or whatever it was, cut away much of the substance of friendship. One was too uncertain. And so one let it all go. Yet I certainly expected that we should meet again next summer, & start fresh. And I was jealous of her writing – the only writing I have ever been jealous of. This made it harder to write to her; & I saw in it, perhaps from jealousy, all the qualities I disliked in her.

For two days I felt that I had grown middle aged, & lost some spur to write. That feeling is going. I no longer keep seeing her with her wreath. I dont pity her so much. Yet I have the feeling that I shall think of her at intervals all through life. Probably we had something in common which I shall never find in anyone else. (This I say in so many words in 1919 again and again.) Moreover I like speculating about her character. I think I never gave her credit for all her physical suffering & the effect it must have had in embittering her.

Katherine Mansfield
by T. S. Eliot (1888–1965)

LETTER TO EZRA POUND, 3 JULY 1920

I have seen Murry and secured a vague understanding that he would print a few of the poems (I said *not more* than five) but he has not read them yet. I must say that he is much more difficult to deal with when K.M. is about, and I have an impression that she terrorises him. He told Ottoline that K.M. was the only living writer of English prose (this is as Ott. reports it). I believe her to be a dangerous WOMAN: and of course two sentimentalists together are more than 2 times as noxious as one.

I am not running the paper [*The Criterion*] for Binyon any more than for K. Mansfield. Of course I don't mind printing a story by K. Mansfield, though I prefer Binyon and have no use for either. I will however suggest to Lady R[othermere]. that she should secure a story from K. Mansfield. I myself should much prefer to have something from Murry; he is at least in every way preferable to his wife. The latter is not by any means the most intelligent woman Lady R. has ever met. She is simply one of the most persistent and thickskinned toadies and one of the vulgarest women Lady R. has ever met and is also a sentimental crank.

T. S. ELIOT (1888–1965)
by Robert Graves (1895–1985)

I first met Eliot in 1916, a startlingly good-looking, Italianate young man, with a shy, hunted look, and a reluctance (which I found charming) to accept the most obvious phenomenon of the day – a world war now entering its bloodiest stage, and showing every sign of going on until it had killed off every man in London but the aged and neutrals. I was due to return to the Somme any day, and delighted to forget the war too in Eliot's gently neutral company.

T. S. Eliot
by Virginia Woolf (1882–1941)

15 NOVEMBER 1918

... I was interrupted somewhere on this page by the arrival of Mr Eliot. Mr Eliot is well expressed by his name – a polished, cultivated, elaborate young American, talking so slow, that each word seems to have special finish allotted it. But beneath the surface, it is fairly evident that he is very intellectual, intolerant, with strong views of his own, & a poetic creed. I'm sorry to say that this sets up Ezra Pound & Wyndham Lewis as great poets, or in the current phrase 'very interesting' writers. He admires Mr Joyce immensely. He produced 3 or 4 poems for us to look at – the fruit of two years, since he works all day in a Bank, & in his reasonable way thinks regular work good for people of nervous constitutions. I became more or less conscious of a very intricate & highly organised framework of poetic belief; owing to his caution & his excessive care in the use of language we did not discover much about it. I think he believes in 'living phrases' & their difference from dead ones; in writing with extreme care, in observing all syntax & grammar; & so making this new poetry flower on the stem of the oldest.

19 SEPTEMBER 1920

Eliot is separated only by the floor from me. Nothing in mans or womans shape is any longer capable of upsetting me. The odd thing about Eliot is that his eyes are lively & youthful when the cast of his face & the shape of his sentences is formal & even heavy. Rather like a sculpted face – no upper lip: formidable, powerful; pale. Then those hazel eyes seeming to escape from the rest of him. We talked – America, Ottoline, aristocracy, printing, Squire, Murry, criticism. 'And I behaved like a priggish pompous little ass' was one of his comments upon his own manner at Garsington. He is decidedly of the generation beneath us – I daresay superior – younger, though.

20 SEPTEMBER 1920

To go on with Eliot, as if one were making out a scientific observation – he left last night directly after dinner. He improved as the day went on; laughed more openly; became nicer. L[eonard]. whose opinion on this matter I respect, found him disappointing in brain – less powerful than he expected, & with little play of mind. I kept myself successfully from being submerged, though feeling the waters rise once or twice. I mean by this that he completely neglected my claims to be a writer, & had I been meek, I suppose I should have gone under – felt him & his views dominant & subversive.

22 MARCH 1921

We had Eliot to dinner on Sunday & went to Love for Love, he & I in the Pit; L. upstairs, with a ticket from the New Statesman. Eliot & I had to drive in to Hammersmith in a taxi, having missed our train. We passed through dark market gardens. 'Missing trains is awful' I said. 'Yes. But humiliation is the worst thing in life' he replied. 'Are you as full of vices as I am?' I demanded. 'Full. Riddled with them.' 'We're not as good as Keats' I said. 'Yes we are' he replied. 'No: we don't write classics straight off as magnanimous people do.' 'We're trying something harder' he said. 'Anyhow our work is streaked with badness' I said. 'Compared with theirs, mine is futile. Negligible. One goes on because of an illusion.' He told me that I talked like that without meaning it. Yet I do mean it. I think one could probably become very intimate with Eliot because of our damned self conscious susceptibility: but I plunge more than he does: perhaps I could learn him to be a frog. He has the advantage of me in laughing out. He laughed at Love for Love: but thinking I must write about it I was a little on the stretch.

29 APRIL 1929

Poor Tom – a true poet, I think; what they will call in a hundred years a man of genius: & this is his life. I stand for half an hour listening while he says that Vivien [his first wife] cant walk. Her legs have gone. But whats the matter? No one knows. And so she lies in bed – cant put a shoe on. And they have difficulties, humiliations, with servants. And after endless quibbling about first cousins come to England, suddenly he appears overcome, moved, tragic, unhappy broken down, because I offer to come to tea on Thursday. Oh but we dont dare ask our friends, he said. We have been deserted. Nobody has been to see us for weeks. Would you really come – all this way? to see us? Yes I said. But what a vision of misery, imagined, but real too. Vivien with her foot on a stool, in bed all day; Tom hurrying back lest she abuse him: this is our man of genius.

10 SEPTEMBER 1933

... Tomorrow, in the divine peace of Monday, I shall walk on the downs & think of Tom & my parched lips with some degree of pleasure ... He is 10 years younger: hard, spry, a glorified boy scout in shorts & yellow shirt. He is enjoying himself very much. He is tight & shiny as a wood louse (I am not writing for publication.) But there is well water in him, cold & pure. Yes I like talking to Tom. But his wing sweeps curved & scimitar-like round to the centre himself. He's settling in with some severity to being a great man.

16 FEBRUARY 1940

Tom's great yellow bronze mask all draped upon an iron framework. An inhibited, nerve drawn: dropped face – as if hung on a scaffold of heavy private brooding; & thought. A very serious face. & broken by the flicker of relief, when other people interrupt.

T. S. Eliot
by Robert Lowell (1917–77)

Caught between two streams of traffic, in the gloom
of Memorial Hall and Harvard's war dead . . . And he:
'Don't you loathe to be compared with your relatives?
I do. I've just found two of mine reviewed by Poe.
He wiped the floor with them . . . and I was *delighted*.'
Then on with warden's pace across the Yard,
talking of Pound, 'It's balls to say he only
pretends to be like Ezra . . . He's better though. This year
he no longer wants to rebuild the Temple at Jerusalem.
Yes, he's better. "*You* speak," he said, when he'd talked two hours.
By then I had absolutely nothing to *say*.'
Ah Tom, one muse, one music, had one the luck –
lost in the dark night of the brilliant talkers,
humor and honor from the everlasting dross!

E. E. CUMMINGS (1894–1962)
by John Dos Passos (1896–1970)

Cummings' delight in certain things was contagious as a child's. Christmas tree balls, stars, snowflakes. Elephants were his totem. I would never have enjoyed snow so much if I hadn't walked around Washington Square with Cummings in a snowstorm. He had a great eye for sparrows and all pert timid brighteyed creatures.

The last time I saw him in the summer before he died he was entertaining a tame chipmunk. We ate supper on the porch of his father's old hilltop house in the woods above Silver Lake. The chipmunk kept popping through the vines and out onto the brick floor of the porch for peanuts.

You couldn't tell whether Cummings or the chipmunk enjoyed the little scene more. They had the same glint in their eyes. They both looked their best.

ROBERT GRAVES (1895–1985)
by Wilfred Owen (1893–1918)

LETTER TO SUSAN OWEN (HIS MOTHER), 14 OCTOBER 1917

On Sat. I met Robert Graves . . . for Sassoon, whom nothing could keep from his morning's golf; & took Graves over to the Course when he arrived. He is a big, rather plain fellow, the last man on earth apparently capable of the extraordinary, delicate fancies in his books.

No doubt he thought me a slacker sort of sub S.S. when they were together showed him my longish war-piece 'Disabled' (you haven't seen it) & it seems Graves was mightily impressed, and considers me a kind of *Find*!! No thanks, Captain Graves! I'll find myself in due time.

LETTER TO SUSAN OWEN, 18 OCTOBER 1917

I think I described you my meeting with Robert Graves, and how S.S. said of him: he is a man one likes better *after* he has been with one.

F. SCOTT FITZGERALD (1896–1940)
by Ernest Hemingway (1899–1961)

Much later in the time after Zelda had what was then called her first nervous breakdown and we happened to be in Paris at the same time, Scott asked me to have lunch with him at Michaud's restaurant on the corner of the rue Jacob and the rue des Saints-Pères. He said he had something very important to ask me that meant more than anything in the world to him and that I must answer absolutely truly. I said that I would do the best that I could. When he would ask me to tell him something absolutely truly, which is very difficult to do, and I would try it, what I said would make him angry, often not when I said it but afterwards, and sometimes long afterwards when he had brooded on it. My words would become something that would have to be destroyed and sometimes, if possible, me with them.

He drank wine at the lunch but it did not affect him and he had not prepared for the lunch by drinking before it. We talked about our work and about people and he asked me about people that we had not seen lately. I knew that he was writing something good and that he was having great trouble with it for many reasons, but that was not what he wanted to talk about. I kept waiting for it to come, the things that I had to tell the absolute truth about; but he would not bring it up until the end of the meal, as though we were having a business lunch.

Finally when we were eating the cherry tart and had a last carafe of wine he said. 'You know I never slept with anyone except Zelda.'

'No, I didn't.'

'I thought I had told you.'

'No. You told me a lot of things but not that.'

'That is what I have to ask you about.'

'Good. Go on.'

'Zelda said that the way I was built I could never make any woman happy and that was what upset her originally. She said it was a matter of measurements. I have never felt the same since she said that and I have to know truly.'

'Come out to the office,' I said.

'Where is the office?'

'*Le water,*' I said. We came back into the room and sat down at the table.

'You're perfectly fine,' I said. 'You are O.K. There's nothing wrong with you. You look at yourself from above and you look foreshortened. Go over to the Louvre and look at the people in the statues and then go home and look at yourself in the mirror in profile.'

'Those statues may not be accurate.'

'They are pretty good. Most people would settle for them.'

'But why would she say it?'

'To put you out of business. That's the oldest way in the world of putting people out of business. Scott, you asked me to tell you the truth and I can tell you a lot more but this is the absolute truth and all you need. You could have gone to see a doctor.'

'I didn't want to. I wanted you to tell me truly.'

'Do you believe me?'

'I don't know,' he said.

'Come on over to the Louvre,' I said. 'It's just down the street and across the river.'

We went over to the Louvre and he looked at the statues but still he was doubtful about himself.

'It is not basically a question of the size in repose,' I said. 'It is the size that it becomes. It is also a question of angle.' I explained to him about using a pillow and a few other things that might be useful for him to know.

'There is one girl,' he said, 'who has been very nice to me. But after what Zelda said –'

'Forget what Zelda said,' I told him. 'Zelda is crazy. There's nothing wrong with you. Just have confidence and do what the girl wants. Zelda just wants to destroy you.'

'You don't know anything about Zelda.'

'All right,' I said. 'Let it go at that. But you came to lunch to ask me a question and I've tried to give you an honest answer.'

But he was still doubtful.

'Should we go and see some pictures?' I asked. 'Have you ever seen anything in here except the Mona Lisa?'

'I'm not in the mood for looking at pictures,' he said. 'I promised to meet some people at the Ritz bar.'

Ernest Hemingway (1899–1961)
by F. Scott Fitzgerald (1896–1940)

In the first published version of 'The Snows of Kilimanjaro' (in Esquire *magazine, August 1936) Hemingway's hero remembers: 'The rich were dull and they drank too much, or they played too much backgammon. They were dull and they were repetitious. He remembered poor Scott Fitzgerald and his romantic awe of them and how he had started a story once that began, "The very rich are different from you and me." And how someone had said to Scott, Yes, they have more money. But that was not humorous to Scott. He thought they were a special glamorous race and when he found they weren't it wrecked him just as much as any other thing that wrecked him.' For the story's book publication Hemingway changed 'Scott Fitzgerald' to 'Julian'.*

I feel that I must tell you something which at first seemed better to leave alone: I wrote Ernest about that story of his, asking him in the most measured terms not to use my name in future pieces of fiction. He wrote me back a crazy letter, telling me about what a great Writer he was and how much he loved his children, but yielding the point – 'If I should outlive him' – which he doubted. To have answered it would have been like fooling with a lit firecracker.

Somehow I love that man, no matter what he says or does, but just one more crack and I think I would have to throw my weight with the gang and lay him. No one could ever hurt him in his first books but he has completely lost his head and the duller he gets about it, the more he is like a punch-drunk pug fighting himself in the movies.

. . . I talk with the authority of failure – Ernest with the authority of success. We could never sit across the same table again.

Ernest Hemingway
by William Faulkner (1897–1962)

I'll write to Hemingway. Poor bloke, to have to marry three times to find out that marriage is a failure, and the only way to get any peace out of it is (if you are fool enough to marry at all) keep the first one and stay as far away from her as much as you can, with the hope of some day outliving her. At least you will be safe then from any other one marrying you – which is bound to happen if you ever divorce her. Apparently man can be cured of drugs, drink, gambling, biting his nails and picking his nose, but not of marrying.

On 14 November 1945, Hemingway wrote to Cowley: 'I'd no idea Faulkner was in that bad shape and very happy you are putting together the Portable of him. He has the most talent of anybody and he just needs a sort of conscience that isn't there. Certainly if no nation can exist half free and half slave no man can write half whore and half straight. But he will write absolutely perfectly straight and then go on and on and not be able to end it. I wish the Christ I owned him like you'd own a horse and train him like a horse and race him like a horse – only in writing. How beautifully he can write and as simple and as complicated as autumn or as spring. I'll try and write him and cheer him up.'

Ernest Hemingway
By John Dos Passos (1896–1970)

Ernest and Pauline bought themselves a lovely highceilinged old stucco house in Key West. Pauline was as much fun as ever . . . but things got rocky between Ernest and me more often than they used to. It may have been as much my fault as his. Katy and I laid it to the literary gaspers. The famous author, the great sportsfisherman, the mighty African hunter: we tried to keep him kidded down to size. We played up to him some at that, particularly nights when he had a sore throat and would retire to bed before supper and we'd all bring him drinks and eat our supper on trays around the bedroom. We called it the *lit royale*. I never knew an athletic vigorous man who spent so much time in bed as Ernest did . . .

Katy and I arrived in Key West one fine day and found that some damn sculptor had done a bust of Ernest. A plaster cast of it stood in the front hall. It was a horrible bust. Looked as if it were made out of soap. We let out a roar of laughter when we first saw it. We couldn't imagine that Ernest could take it seriously. That winter I developed the habit of trying to ring it with my panama hat when I stepped in the door. Ernest caught me at it one day, gave me a sour look and took the hat off the bust's head. He was grouchy for the rest of the day. Nobody said anything but after that things were never quite so good.

ELIZABETH BOWEN (1899–1973)
by Virginia Woolf (1882–1941)

TUESDAY, 12 APRIL 1938

. . . E. Bowen to tea; cut out of coloured cardboard but sterling & sharpedged . . .

VLADIMIR NABOKOV (1899–1977)
by Edmund Wilson (1895–1972)

When Nabokov emigrated to the United States in 1940, Wilson provided valuable help in securing work and contacts in the American literary world and they became close friends. As Nabokov later recalled: 'When I first came to America a quarter of a century ago, he wrote to me, and called on me, and was most kind to me in various matters, not necessarily pertaining to his profession. I have always been grateful to him for the tact he showed in not reviewing any of my novels while constantly saying flattering things about me in the so-called literary circles where I seldom revolve.' The friendship was constantly shaken by disagreements over Russian prosody and the character of Lenin; by Wilson's diminishing enthusiasm for Nabokov's work, most publicly his four-volume trans-lation of Pushkin's Eugene Onegin. *In Wilson's last letter to Nabokov, dated 8 March 1971, he wrote: 'I have included an account of my visit to you in Ithaca that will be out this spring, . . . based on twenty years of Talcottville diary. I hope it will not again impair our personal relations. (It shouldn't).' This is that account:*

Visit to Ithaca, May 25–8 [1957]: . . . Volodya was playing the host with a good humour, even joviality, which I had never seen him display before and which I believe is rather alien to him. The success of *Pnin* and the acclaim of *Lolita*, with the fuss about its suppression in Paris, have had upon him a stimulating effect. With no necktie and his hair *ébouriffé*, consuming his little glasses of 'faculty' port and sherry (as Frohock at Harvard calls them), he was genial with everybody and seemed full of high spirits. But when I saw him the next day after supervising his two-hour examination – at which Vera, of course, had helped him, he was fatigued, rather depressed and irritable. He said that Roman Jakobson, the philologist, who had just visited Russia, had been trying to induce him to go back and lecture; but that he would never go back to Russia, that his disgust at what had been happening there had become for him an obsession. He is undoubtedly overworked here, with his academic duties and writing his books. Just now he has a hundred and fifty papers to correct. That night his nerves were still on edge but he exhilarated himself with drinks – in which, in spite of my gout, I joined him – and was at first amusing and charming, then relapsed into his semi-humorous, semi-disagreeable mood, when he is always contradicting and always trying to score, though his statements may be quite absurd – as when he asserts, on no evidence whatever and contrary to the well-known facts, that Mérimée knew no Russian and that Turgenev knew only enough English to enable him to read a newspaper. He denies that Russians deserve their reputation of being remarkably good linguists and says of every Russian who speaks good English that he or she had had the advantage of a governess or a tutor – though I met in the Soviet Union a number of young Russians who had learned to speak excellent English without ever having been out of Russia. These false ideas, of course, are prompted by his compulsion to think of himself as the only writer in history who has been equally proficient in Russian, English and French, and he is always hopping on people, with accents of outrage, for the pettiest kind of mistakes such as Steegmuller's *verre à vin* translated as if it were *verre de vin* – when he himself occasionally makes mistakes in English and French and is even in error about Russian. He and Vera would not believe me two summers ago when I told them that *fastidieux* in French meant tiresome and not fastidious, and Volodya declared with emphasis – contrary to the authority of Dahl, the great Russian lexicographer – that *samodur* had nothing in common with the root of *durak*. He tried to tell me just now that *nihilist* in English was pronounced *neehilist*. It is, of course, very difficult to function as resourcefully as he does between two such different languages, and the task is made even more difficult by the differences between English and American English.

Vera always sides with Volodya, and one seems to feel her bristling with hostility if, in her presence, one argues with him. She had revived our discussion of metrics by inquiring, with a certain deadliness, whether it wasn't true that I had said that *Evgeni Onegin* was written in syllabic verse, and when I answered that this was absurd, she seemed to intimate that they had letters of mine which could prove the untruth of this disclaimer. When I attacked the subject of controversy from some angle – such as Greek and Latin – about which Volodya knows nothing, he assumes an ironical expression. I had brought Volodya *Histoire d'O*, that highly sophisticated and amusing pornographic work, and in return he sent me in my quarters a collection of French and Italian poems of a more or less licentious character, which I think he had been consulting in connection with his translation of Pushkin. I had a very bad attack of gout and had to sit with my foot up, and even during meals had to eat away from the table. I think it irked Vera a little to have to serve me thus.

She so concentrates on Volodya that she grudges special attention to anyone else, and she does not like my bringing him pornographic books and, as I once did, a magnum of champagne, which we merrily consumed on the porch. The next morning after the gout-harried dinner, when I was leaving and he came out to say goodbye, I congratulated him on his appearance after his bath. He leaned into the car and murmured, burlesquing a feature of *Histoire d'O*, '*Je mettais du rouge sur les lèvres de mon ventre.*' Vera had just asked me, 'Did he give you back that little horror?' She had evidently looked into it. When she had found us talking about it, she said with disgust that we had been giggling like schoolboys. In the book, there is inserted a more or less realistic picture of a Russian family in exile living in Paris which reminded me of Elena's relatives. I asked Volodya whether it seemed to him that there was something a little queer about the French, and suggested that the book might have been written by a Russian. He answered, 'A Pole, perhaps.'

I always enjoy seeing them – what we have are really intellectual romps, sometimes accompanied by mauling – and I am always afterwards left with a somewhat uncomfortable impression. The element in his work that I find repellent is his addiction to *Schadenfreude*. Everybody is always being humiliated. He himself, since he left Russia and as a result of the assassination of his father, must have suffered a good deal of humiliation and suffered it more acutely because there is something in him of the arrogance of the rich young man. As the son of a liberal who defied the Tsar, he has not really been accepted by the old-line and strictly illiberal nobility. He has now at least his characters at his mercy and at the same time subjects them to torments and identifies with them. And yet he is in many ways an admirable person, a strong character, a terrific worker, unwavering in his devotion to his family, with a rigour in his devotion to his art which has something in common with Joyce's – Joyce is one of his few genuine admirations. The miseries, horrors and handicaps that he has had to confront in his exile would have degraded or broken many, but these have been overcome by his fortitude and his talent.

The New York Times Book Review *published the following letter from Nabokov in its issue of 7 November 1971:*

I seek the shelter of your columns to help me establish the truth in the following case:

A kind correspondent Xeroxed and mailed me pp. 154–162 referring to my person as imagined by Edmund Wilson in his recent work *Upstate*. Since a number of statements therein wobble on the brink of libel, I must clear up some matters that might mislead trustful readers.

First of all, the 'miseries, horrors, and handicaps' that he assumes I was subjected to during forty years before we first met in New York are mostly figments of his warped fancy. He has no direct knowledge of my past. He has not even bothered to read my *Speak, Memory,* the records and recollections of a happy expatriation that began practically on the day of my birth. The method he favours is gleaning from my fiction what he supposes to be actual, 'real-life' impressions and then popping them back into my novels and considering my characters in that inept light – rather like the Shakespearian scholar who deduced Shakespeare's mother from the plays and then discovered allusions to her in the very passages he had twisted to manufacture the lady. What surprises me, however, is not so much Wilson's aplomb as the fact that in the diary he kept while he was my guest in Ithaca he pictures himself as nursing feelings and ideas so vindictive and fatuous that if expressed they should have made me demand his immediate departure. . . .

I am aware that my former friend is in poor health but in the struggle between the dictates of compassion and those of personal honour the latter wins. Indeed, the publication of those 'old diaries' (doctored, I hope, to fit the present requirements of what was then the future), in which living persons are but the performing poodles of the diarist's act, should be subject to a rule or law that would require some kind of formal consent from the victims of conjecture, ignorance, and invention.'

ALLEN TATE (1899–1979)
by Stephen Spender (1909–95)

I went to visit Allen Tate in hospital. He was lying in bed, extremely emaciated, with one thin arm outstretched. The skin along the length of the bone seemed like white tape. The first question he asked me was whether I had received his *Collected Poems*. Not quite remembering, I said 'yes' and then felt embarrassed lest if I said I had enjoyed them he would then ask me which I like most and I might stumble in answering. (I don't really like his poems – they seem to me terribly self-conscious and what Lawrence calls 'would-be'.) He then asked me about Mac-Neice and how his reputation was doing. I said I thought students were very admiring of Louis. I must have told him I was shortly going to see E. He said E. had written two early poems praised by I. A. Richards but not much to care for since. He asked me how they were treating me at Vanderbilt. He asked about Natasha. Altogether our conversation was very normal, as it has always been, showing his interest in literary news, gossip, reputations. I thought I might be tiring him, also felt he wanted me to stay, also, ignobly wanted to get away as soon as possible. After fifteen minutes I said I had to go, I felt guilty that I was using the convention that I really despise. If I had exhausted Allen or even killed him with shock by saying something outrageous it would not have mattered. I realized that he had only a few days to live.

GRAHAM GREENE (1904–91)
by Evelyn Waugh (1903–66)

SUNDAY 11 JANUARY 1948

Mass at 12 at Farm Street where I met the shambling, unshaven and as it happened quite penniless figure of Graham Greene. Took him to the Ritz for a cocktail and gave him 6d for his hat. He had suddenly been moved by love of Africa and emptied his pockets into the box for African missions.

THURSDAY 28 JULY 1955

. . . Graham was genial and full of repose, deep in a condemned book by an Italian theologian who holds that mankind was created to redeem the Devil.

LETTER TO ANN FLEMING, 5 SEPTEMBER 1960

Many men like large beds even if they sleep alone. I do myself & Graham Greene is much taller than I am. There is no evidence of adultery in his preference. There is indeed an element of ostentation . . . He is a great one for practical jokes. I think also he is a secret agent on our side and all his buttering up of the Russians is 'cover'.

HENRY GREEN (1905–73)
by Evelyn Waugh (1903–65)

'Henry Green' was the pseudonym of Henry Yorke.

LETTER TO NANCY MITFORD, 16 MAY 1951

He was here for a very long week-end. In London, where everyone is seedy, he did not appear notable. Here in the country he looked GHASTLY. Very long black dirty hair, one brown tooth, pallid puffy face, trembling hands, stone deaf, smoking continuously throughout meals, picking up books in the middle of conversations & falling into maniac giggles, drinking a lot of raw spirits, hating the country & everything good. If you mention Forthampton [Yorke's family home] to him he shies with embarrassment as business people used to do if their business were mentioned.

LETTER TO MAURICE BOWRA, 29 NOVEMBER 1951

Do you think Henry is a communist? Evidence: love of false names and clandestine travel; membership of Fire Brigade [during World War II]; insistence in all his works that social distinctions depend solely on cash; close trade relations, introducing water-closets to the Kremlin; dependence on jazz bands; ostentatious poverty (mulcted for party funds); hatred of architecture, wine and poetry; elaborate code of conventional bad-manners in dress, opening doors to women, etc; obsession with royal family (most disrespectful).

LETTER TO LORD KINROSS, 31 DECEMBER 1958

The major humiliations suffered by Yorke after your luncheon do not directly involve Dame Rose [Macaulay]. She, you may remember, was without water at her flat. Yorke claimed acquaintance with a dignitary called 'Stop Cock' or 'Turn Cock' whom we pursued through a number of fire stations at each of which Yorke's efforts to pass himself off as a proletarian met ludicrous rebuffs. Yorke then reverted from fireman to engineer & said he would mend Dame Rose's cistern himself. (He had been telling some pretty tall stories of his intrepidity on roofs during the 'blitz'.) When we got to Dame Rose's flat we found the cistern was on the roof approached by a rather steep iron ladder. Dame R. shinned up it like a monkey. Yorke trembled below. Only my taunts made him climb. He got to the top, panting & groaning, clung to the tank for a few moments then came down. He had some sort of spasm, seizure or collapse at the foot.

Henry Green
by *Anthony Powell* (1905–)

Throughout his life elements of a success-story were not lacking in Yorke's career, yet he never felt he had been a success; except perhaps briefly when his novel, *Loving* (1945), showed considerable improvement on earlier (and later) sales. To the last he was complaining that he had failed to achieve recognition, though he appears in standard works of reference on writers of his period; perhaps a small recompense for a life's work, but one writers of respectable distinction often fail to pull off. Certainly Yorke was disappointed. In the latter part of his life he withdrew from many people – myself among them – he had formerly known, becoming something of a hermit. There had never been any specific coldness or rift between us, or, for that matter, regarding many other friends he had ceased to see.

Towards the end of the 1950s (the moment dated by the new US Embassy being not yet quite ready for use), I went to a large party given by the American Institute in a house on the south side of Grosvenor Square. There were a few chairs round the walls, but almost everyone was standing up, and, acoustics being not of the best, the noise made by concentrated literary conversation was even more resonant than usual. A long way off I saw a hand feebly waving from a chair, but could not discern, from where I stood, who was sitting there. It turned out to be Yorke.

He began to speak excitedly. He was not in very good shape. We talked for a while, the row going on round about making his words hard to catch. In one of his old bursts of volubility, he began to pour out a lot of memories of the past we had experienced together: our prep school; how his uncle, the General, had shown him campaign maps of France; names of people we had known at Eton, whom he now never saw. In the end he was almost in tears of emotion. 'I'm not well,' he said. 'People say it's drink. It's not that. I'm not well. I think I'm going to die.' I felt rather upset after this encounter. It was the last time I saw him.

W. H. Auden (1907–73)
by Wyndham Lewis (1882–1957)

Nearly ten years ago, before Auden left Oxford, he came to see me in Ossington Street, and I got to know Stephen Spender at the same time. Spender, who is half a Schuster, and combines great practical ability with great liberal charm, showed me a lot of jolly poems, mostly about Auden – he said modestly, a much better poet than himself. And then Auden came himself. He was very crafty and solemn: I felt I was being interviewed by an emissary of some highly civilized power – perhaps over-civilized – who had considered that something had to be done about me and so one of its most able negotiators had been sent along to sound me. The author of *The Dog Beneath the Skin* is, I understand, Icelandic in origin. This causes him to be absurdly fair – or he was then, those blondes darken quickly: I always think of him as a rather *psychic* phenomenon. I should not be surprised if he were 'fey'.

W. H. Auden
by Paul Bowles (1911–)

Lincoln [Kirstein] had made it possible for George Davis, who at that time was fiction editor of *Harper's Bazaar*, to sign a lease on an old brownstone house on Middagh Street in Brooklyn Heights. The purpose of his gesture was to provide reasonably priced living quarters for a group of people working in the arts. Gypsy Rose Lee had taken up residence in the house while writing a mystery called *The G-String Murders* (which George Davis always claimed he wrote), and having finished the book, she had moved out. Jane and I occupied the two empty rooms.

To me the house was a model of *Gemütlichkeit*. It was furnished with what are now called antiques: examples of nineteenth-century American Ugly which George had picked up on Third Avenue and on Brooklyn's Fulton Street and combined with capricious perversity to make a comic facsimile of his grandmother's house in Michigan. It was well heated, and it was quiet, save when Benjamin Britten was working in the first-floor parlour, where he had installed a big black Steinway. George lived on the first floor, Oliver Smith, Jane and I on the second, Britten Auden and Peter Pears, the British tenor, on the third, and Thomas Mann's younger son Golo lived in the attic. Later, when we moved out, Carson McCullers took our rooms and Richard Wright moved in with his wife and child. It was an experiment, and I think a successful one, in communal living. It worked largely because Auden ran it; he was exceptionally adept at getting the necessary money out of us when it was due. We had a good cook and an impossible maid (except that I doubt that any maid could ever have kept that house completely clean and neat), and we ate steaming meals that were served regularly and punctually in the dim, street-floor dining room, with Auden sitting at the head of the table. He would preface a meal by announcing: 'We've got a roast and two veg, salad and savoury, and there will be no political discussion.' He had enough of the don about him to keep us all in order; quite rightly he would not tolerate argument or bickering during mealtime. He exercised a peculiar fascination over Jane [Bowles], who offered to do his typing for him; astonishingly enough, he accepted, and she had to get up every morning at six o'clock and go downstairs to meet him in the dining room, where they would work for three hours or so before breakfast, calling out from time to time for more coffee from the kitchen.

RICHARD WRIGHT (1908–60)
by James Baldwin (1924–87)

The day I got to Paris, before I even checked in at a hotel, I was carried to the Deux Magots, where Richard sat, with the editors of *Zero* magazine. 'Hey, boy!' he cried, looking more surprised and pleased and conspiratorial than ever, and younger and happier. I took this meeting as a good omen, and I could not possibly have been more wrong.

I later became rather closely associated with *Zero* magazine, and wrote for them the essay called 'Everybody's Protest Novel.' On the day the magazine was published, and before I had seen it, I walked into the Brasserie Lipp. Richard was there, and he called me over. I will never forget that interview, but I doubt that I will ever be able to re-create it.

Richard accused me of having betrayed him, and not only him but all American Negroes by attacking the idea of protest literature. It simply had not occurred to me that the essay could be interpreted in that way. I was still in that stage when I imagined that whatever was clear to me had only to be pointed out to become immediately clear to everyone. I was young enough to be proud of the essay and, sad and incomprehensible as it now sounds, I really think that I had rather expected to be patted on the head for my original point of view. It had not occurred to me that this point of view, which I had come to, after all, with some effort and some pain, could be looked on as treacherous or subversive. Again, I had mentioned Richard's *Native Son* at the end of the essay because it was the most important and most celebrated novel of Negro life to have appeared in America. Richard thought that I had attacked it, whereas, as far as I was concerned, I had scarcely even criticized it. And Richard thought that I was trying to destroy his novel and his reputation; but it had not entered my mind that either of these *could* be destroyed, and certainly not by me. And yet, what made the interview so ghastly was not merely the foregoing or the fact that I could find no words with which to defend myself. What made it most painful was that Richard was right to be hurt, I was wrong to have hurt him. He saw clearly enough, far more clearly than I had dared to allow myself to see, what I had done: I had used his work as a kind of springboard into my own. His work was a road-block in my road, the sphinx, really, whose riddles I had to answer before I could become myself. I thought confusedly then, and feel very definitely now, that this was the greatest tribute I could have paid him. But it is not an easy tribute to bear and I do not know how I will take it when my time comes. For, finally, Richard was hurt because I had not given him credit for any human feelings or failings. And indeed I had not, he had never really been a human being for me, he had been an idol. And idols are created in order to be destroyed.

This quarrel was never really patched up, though it must be said that, over a period of years, we tried. 'What do you mean, *protest*!' Richard cried. '*All* literature is protest. You can't name a single novel that isn't protest.' To this I could only weakly protest that all literature might be protest but all protest was not literature. 'Oh,' he would say then, looking, as he so often did, bewilderingly juvenile, 'here you come again with all that art for art's sake crap.' This never failed to make me furious, and my anger, for some reason, always seemed to amuse him. Our rare, best times came when we managed to exasperate each other to the point of helpless hilarity. 'Roots,' Richard would snort, when I had finally worked my way around to this dreary subject, 'what – roots! Next thing you'll be telling me is that all coloured folks have rhythm.' Once, one evening, we managed to throw the whole terrifying subject to the winds, and Richard, Chester Himes, and myself went out and got drunk. It was a good night, perhaps the best I remember in all the time I knew Richard.

For he and Chester were friends, they brought out the best in each other, and the atmosphere they created brought out the best in me. Three absolutely tense, unrelentingly egotistical, and driven people, free in Paris but far from home, with so much to be said and so little time in which to say it!

NELSON ALGREN (1909–81)
by Norman Mailer (1923–)

A couple of months ago Nelson Algren brought out a book called *Who Lost an American?* It's a work which gets better as it goes along, but the worst to be said about the first chapter is that somebody might read it. It has a parody of James Baldwin and myself which hits everybody but the ring rope, and keeps missing altogether. I don't know about Baldwin, but it ought to be relatively easy to do a job on me. Only Algren was throwing too hard. The first chapter read like the prose of a girl who has broken into hysteria trying to beat up her big big boyfriend. Indeed it was so bad it sounded like a parody of what one's best friend on *Time* might write.

I went through these pages the night before I was scheduled to go on a television show with Algren. This act of reading startled me. What had I done to Nelson? We hardly knew each other. The only crime I could remember was that once some years ago in *Advertisements for Myself* I had shaded lukewarm praise for Algren's books with a few tart remarks, the worst of which maybe in Nelson's eyes was to call him 'The Grand Odd-Ball' of American letters. Of course 'odd-ball' was not an altogether unsympathetic word, and 'grand' was fine, but then Algren's eye might see it in other focus. Still? The parody was frantic, I decided, too frantic to keep one awake. I went to bed pleased (about something else, naturally) and aroused myself at six-thirty with four hours of sleep, to make my way to the television studio. Our show was *Calendar*, Harry Reasoner's C.B.S. morning production; they tape early. To my surprise, I was not suffering. I had had a good night and a good four hours of sleep, and I was alert. Which put me in a most excellent mood. I hadn't felt this good with four hours of sleep in quite a while.

Algren, when I saw him, was not looking his best. He too obviously had had four hours of sleep, but he looked like he'd awakened with somebody else's liver in his windpipe. Nelson has an interesting face when you get a chance to study it, but at first sight he slides into your vision like an ex-con who's put twenty years in the can. Pallor for one thing, and a skinny flick in his eyes which promises nothing but angles.

'You're looking well, Norman,' was his formal greeting.

'Fat and pretty.' I was feeling genial and I was acting even more genial than I felt. I think he was feeling a classic embarrassment. There's nothing exactly so dim as meeting somebody you've written about savagely if you no longer feel savage.

Perhaps the television promoters of this show had the idea we would offer a literary war for their camera – their introduction was calculated to nip the tail feathers of two fighting cocks, which is what novelists usually are not – but in any case Reasoner's questions cast Algren and me willy-nilly together. We expended most of our first ten minutes in defense of authors who write about the 'seamy side of life.' Since we were banded together against the common enemy – most of America out there in televisionland – we could hardly throw any roundhouses at each other. Occasionally I'd stick a jab at Algren, but he was on his bicycle. Nelson seemed to be looking for no fight. If it were going to be a personality contest, obviously I was going to win going away. One of things I some-times distrust about myself is that I'm fairly good on television. Nelson isn't. He's a gentle voice, and needs time and a coterie around him to be very funny. Then he can be so funny. This morning he was just doing his hangover best, a club fighter out of training who would like to go the distance, pick up his paycheck and not get hurt.

But he dropped a bomb on me. The show was a half-hour offering, with two stops for commercials. Just before the second half Algren was asked who he considered the best writer around, and he said William Styron was far and away the best because Styron'd written two major novels which nobody else in the generation had done. Yes, said Algren queried by Harry Reasoner, Styron was better than say a writer like Scott Fitzgerald. Came the commercial. Silence.

My feud with Styron was not exactly a young widow's secret. During the break for the product, I realized Algren had done it. I had the choice of keeping my mouth shut, or shoving it into a back-and-forth. (I don't think he's that good – I say he is.) I took the first option. Nobody up at that hour would be able to remember Styron's name anyway. Best to drop the matter cold. Only I was mad. Algren had gotten into me. That tired hungover club fighter had studied me enough to know where my guard was cute, and he dropped a big one in. I was as mad as a lazybitch boxer (a cassiusclay so to speak) who has been winning every round by a fraction and gets decked in the ninth with a manager's punch. That is to say, a punch which was conceived in training camp before the fight. I was mad enough to ignore my own decision and talk about Styron, but the questions went to another direction and we rode out the rest of the show with nothing further for a happening.

I told myself to hold my temper, but succeeded merely by half. 'Listen,' I said, coming on Algren the moment the cameras were done, 'you're twice the writer Styron is, and you aren't even that good.'

'Well, I was impressed with him,' Algren said.

'Come on.' We were talking with the quick intricacy of cellmates. 'You know that second novel is as full of shit as a Yuletide turkey.'

'But the first is good,' said Algren. 'I just read *Lie Down in Darkness* last summer. It's a most remarkable book.'

'It is,' I said, 'but the second . . .'

'Well . . .' said Algren. I had the feeling he didn't necessarily disagree with me. Nelson put on his twenty-years-in-the-pen look again. 'Tell you,' he said, 'you know what I admire about Styron. He gets a picture taken of Mr and Mrs William Styron on the S.S. *United States* that the S.S. *United States* puts in its ads in all the magazines. I got to admire that,' said Nelson out of the side of his mouth. 'I always got to slink over.'

'Nelson, you'd give a testimonial to the Miami Hilton if they put your picture in a magazine.'

Algren looked hurt. He shook his head quietly as if to say, 'You're going too far,' but he ended with a carny grin. 'I think I'll call Styron up the day this show goes on, tell him to look at it, and then pay him a visit for a month.'

'After he sees the show, Styron'll put you up for a year.'

Well, there we were. I couldn't help it. I liked Algren.

We started to talk about middleweight prizefighters. We talked of Henry Hank for a while, and of Reuben Carter who Nelson was certain could take Dick Tiger. I told him Tiger was the best fighter pound for pound in the world. 'He was,' said Algren, 'but Fullmer took a lot out of him.'

'Well, we'll see.'

'Yes.'

We stepped out of the studio together. Algren was going to get an hour of sleep before taking off to Aqueduct for the day. I had an impression he was wondering whether to ask me along. On the street, we hesitated.

Then I stuck out my arm and we shook hands. Two middleweight artists had fought a draw in Baltimore.

STEPHEN SPENDER (1909–95)
by George Orwell (1903–50)

LETTER TO STEPHEN SPENDER, 15 APRIL 1938

You ask how it is that I attacked you not having met you, & on the other hand changed my mind after meeting you. I don't know that I had exactly attacked you, but I had certainly in passing made offensive remarks about 'parlour Bolsheviks such as Auden & Spender' or words to that effect. I was willing to use you as a symbol of the parlour Bolshie because *a.* your verse, what I had read of it, did not mean very much to me, *b.* I looked upon you as a sort of fashionable successful person, also a Communist or Communist sympathizer, & I have been very hostile to the C.P. since about 1935, & *c.* because not having met you I could regard you as a type & also an abstraction. Even if when I met you I had not happened to like you, I should still have been bound to change my attitude, because when you meet anyone in the flesh you realize immediately that he is a human being & not a sort of caricature embodying certain ideas. It is partly for this reason that I don't mix much in literary circles, because I know from experience that once I have met & spoken to anyone I shall never again be able to show any intellectual brutality towards him, even when I feel that I ought to, like the Labour M.P.s who get patted on the back by dukes & are lost forever more.

WILLIAM GOLDING (1911–93)
by John Fowles (1926–)

I have met William Golding only once, at a pleasant small private occasion in the autumn of 1983, just three weeks before the announcement that he had won the Nobel Prize; a coming honour he must have known, but breathed not a word of at our lunch. We were both outshone by David Cecil, who was also there. It is rather difficult to be anything else before someone with amusing memories of being snubbed by Virginia Woolf in her own drawing room, and the like; but I think our being outshone by a skilled conversationalist and raconteur is fairly typical of most novelists in such situations. Our talent seldom lies in the spoken, or in the leaving, after such informal encounters, an indelible impression. I hasten to add I was not disappointed in my famous fellow author; much more, slightly dislocated. Somehow Golding the man, the presence that day, did not quite hit how I had supposed he might be either from his books or from what small gossip I had heard of him – did not fit what I need really to put in inverted commas, an entity made purely of words, 'Golding'.

This must seem naive and foolish in me, since I have long had to realize that I share my own life with just such an entity as 'Golding'. In an extremely unfair kind of way something called 'Fowles' has become my representative in the public world, a kind of vulgar waxwork figure with (it seems to me) only a crude caricature resemblance to the original. I believe the Japanese set up stuffed hate figures in their factory gymnasiums, for the workers to take out their resentments on; that is 'Fowles'. Occasionally this monstrously insufficient surrogate provokes something rather different, a kind of foolish idolatry, like some sort of obscure local saint in Catholic countries ... but in both simulacra remains equally remote from recognizable life.

The real Golding: an affable, gentle man in all outward respects, though not without the bluff asperity or disagreement now and then. Had I not known who he was, I might have guessed a spry retired admiral, as indeed he appears (with clearly comic intention) in one of the crew photographs in the very recent *An Egyptian Journal*. In the flesh he shows a mixture of authority and reserve, with a distinct dry humour, a tiny hint of buried demon; a man still with a touch of the ancient schoolmaster, and also of what years ago in the Marines we used to call the matlows ... as anyone who has read the potted biography on one of the backs of his books could foresee. He looked older than I expected. I had always thought of him as of my own age; not of his being a decade and a half my senior, white-bearded, as he is in reality.

For some reason he reminded me that day – it must seem absurdly – on the one hand of an Elizabethan bishop-scholar of the more tolerant, humanist kind, a sort of quietist Sarum that never was; on the other, of a Slocum, someone who had done long voyages single-handed, metaphorically at least, but preferred now not to talk of them. We managed one or two compliments, when attention was elsewhere. He told me his new novel (*The Paper Men*, not then published) was to be about a novelist being persecuted by a literary researcher, and we discussed briefly that aspect of both our lives; the letters, the academic visitors, the thesis writers. We chatted about his interest in small boats and sailing (which I understood) and a lesser one for horses and riding (which I did not, my dislike for the animal being exceeded only by suspicion of its human admirers). It would have been a very flat occasion for anyone present that had swallowed the old myth, that novelist must equal brilliant talker . . . wit, outrageous gossip, profound intellectual discourse, all the rest of it. I am (temperamentally, and now upon something like principle) a complete failure in that line, and I sensed that Golding felt no need to excel in it, either. But what really that meeting most brought to me was how little I knew of Golding, this agreeable elderly man beside me; and how much more of 'Golding', that is, a semi-mythical, semi-fictional figure. In plain English, not of him as he is, but as I imagined him.

I know the friends who hospitably brought us and our wives, and Lord David, together did so with the kindest intentions. But I must confess that I have a long distaste for literary meetings of any kind, however congenial and well meant in other ways, and fascinating to spectators. In my admittedly very limited experience there is an essential precondition if they are to succeed. It is that the two writers are alone . . . no wives or husbands, no third parties, above all no other literary person, no bookish audience. Perhaps some writers do meet each other for the first time with pleasure and enjoyment, something beyond idle or cautious curiosity; but I must beg leave to doubt it.

Both parties know too much, for a start, of the very special nature of their joint pursuit. They may know very little of each other's private triumphs and disasters, of their dark nights and sunlit days, their fair winds and foul, of their experience on the voyage; but at least they know they are with someone who has also been at sea. They know what havoc their solitary profession performs on the private psyche; of its guilts and anxieties, its vices and egocentricities, its secret pleasures, its sloughs of despond, its often appalling personal costs; of what they are in reality, and what they have become, in quotes. I remember meeting a young American writer years ago (a would-be Hemingway, needless to say) who demanded to know how many times a day I pulled myself off. He meant, how many hours I spent writing. His metaphor, as every writer knows, has a certain truth, whatever it lacks elsewhere. One can no more think of making fiction without onanism, or selfishness (ask our wives), than of the sea without waves.

Nor usually can we writers ever meet each other without a sense, however subdued, of rivalry. The absurd model of the beauty contest or the athletics race haunts such occasions; or perhaps I should liken the ghost to that of a sinister and irrational football league, where the place, even the division, of one's own club is never fixed, the standards of judgement never clear, and in any case always fluctuating in themselves. Most older writers are, I think, wise enough not to lose sleep over this; they know they will be asleep for ever, well out of the stadium, by the time the final match is decided. It is only face to face with each other that the question of comparative status threatens to raise its ugly head.

TENNESSEE WILLIAMS (1911–83)
by Truman Capote (1924–84)

My funniest memory, though, is of four or five years ago, when I was staying with Tennessee in Key West. We were in a terrifically crowded bar – there were probably three hundred people in it, both gays and straights. A husband and wife were sitting at a little table in the corner, and they were both quite drunk. She had on a pair of slacks and a halter top, and she approached our table and held out an eyebrow pencil. She wanted me to autograph her belly button.

I just laughed and said, 'Oh, no. Leave me alone.'

'How can you be so cruel?' Tennessee said to me, and as everyone in the place watched, he took the eyebrow pencil and wrote my name around her navel. When she got back to her table, her husband was furious. Before we knew it, he had grabbed the eyebrow pencil out of her hand and walked over to where we were sitting, whereupon he unzipped his pants and pulled out his cock and said – to me – 'Since you're auto-graphing everything today, would you mind autographing *mine*?' I had never heard a place with three hundred people in it get that quiet. I didn't know what to say – I just looked at him.

Then Tennessee reached up and took the eyebrow pencil out of the stranger's hand. 'I don't know that there's room for Truman to autograph it,' he said, giving me a wink, 'but I'll initial it.'

It brought down the house.

DYLAN THOMAS (1914–53)
by Kingsley Amis (1922–95)

In the Spring of 1951 Dylan Thomas accepted an invitation to give a talk
to the English Society of the University College of Swansea. The society's
secretary, a pupil of mine, asked me if I would like to come along to the
pub and meet Thomas before the official proceedings opened. I said I
would like to very much, for although I was not at this time an enthusiast
for his verse, I had heard a great deal, in Swansea and elsewhere, of his
abilities as a talker and entertainer of his friends. And after all, the fellow
was an eminent poet and had written at least one book, the *Portrait of
the Artist as a Young Dog*, for which my admiration had never wavered.
I arranged with my wife and some of my friends that we would try to get
Thomas back into the pub after his talk (we anticipated little difficulty
here), and thereafter to our house for coffee and a few bottles of beer. I
got down to the pub about six, feeling expectant.

Thomas was already there, a glass of light ale before him and a half
circle of students round him. Also in attendance was a Welsh painter of
small eminence whom I will call Griffiths; in the course of the evening he
told us several times that he had that day driven all the way down from
his home in Merionethshire on purpose to meet Thomas, whom he had
known, he said, for some years. Except for Griffiths, I think we all felt
rather overawed in the presence of the master, and the conversation hung
fire a little for some time. Thomas looked tired and a bit puffy, though
not in any way ill, and if, as I was told later, he had already been drinking
for some time he gave no sign of it. He was in fact very sedate, perhaps
because of the tiredness or, what would have been perfectly explicable,
through boredom. He was putting the light ales down with regularity but
without hurry; I congratulated myself on having bought one of them for
him. There was some uninspired talk about his recent visit to America.
Then he announced, in his clear, slow, slightly haughty, cut-glass Welsh
voice: 'I've just come back from Persia, where I've been pouring water on
troubled oil.'

Making what was in those days my stock retort to the prepared
epigram, I said: 'I say, I must go and write that down.'

He looked round the circle, grinning. 'I have,' he said.

After a few more remarks about Persia had been exchanged, Griffiths,
who had been getting restless, shifted his buttocks along the leatherette

bench, raised his bearded chin and asked: 'What about a few of the old limericks, Dylan?'

Thomas agreed, though without the slightest enthusiasm. I thought it possible that he was not greatly attached to Griffiths, who now began to recite a long string of limericks, bending forward along the seat and addressing himself exclusively to Thomas, indeed at times fairly hissing them into his ear. The content was scatological rather than obscene, with a few references to vomiting and dirty socks thrown in.

Thomas went on apparently ignoring Griffiths, sitting there placidly drinking and smoking, gazing over our heads and occasionally wrinkling his parted lips, no doubt a habit of his. When he did this he lost his faintly statuesque appearance and became a dissolute but very amiable frog. All at once he roused himself and told some limericks back to his associate. They barred a few more holds than the other's, but not many. They were, however, distinctly funnier. The only one I remember cannot be reproduced here, on grounds of possible offence to the Crown. Griffiths said he had heard it before.

After some minutes of this antiphon, the secretary, speaking I think for the first time since introducing me, told us it was time to get along to the meeting. Thomas jumped up and bought a number of bottles of beer, two of which he stuffed into his coat pockets. He gave the others to Griffiths to carry. 'No need to worry, man,' Griffiths kept saying. 'Plenty of time afterwards.'

'I've been caught that way before.'

The bottles were still in his pockets – he checked up on this several times – when in due course he sat rather balefully facing his audience in a room in the Students' Union. About fifty or sixty people had turned up: students and lecturers from the college mainly, but with a good sprinkling of persons who looked as if they were implicated in some way with the ulocal Bookmen's Society. With a puzzled expression, as if he wondered who its author could be, Thomas took from his breast pocket and sorted through an ample typescript, which had evidently been used many times before.

His first words were: 'I can't manage a proper talk. I might just manage an improper one.' Some of the female Bookmen glanced at one another apprehensively. The rest of the talk I forget *in toto*, except for a reference to 'crew-cut sophomores from the quarterback division', and something about the fierce, huge matrons who, according to him, infested American literary clubs. His theme, in so far as he had one, was indeed his experiences while lecturing on and reading poetry in the United States, and his tone was one of pretty strong contempt. Aside from this, much of what he said seemed good sense and was phrased as such, but rather more was couched in his vein of sonorous whimsy, well tricked out with long impressionistic catalogues, strings of compound adjectives, and puns, or rather bits of homophone play – the vein he used in his broadcasts. Stopping this rather than concluding it, he said he would read some poems.

The one that sticks in my mind most was 'Fern Hill', which he recited with a kind of controlled passion that communicated itself to every person in the room. For the most part, though, he read the works of other poets: Auden's 'The Unknown Citizen', Plomer's 'The Flying Bum' (the Bookmen got a little glassy-eyed about that one) and Yeats's 'Lapis Lazuli'. His voice was magnificent, and his belief in what he read was so patent as to be immediately infectious, yet there was something vaguely discomforting about it too, not only to me. Although obviously without all charlatanry, he did here and there sound or behave like a charlatan. This feeling was crystallized for me when he came to the end of 'Lapis Lazuli'. He went normally enough, if rather slowly, as far as:

> Their eyes mid many wrinkles, their eyes,
> Their ancient, glittering eyes . . .

and then fell silent for a full ten seconds. This, as can readily be checked, is a very long time, and since his still rather baleful glare at his audience did not flicker, nor his frame move a hair's breadth, it certainly bore its full value on this occasion. At the end of this period his mouth dropped slowly and widely open, his lips crinkled like a child's who is going to cry, and he said in a tremulous half-whisper:

> . . . are gay.

He held it for another ten seconds or so, still staring and immobile, his mouth still open and crinkled. It was magnificent and the silence of the room was absolute, but . . .

Not very long afterwards we were all back in the pub, Griffiths included. With his performance over, Thomas's constraint had disappeared and he was clearly beginning to enjoy himself. Griffiths, however, was monopolizing him more and more and exchanging a kind of cryptic badinage with him that soon became hard to listen to, especially on one's feet. The pub, too, had filled up and was by now so crowded that the large group round Thomas soon lost all cohesion and started to melt away. I was not sorry to go and sit down at the other end of the room when the chance came.

It was at this time that my friends and I finally abandoned our scheme of trying to get Thomas up to my house when the pub shut. After a time the girl student who had been with us earlier, and who had stayed with Thomas longer than most, came over and said: 'You know, nobody's talking to him now, except that Griffiths chap.'

'Why don't you stay and talk to him?'

'Too boring. And he wasn't talking to any of us. Still, poor dab, he does look out of it. He was in a real state a while ago.'

'How do you mean?'

'All sorry for himself. Complaining that everybody'd gone and left him.'

We all felt rather uncomfortable, and rightly. Although I can vividly recall how tedious, and how unsharable, his conversation with Griffiths was, I am ashamed now to think how openly we must have seemed to be dropping Thomas, how plain was our duty not to drop him at all. Our general disappointment goes to explain our behaviour, but does not excuse it. We were unlucky, too, in encountering him when he was off form and accompanied by Griffiths. At the time I thought that if he had wanted to detach himself and talk to the students he would have found some means of doing so: I have since realized that he was far too good-natured ever to contemplate giving anybody the cold shoulder, and I wonder whether a talent for doing that might not have been something that he badly needed. One of us, at any rate, should have found a way of assuring him that he was being regarded that evening, not with a coltish mixture of awe and suspicion, but sympathetically. Then, I think, we should have seen that his attitude was the product of nothing more self-aware or self-regarding than shyness.

JOHN BERRYMAN (1914–72)
by Saul Bellow (1915–)

I would visit John at an institution (not the one in this novel) called, I believe, The Golden Valley. He was not there because he had broken his leg. The setting of The Golden Valley was indeed golden. It was early autumn, and the blond stubble fields shone. John's room was furnished simply. On the floor was the straw *tatami* mat on which he performed his Yoga exercises. At a collapsible bridge table he wrote Dream Songs. He said, 'As you can see they keep me in a baby crib. They raise the sides at night to keep me from falling out. It is Humiliating! Listen, pal, I have written something new. It is,' he assured me, raising hands that shook, 'absolutely a knockout.'

He put a finger to the bridge of his glasses, for nothing was steady here. Things shook and dropped. Inside and outside they wavered and flew. The straw of Golden Valley swirled on the hills.

John had waited a long time for this poet's happiness. He had suffered agonies of delay. Now came the poems. They were killing him.

> Nitid. They are shooting me full of sings.
> I give no rules. Write as short as you can, in order,
> of what matters.

Inspiration contained a death threat. He would, as he wrote the things he had waited and prayed for, fall apart. Drink was a stabilizer. It somewhat reduced the fatal intensity. Perhaps it replaced the public sanction which poets in the Twin Cities (or in Chicago, in Washington or New York) had to do without. This sanction was not wickedly withheld. It simply did not exist. No one minded if you bred poodles. No one objected if you wrote Dream Songs. Some men of genius were fortunate. They could somehow come to terms with their respective countries. Others had women, the bottle, the hospital. Even in France, far from the Twin Cities, a Verlaine had counted heavily on hospitals and prisons.

John drank, of course, and he took refuge in hospitals, but he also studied and taught. The teaching was important. His lectures were conscientiously, even pedantically prepared. He gave them everything he had. He came in from Golden Valley by cab to address his Humanities class.

He walked up the stone stairs of the University building looking very bad. He wore a huge Western sort of hat. Under the flare of the brim his pale face was long and thin. With tremulous composure, shoulders high, he stalked into the classroom. While the taxi waited, he gave his lecture. His first words were shaky, inaudible, but very soon other instructors had shut their doors against his penetrating voice. He sweated heavily, his shaky fingers turned the numbered cards of his full and careful lecture outline but he was extremely proud of his dependability and of his power to perform. 'Henry' was indeed one of the steadiest men on the block, as faithful to his schedule as Kant, as precise and reliable as a Honeywell product. His talk ended. Then, peanut-faced under the enormous hat and soaked in sweat, he entered the cab and was returned to The Golden Valley, to the *tatami* mat and the bridge table, to the penitential barrenness of the cure. No wonder after these solitary horrors that he was later grateful for group therapy, submitting democratically and eagerly to the criticisms of wacky truckers, graceful under the correction of drinking plumbers and mentally disturbed housewives. In hospitals he found his society. University colleagues were often more philistine, less tolerant of poets than alcoholics or suicidal girls. About *these* passioning countrymen he did not need to be ironical. Here his heart was open.

But everything went into his poems. His poems said everything. He himself said remarkably little. His songs were his love offerings. These offerings were not always accepted. Laid on the altar of, say, an Edmund Wilson, they sometimes were refused. Wilson, greatly respected by John, had written him a harsh letter about his later poems and John was wounded by this the last time I saw him. I read Wilson's letter. John sat at my table, meteor-bearded like John Brown, coughing softly and muttering that he couldn't understand – these were some of his best things. Then he snatched up the copy of *Love & Fame* which he had brought me and struck out certain poems, scribbling in the margins, 'Crap!', 'Disgusting!' But of one poem, 'Surprise Me,' he wrote shakily, 'This is certainly one of the truest things I've been gifted with.'

I read it again now and see what he meant. I am moved by the life of a man I loved. He prays to be surprised by the 'blessing gratuitous' 'on some ordinary day.' It would have to be an ordinary day, of course, an ordinary American day. The ordinariness of days was what it was all about.

He had arrived during a sub-zero wave to give a reading in Chicago. High-shouldered in his thin coat and big Homburg, bearded, he coughed up phlegm. He looked decayed. He had been drinking and the reading was a disaster. His Princeton stutter, once an affectation, had become a vice. People strained to hear a word. Except when, following some arbitrary system of dynamics, he shouted loudly, we could hear nothing. We left a disappointed, bewildered, angry audience. Dignified, he entered a waiting car, sat down, and vomited. He passed out in his room at the Quadrangle Club and slept through the faculty party given in his honour. But in the morning he was full of innocent cheer. He was chirping. It had been a great evening. He recalled an immense success. His cab came, we hugged each other, and he was off for the airport under a frozen sun.

He was a full professor now, and a celebrity. *Life* interviewed him. The *Life* photographer took ten thousand shots of him in Dublin. But John's human setting was oddly thin. He had, instead of a society, the ruined drunken poet's God to whom he prayed over his shoulder. Out of affection and goodwill he made gestures of normalcy. He was a husband, a citizen, a father, a householder, he went on the wagon, he fell off, he joined AA. He knocked himself out to be like everybody else – he liked, he loved, he cared, but he was aware that there was something peculiarly comical in all this. And at last it must have seemed that he had used up all his resources. Faith against despair, love versus nihilism had been the themes of his struggles and his poems. What he needed for his art had been supplied by his person, by his mind, his wit. He drew it out of his vital organs, out of his very skin. At last there was no more. Reinforcements failed to arrive. Forces were not joined. The cycle of resolution, reform and relapse had become a bad joke which could not continue.

John Berryman
by Robert Lowell (1917–77)

I sit looking out a window at 3:30 this February afternoon. I see a pasture, green out of season and sunlit; in an hour or more or less, it will be black. John Berryman walks brightly out of my memory. We met at Princeton through Caroline Gordon, in 1944, the wane of the war. The moment was troubled; my wife, Jean Stafford, and I were introduced to the Berrymans for youth and diversion. I remember expected, probably false, images, the hospital-white tablecloth, the clear martinis, the green antiquing of an Ivy League college faculty club. What college? Not Princeton, but the less spruce Cambridge, England, John carried with him in his speech rhythms and dress. He had a casual intensity, the almost intimate mumble of a don. For life, he was to be a student, scholar, and teacher. I think he was almost *the* student-friend I've had, the one who was the student in essence. An indignant spirit was born in him; his life was a cruel fight to set it free. Is the word for him courage or generosity or loyalty? He had these. And he was always a performer, a prima donna; at first to those he scorned, later to everyone, except perhaps students, his family, and Saul Bellow.

From the first, John was humorous, learned, thrustingly vehement in liking . . . more adolescent than boyish. He and I preferred critics who were writers to critics who were not writers. We hated literary discussions animated by jealousy and pushed by caution. John's own criticism, mostly spoken, had a poetry. Hyper-enthusiasms made him a hot friend, and could also make him wearing to friends – one of his dearest, Delmore

Schwartz, used to say no one had John's loyalty, but you liked him to live in another city. John had fire then, but not the fire of Byron or Yevtushenko. He clung so keenly to Hopkins, Yeats, and Auden that their shadows paled him.

Later, the Berrymans (the first Berrymans, the first Lowells) stayed with us in Damariscotta Mills, Maine. Too many guests had accepted. We were inept and uncouth at getting the most out of the country; we didn't own or drive a car. This gloomed and needled the guests. John was ease and light. We gossiped on the rocks of the millpond, baked things in shells on the sand, and drank, as was the appetite of our age, much less than now. John could quote with vibrance to all lengths, even prose, even late Shakespeare, to show me what could be done with disrupted and mended syntax. This was the start of his real style. At first he wrote with great brio bristles of clauses, all breaks and with little style to break off from. Someone said this style was like Emily Dickinson's mad-dash punctuation without the words. I copied, and arrived at a manner that made even the verses I wrote for my cousins' *bouts rimés* (with 'floor,' 'door,' 'whore,' and 'more' for the fixed rhymes) leaden and unintelligible. Nets so grandly knotted could only catch logs – our first harsh, inarticulate cry of truth.

My pilgrimage to Princeton with Randall Jarrell to have dinner with the Berrymans was not happy. Compared with other poets, John was a prodigy; compared with Randall, a slow starter. Perpetrators of such miscounters usually confess their bewilderment that two talents with so much in common failed to jell. So much in common – both were slightly heretical disciples of Bernard Haggin, the music and record critic. But John jarred the evening by playing his own favourite recordings on an immense machine constructed and formerly used by Haggin. This didn't animate things; they tried ballet. One liked Covent Garden, the other Danilova, Markova, and the latest New York Balanchine. Berryman unfolded leather photograph books of enlarged British ballerinas he had almost dated. Jarrell made cool, odd evaluations drawn from his forty, recent, consecutive nights of New York ballet. He hinted that the English dancers he had never seen were on a level with the Danes. I suffered more than the fighters, and lost authority by trying not to take sides.

Both poet-critics had just written definitive essay-reviews of my first book, *Lord Weary's Castle*. To a myopic eye, they seemed to harmonize. So much the worse. Truth is in minute particulars; here, in the minutiae, nothing meshed. Earlier in the night, Berryman made the tactical mistake of complimenting Jarrell on his essay. This was accepted with a hurt, glib croak, 'Oh, thanks.' The flattery was not returned, not a muscle smiled. I realized that if the essays were to be written again ... On the horrible New Jersey midnight local to Pennsylvania Station, Randall analyzed John's high, intense voice with surprise and coldness. 'Why hasn't anyone told him?' Randall had the same high, keyed-up voice he criticized. Soon he developed chills and fevers, ever more violent, and I took my suit coat and covered him. He might have been a child. John, the host, the insulted one, recovered sooner. His admiration for Randall remained unsoured, but the dinner was never repeated.

Our trip a year later to Ezra Pound at St Elizabeths Hospital near Washington was softer, so soft I remember nothing except a surely mis-placed image of John sitting on the floor hugging his knees and asking with shining cheeks for Pound to sing an aria from his opera *Villon*. He saw nothing nutty about Pound, or maybe it was the opposite. Anyway, his instincts were true – serene, ungrudging, buoyant. Few people, even modern poets, felt carefree and happy with Pound then ... When we came back to my room, I made the mistake of thinking that John was less interested in his new poems than in mine ... Another opera. Much later, in the ragged days of John's first divorce, we went to the Met Opera Club, and had to borrow Robert Giroux's dinner jacket and tails. I see John dancing in the street shouting, 'I don't know you, Elizabeth wouldn't know you, only your mother would.'

Pound, Jarrell, and Berryman had the same marvellous and maddening characteristic: they were self-centred and unselfish. This gave that breath-less, commanding rush to their amusements and controversies – to Jarrell's cool and glowing critical appreciations, to Berryman's quotations and gossip. His taste for what he despised was infallible; but he could outrage-ously hero-worship living and dead, most of all writers his own age. Few have died without his defiant, heroic dirge. I think he sees them rise from their graves like soldiers to answer him.

Jarrell's death was the sadder. If it hadn't happened, it wouldn't have happened. He would be with me now, in full power, as far as one may at fifty. This might-have-been (it's a frequent thought) stings my eyes. John, with pain and joy like his friend Dylan Thomas, almost won what he gambled for. He was more eccentric than Thomas, less the natural poet of natural force, yet had less need to be first actor. He grew older, drier, more toughly twisted into the varieties of experience.

I must say something of death and the *extremist poets*, as we are named in often pre-funerary tributes. Except for Weldon Kees and Sylvia Plath, they lived as long as Shakespeare, outlived Wyatt, Baudelaire and Hopkins, and long outlived the forever Romantics, those who really died young. John himself lived to the age of Beethoven, whom he celebrates in the most ambitious and perhaps finest of his late poems, a monument to his long love, unhampered expression and subtle criticism. John died with fewer infirmities than Beethoven. The consolation somehow doesn't wash. I feel the jagged gash with which my contemporaries died, with which we were to die. Were they killed, as standard radicals say, by our corrupted society? Was their success an aspect of their destruction? Were we uncomfortable epigoni of Frost, Pound, Eliot, Marianne Moore, etc.? This bitter possibility came to us at the moment of our *arrival*. Death comes sooner or later, these made it sooner. I somehow smile, though a bit crookedly, when I think of John's whole life, and even of the icy leap from the bridge to the hard ground. He was springy to the end, and on his feet. The cost of his career is shown by an anecdote he tells in one of the earlier *Dream Songs* – as a boy the sliding seat in his shell slipped as he was rowing a race, and he had to push back and forth, bleeding his bottom on the runners, till the race was finished. The bravery is ignominious and screams. John kept rowing; maybe at the dock no one noticed the blood on his shorts – his injury wasn't maiming. Going to one of his later Minnesota classes, he stumbled down the corridor, unhelped, though steadying himself step by step on the wall, then taught his allotted hour, and walked to the ambulance he had ordered, certain he would die of a stroke while teaching. He was sick a few weeks, then returned to his old courses – as good as before.

The brighter side is in his hilarious, mocking stories, times with wives, children, and friends, and surely in some of the sprinted affairs he fabled. As he became more inspired and famous and drunk, more and more John Berryman, he became less good company and more a happening – slashing eloquence in undertones, amber tumblers of bourbon, a stony pyramid talking down a rugful of admirers. His almost inhuman generosity sweetened this, but as the heart grew larger, the hide grew thicker. Is his work worth it to us? Of course; though the life of the ant is more to the ant than the health of his anthill. He never stopped fighting and moving all his life; at first, expert and derivative, later the full output, more juice, more pages, more strange words on the page, more simplicity, more obscurity. I am afraid I mistook it for forcing, when he came into his own. No voice now or persona sticks in my ear as his. It is poignant, abrasive, anguished, humorous. A voice on the page, identified as my friend's on the telephone, though lost now to mimicry. We should hear him read aloud. It is we who are laboured and private, when he is smiling.

I met John last a year or so ago at Christmas in New York. He had been phoning poems and invitations to people at three in the morning, and I felt a weariness about seeing him. Since he had let me sleep uncalled, I guessed he felt numbness to me. We met one noon during the taxi strike at the Chelsea Hotel, dusty with donated, avant-garde constructs, and dismal with personal recollections, Bohemia, and the death of Thomas. There was no cheerful restaurant within walking distance, and the seven best bad ones were closed. We settled for the huge, varnished unwelcome of an empty cafeteria-bar. John addressed me with an awareness of his dignity, as if he were Ezra Pound at St Elizabeths, emphatic without pertinence, then brownly inaudible.

His remarks seemed guarded, then softened into sounds that only he could understand or hear. At first John was ascetically hung over, at the end we were high without assurance, and speechless. I said, 'When will I see you again?' meaning, in the next few days before I flew to England. John said, 'Cal, I was thinking through lunch that I'll never see you again.' I wondered how in the murk of our conversation I had hurt him, but he explained that his doctor had told him one more drunken binge would kill him. Choice? It is blighting to know that this fear was the beginning of eleven months of abstinence . . . half a year of prolific rebirth, then suicide.

BERNARD MALAMUD (1914–86)
by Philip Roth (1933–)

In July 1985, just back from England, Claire [Bloom] and I drove north from Connecticut to have lunch and spend the afternoon with the Malamuds in Bennington. The summer before they had made the two-and-a-half-hour trip down to us and then spent the night, but Bern wasn't equal to the journey now. The debilitating after-effects of the bypass surgery and stroke of three years earlier had begun increasingly to sap his strength, and the effort not to submit without a fight to all the disabling physical problems had begun to beat him down. I saw how weak he'd got as soon as we drove up. Bern, who always managed, regardless of the weather, to be waiting in the driveway to greet you and see you off, was out there all right in his poplin jacket, but as he nodded a rather grim welcome, he looked to be listing slightly to one side at the same time that he seemed to be holding himself, by dint of will power alone, absolutely still, as though the least movement would bring him down. It was impossible to discern in him even a remnant of the stolid, resolute insurance agent I'd envisaged years ago. The 46–year-old transplanted Brooklynite that I'd met in the Far West, that undiscourageable round-the-clock worker with the serious, attentive face and the balding crown and the pitiless Eugene, Oregon haircut, whose serviceable, surface mild-ness was in no way intended to mislead anyone about the molten obstinacy at the core, was now, without question, a frail and very sick old man, whose tenacity was just about used up.

It was his heart and the stroke and all the medication that had done the damage, but to a long-time reader of the man and his fiction it couldn't help but appear as though the pursuit of that unremitting aspiration that he shared with so many of his characters – to break down the iron limits of circumstance and self in order to live a better life – had finally taken its toll. Though he'd never said much to me about his childhood, from the little I knew about his mother's death when he was still a boy, and about the father's poverty and the handicapped brother whose lamentable fate had become Bern's responsibility, I imagined that he'd had no choice but to forgo youth and accept adulthood at a very early age. And now he looked it – like a man who'd had to be a man for just too long a time . . .

It was a very sad afternoon. We talked in the living-room before lunch; Bern asked Claire about her daughter's opera career, they talked about singers and singing, and then he went on to speak about his own two children, but concentration was a struggle for him, and though his was a will powerless to back away from any difficult task, it was disheartening to realise how imposing a challenge just pursuing a conversation with friends had become.

As we were leaving the living-room to have lunch outdoors on the back porch, Bern asked if he might read aloud to me later the opening chapters of a first draft of a novel. He'd never before read to me or asked my opinion of a work-in-progress and I was surprised by the request. I was also a little perturbed, and wondered throughout lunch what sort of book it could be, conceived and begun in the midst of all this hardship by a writer whose memory of even the multiplication tables had been clouded now for several years and whose vision, also impaired by the stroke, made shaving every morning what he'd wryly described to me as 'an adventure'.

After coffee Bern went to his study for the manuscript, a thin sheaf of pages perfectly typed and neatly clipped together. Ann, whose back had been bothering her, excused herself to take a rest, and when Bern settled back at the table it was to begin to read, a little formally, in his quiet insistent way, to just Claire and me.

I noticed when he sat down that all round his chair, on the porch floor, were scattered crumbs from his lunch. A tremor had made eating a little bit of an adventure too, and yet he had driven himself to write these pages, to undertake once again this ordeal . . .

It turned out that not too many words were typed on each page and that the first-draft chapters were extremely brief. I didn't dislike what I heard because there was nothing yet to like or dislike – he hadn't got started, really, however much he wanted to think otherwise. It was like having been led into a dark hole to see by torchlight the first Malamud story ever scratched upon a cave wall. What was awesome wasn't what was on the wall but, rather, contemplating the power of the art that had been generated by such simple markings.

I didn't want to lie to him but, looking at the thin sheaf of pages in the hands of that very frail man, I couldn't tell the truth, even if he was expecting it of me. I said simply, and only a little evasively, that it seemed to me a beginning like all beginnings. That was quite truthful enough for a man of 71 who had published twelve of the most original works of fiction written by an American in the past thirty-five years. Trying to be constructive, I suggested that perhaps the narrative opened too slowly and that he might better begin further on, with one of the later chapters. Then I asked where it was all going. 'What comes next?' I said, hoping we could pass on to what it was he had in mind if not yet down on the page. But he wouldn't let go of what he had written, at such cost, as easily as that. Nothing was ever as easy as that, least of all the end of things. In a soft voice suffused with fury, he said: 'What's next isn't the point.'

In the silence that followed, before Claire eased him gently into a discussion of the kind of character he was imagining as his hero, he was perhaps as angry at failing to master the need for assurance so nakedly displayed as he was with me for having nothing good to say. He wanted to be told that what he had painfully composed while enduring all his burdens was something more than he himself must have known it to be in his heart. He was suffering so, I wished I could have said that it *was* something more, and that if I'd said it, he could have believed me.

Before I left for England in the fall I wrote him a note telling him that I was off, and inviting him and Ann to come down to Connecticut the next summer – it was our turn to entertain them. The response that reached me in London some weeks later was pure, laconic Malamudese. They'd be delighted to visit, but, he reminded me, 'next summer is next summer.'

He died on 18 March, three days before spring.

SAUL BELLOW (1915–)
by Arthur Miller (1915–)

Pyramid Lake, Nevada, was a piece of the moon in 1956, long before the marina, the hotdog stands, and the roar of outboards blasted away its uninhabited, enigmatic enchantment. It was a gray, salty lake miles long, surrounded by a Paiute Indian reservation, a forbidding but beautiful place occasionally favoured by movie companies shooting scenes of weird monsters in outer space. I had come here to live out the six-week residency required for the otherwise easy Nevada divorce, the New York State law still requiring a finding of adultery. Saul Bellow, with whom I shared an editor, Pascal Covici of Viking Press, was in Nevada for the same reason, and Covici had asked his help in finding me a place to stay. Bellow had taken one of the two cottages facing the lake. I took the other. He was then working on his novel *Henderson the Rain King*. I was trying to make some personal contact with the terrain where I had landed after exploding my life.

Fittingly, this being Nevada, home of the rootless, the wanderers, and the misfits, the only phone between our cottages and Reno, some forty miles away, was in a lone booth standing beside the highway, a road travelled by perhaps three vehicles a day and none at night. Nearby were the empty cottages of an abandoned motel for people waiting out their divorces. Only its owners lived there now, a troubled couple, the man a fairly scrupulous horse breeder whose half-dozen thoroughbreds grazed untied along the lakeshore. He, his wife, or their hired man would drive over to summon one or the other of us to the phone booth for one of our rare calls from what had come to seem an increasingly remote United States. Surrounding us was a range of low, iron-stained mountains per-petually changing their magenta colours through the unbroken silence of the days. Saul would sometimes spend half an hour up behind a hill a half-mile from the cottages emptying his lungs roaring at the stillness, an exercise in self-contact, I supposed, and the day's biggest event. He had already accumulated a library here large enough for a small college.

ROBERT LOWELL (1917–77)
by Arthur Miller (1915–)

But in the sixties everything one thought one knew was up for grabs. Robert Lowell, his wife, Elizabeth Hardwick, and their eleven-year-old daughter came by for a few hours with our neighbours, Henry and Olga Carlisle, longtime friends of theirs. It was a grey November day, all the leaves were down. Still in the car, he feigned not to see me emerging from the house and kept fussing with his daughter as she got out. Finally we shook hands. His thinning hair was wetted down crossways on his scalp. He was quick to say that my speech at the Bled, Yugoslavia, International PEN Congress had moved him – I had praised his refusal, in protest against the war, of President Johnson's invitation to a festival of the arts at the White House.

He asked about the varieties of trees I was raising, and I got on the tractor to show him how I pruned the roots with a device I had fashioned and attached to the cultivator bar. He leaned far down to his daughter and gently said, 'You can't imagine me pruning tree roots, can you?' The girl barely shook her head, her expression uncomfortable.

We walked down toward the pond side by side, he turning when I turned and halting when I did. He hardly paused in his talking.

'I like Kazan, he has enormous charisma, but I wouldn't let him put on my Greek trilogy; *The Changeling* is a masterpiece, and he ruined it for years to come.' 'I'm not sure it's a masterpiece.'

'It is. Eliot said so.'

I would have liked to argue T. S. Eliot's theatrical credentials, but Lowell was forging ahead and would not have listened, could not. Everything Chinese was astonishing, even perfect. He had considered attending the White House function, falling to his knees at the appropriate moment, and praying for America's mercy upon Vietnam. Roosevelt was a fraud and a liar; Kennedy read a lot.

'Roosevelt,' I said, 'regretted not having helped Spain, you know.'

'He did?' This was the first thing that stopped him, and he looked eager and happy to hear it. 'Why do you say that?'

'It's in Harold Ickes's diary. He told Ickes it was one of the greatest mistakes of his life not to have supported the Loyalists against Franco.'

Lowell brightened. He loved gossip, concealed facts, and I think he rather liked the idea of Roosevelt feeling a stab of remorse. Then he was off again, quite calmly referring to 'my manic phase at the time' – presumably of the White House affair. He must be brave, I thought, to be able to endure the wreckage of his attention like this. It was as though uninterrupted talking kept reality both together and at bay.

It was painful to think what would have happened had his courageous pacifist view prevailed and kept us from entering the war against Hitler, during which he had gone to prison as a conscientious objector. As I sat on the grass with him looking at the pond, trying to follow his rush of barely connected unequivocal ideas, he seemed to symbolize our time, its immensities, its free-floating streams of aspiration and its murdered rationality. It suddenly occurred to me that we resembled one another – we were about the same age and about the same height, wore the same tortoiseshell glasses, and were balding in the same way – but I had no demon in me that was so careless about surviving. His views, however they functioned in his work, were so absolute as to be pretty useless in reality, while I could not long commit myself to anything I did not consider somehow useful in living one's life. He flew high toward his visions, I felt bound to persuade an audience equipped with nothing but common sense at best. Despite everything, I still thought writing had to try to save America, and that meant grabbing people and shaking them by the back of the neck.

Robert Lowell
by Norman Mailer (1923–)

On the weekend of October 21–22, 1967, a major march was arranged in Washington DC as a protest against the US government's escalation of the war in Vietnam. On the Thursday before, four writers who were to participate in the demonstration – Mailer, Lowell, Dwight Macdonald and Paul Goodman – gave a reading at the Ambassador's theatre. This account is of the dinner before the reading and the performance itself. After the march (at which Mailer was arrested), Mailer was commissioned by Harper's *magazine to write a 20,000-word article about the event for the almost unprecedented fee of $10,000. In fact, Mailer's resulting piece* *was 90,000 words long and the magazine's new editor, Willie Morris, devoted a whole issue to it. With an added epilogue, this was published in book form as* The Armies of the Night *and in May 1969 it won Mailer a Pulitzer Prize.*

. . . Mailer gave up quickly any thought of circulation. Rather, he huddled first with Dwight Macdonald, but Macdonald was the operative definition of the gregarious and could talk with equal facility and equal lack of personal observation to an Eskimo, a collector from the New York Department of Sanitation, or a UN diplomat – therefore was chatting happily with the world fifteen minutes after his entrance. Hence Mailer and Robert Lowell got into what was by all appearances a deep conversation at the dinner table sometime before food was laid out, Mailer thus doubly wounding the hostess with his later refusal.

We find, therefore, Lowell and Mailer ostensibly locked in converse. In fact, out of the thousand separate enclaves of their very separate personalities, they sensed quickly that they now shared one enclave to the hilt: their secret detestation of liberal academic parties to accompany worthy causes. Yes, their snobbery was on this mountainous face close to identical – each had a delight in exactly the other kind of party, a posh evil social affair, they even supported a similar vein of vanity (Lowell with considerably more justice) that if they were doomed to be revolutionaries, rebels, dissenters, anarchists, protesters, and general champions of one Left cause or another, they were also, in private, *grands conservateurs*, and if the truth be told, poor damn émigré princes. They were willing if necessary (probably) to die for the cause – one could hope the cause might finally at the end have an unexpected hint of wit, a touch of the Lord's last grace – but wit or no, grace or grace failing, it was bitter rue to have to root up one's occupations of the day, the week, and the weekend and trot down to Washington for idiot mass manifestations which could only drench one in the most ineradicable kind of mucked-up publicity and have for compensation nothing at this party which might be representative of some of the Devil's better creations. So Robert Lowell and Normal Mailer feigned deep conversation. They turned their heads to one another at the empty table, ignoring the potentially acolytic drinkers at either elbow, they projected their elbows out in fact like flying buttresses or old Republicans, they exuded waves of Interruption Repellent from the posture of their backs, and concentrated on their conversation, for indeed they were the only two men of remotely similar status in the room. . . .

Lowell, whose personal attractiveness was immense (since his features were at once virile and patrician and his characteristic manner turned up facets of the grim, the gallant, the tender and the solicitous as if he were the nicest Boston banker one had ever hoped to meet) was not concerned too much about the evening at the theatre. 'I'm just going to read some poems,' he said. 'I suppose you're going to speak, Norman.'

'Well, I will.'

'Yes, you're awfully good at that.'

'Not really.' Harumphs, modifications, protestations and denials of the virtue of the ability to speak.

'I'm no good at all at public speaking,' said Lowell in the kindest voice. He had indisputably won the first round. Mailer the younger presumptive, and self-elected prince was left to his great surprise – for he had been exercised this way many times before – with the unmistakeable feeling that there was some faint strain of the second-rate in this ability to speak on your feet.

Then they moved on to talk of what concerned them more. It was the subject first introduced to Mailer by Mitch Goodman. Tomorrow, a group of draft resisters, led by William Sloane Coffin, Jr., Chaplain at Yale, were going to march from their meeting place at a church basement, to the Department of Justice, and there a considerable number of draft cards would be deposited in a bag by individual students representing themselves, or their groups at different colleges, at which point Coffin and a selected few would walk into the Department of Justice, turn the cards over to the Attorney General, and await his reply.

'I don't think there'll be much trouble at this, do you?' asked Lowell.

'No, I think it'll be dull, and there'll be a lot of speeches.'

'Oh, no,' said Lowell with genuine pain, 'Coffin's not that kind of fool.'

'It's hard to keep people from making speeches.'

'Well, you know what they want us to do?' Lowell explained. He had been asked to accompany a draft resister up to the bag in which the draft cards were being dropped. 'It seems,' said Lowell, with a glint of the oldest Yankee light winging off like a mad laser from his eye, 'that they want us to be *big buddy*.' It was agreed this was unsuitable. No, Lowell suggested, it would be better if they each just made a few remarks. 'I mean,' said Lowell, beginning to stammer a little, 'we could just get up and say we respect their action and support it, just to establish, I suppose, that we're there and behind them and so forth.'

Mailer nodded. He felt no ease for any of these suggestions. He did not even know if he truly supported the turning in of draft cards. It seemed to him at times that the students who disliked the war most should perhaps be the first to volunteer for the Army in order that their ideas have currency in the Army as well. Without them, the armed forces could more easily become Glamour State for the more mindless regions of the proletariat if indeed the proletariat was not halfway to Storm Troop Junction already. The military could make an elite corps best when the troops were homogenized. On the other hand, no soldier could go into combat with the secret idea that he would not fire a gun. If nothing else, it was unfair to friends in his outfit; besides it suggested the suicidal. No, the iron of the logic doubtless demanded that if you disapproved of the war too much to shoot Vietcong, then your draft card was for burning. But Mailer arrived at this conclusion somewhat used up as we have learned from the number of decisions he had to make at various moral crossroads en route and so felt no enthusiasm whatsoever for the preliminary demonstration at the Department of Justice tomorrow in which he would take part. To the contrary, he wondered if he would burn or surrender his own draft card if he were young enough to own one, and he did not really know the answer. How then could he advise others to take the action, or even associate his name? Still, he was going to be there.

He started to talk of these doubts with Lowell, but he could hear the sound of his own voice, and it offended him. It seemed weak, plaintive, as if his case were – no less incriminating word – phony, he did not quite know why. So he shut up.

A silence.

'You know, Norman,' said Lowell in his fondest voice, 'Elizabeth and I really think you're the finest journalist in America.'

Mailer knew Lowell thought this – Lowell had even sent him a postcard once to state the enthusiasm. But the novelist had been shrewd enough to judge that Lowell sent many postcards to many people – it did not matter that Lowell was by overwhelming consensus judged to be the best, most talented, and most distinguished poet in America – it was still necessary to keep the defense lines in good working order. A good word on a card could keep many a dangerous recalcitrant in the ranks.

Therefore, this practice annoyed Mailer. The first card he'd ever received from Lowell was on a book of poems, *Deaths for the Ladies and other disasters* it had been called, and many people had thought the book a joke which whatever its endless demerits, it was not. Not to the novice poet at least. When Lowell had written that he liked the book, Mailer next waited for some word in print to canonize his thin tome; of course it never came. If Lowell were to begin to award living American poets in critical print, two hundred starving worthies could with fairness hold out their bowl before the escaped Novelist would deserve his turn. Still, Mailer was irked. He felt he had been part of a literary game. When the second card came a few years later telling him he was the best journalist in America, he did not answer. Elizabeth Hardwick, Lowell's wife, had just published a review of *An American Dream* in *Partisan Review* which had done its best to disembowel the novel. Lowell's card might have arrived with the best of motives, but its timing suggested to Mailer an exercise in neutralsmanship – neutralize the maximum of possible future risks. Mailer was not critically equipped for the task, but there was always the distant danger that some bright and not unauthoritative voice, irked at Lowell's enduring hegemony, might come along with a long lance and presume to tell America that posterity would judge Allen Ginsberg the greater poet.

This was all doubtless desperately unfair to Lowell who, on the basis of two kind cards, was now judged by Mailer to possess an undue unchristian talent for literary logrolling. But then Mailer was prickly. Let us hope it was not because he had been beaten a little too often by book reviewers, since the fruit of specific brutality is general suspicion.

Still Lowell now made the mistake of repeating his remark. 'Yes, Norman, I really think you are the best journalist in America.'

The pen may be mightier than the sword, yet at their best, each belong to extravagant men. 'Well, Cal,' said Mailer, using Lowell's nickname for the first time, 'there are days when I think of myself as being the best writer in America.'

The effect was equal to walloping a roundhouse right into the heart of an English boxer who had been hitherto right up on his toes. Consternation, not Britannia, now ruled the waves. Perhaps Lowell had a moment when he wondered who was guilty of declaring war on the minuet. 'Oh, Norman, oh, certainly,' he said, 'I didn't mean to imply, heavens no, it's just I have such *respect* for good journalism.' 'Well, I don't know that I do,' said Mailer. It's much harder to write' – the next said with great and false graciousness – 'a good poem.'

'Yes, of course.'

Chuckles. Headmastermanship.

Chuckles. Fellow headmastermanship.

They were both now somewhat spoiled for each other. Mailer got up abruptly to get a drink. He was shrewd enough to know that Lowell, like many another aristocrat before him, respected abrupt departures. The pain of unexpected rejection is the last sweet vice left to an aristocrat (unless they should happen to be not aristocrats, but secret monarchs – then watch for your head!). . . .

Lowell's turn had arrived. Mailer stood up to introduce him.

The novelist gave a fulsome welcome to the poet. He did not speak of his poetry (with which he was not conspicuously familiar) nor of his prose which he thought excellent – Mailer told instead of why he had respect for Lowell as a man. A couple of years ago, the poet had refused an invitation from President Johnson to attend a garden party for artists and intellectuals, and it had attracted much attention at the time for it was one of the first dramatic acts of protest against the war in Vietnam, and Lowell was the only invited artist of first rank who had refused. Saul Bellow, for example, had attended the garden party. Lowell's refusal could not have been easy, the novelist suggested, because that kind of experience was often stimulating to new perception and new work. So, an honorific occasion in full panoply was not easy for the mature artist to eschew. Capital! Lowell had therefore bypassed the most direct sort of literary capital. Ergo, Mailer respected him – he could not be certain he would have done the same himself, although, of course, he assured the audience he would not probably have ever had the opportunity to refuse. (Hints of merriment in the crowd at the thought of Mailer on the White House lawn.)

If the presentation had been formal up to here, it had also been some-what graceless. On the consequence, our audience's amusement tipped the slumbering Beast. Mailer now cranked up a vaudeville clown for finale to Lowell's introduction. 'Ladies and gentlemen, if novelists come from the middle class, poets tend to derive from the bottom and the top. We all know good poets at the bottom – ladies and gentlemen, here is a poet from the top, Mr Robert Lowell.' A large vigorous hand of applause, genuine enthusiasm for Lowell, some standing ovation.

But Mailer was depressed. He had betrayed himself again. The end of the introduction belonged in a burlesque house – he worked his own worst veins, like a man on the edge of bankruptcy trying to collect hopeless debts. He was fatally vulgar! Lowell passing him on the stage had recovered sufficiently to cast him a nullifying look. At this moment, they were obviously far from friends.

Lowell's shoulders had a slump, his modest stomach was pushed forward a hint, his chin was dropped to his chest as he stood at the microphone pondering for a moment. One did not achieve the languid grandeurs of that slouch in one generation – the grandsons of the first sons had best go through the best troughs in the best eating clubs at Harvard before anyone in the family could try for such elegant note. It was now apparent to Mailer that Lowell would move by instinct, ability, and certainly by choice, in the direction most opposite from himself.

'Well,' said Lowell softly to the audience, his voice dry and gentle as any New England executioner might ever hope to be, 'this has been a zany evening.' Laughter came back, perhaps a little too much. It was as if Lowell wished to reprove Mailer, not humiliate him. So he shifted, and talked a bit uneasily for perhaps a minute about very little. Perhaps it was too little. Some of the audience, encouraged by earlier examples, now whistled. 'We can't hear you,' they shouted, 'speak louder.'

Lowell was annoyed. 'I'll bellow,' he said, 'but it won't do any good.' His firmness, his distaste for the occasion, communicated some subtle but impressive sense of his superiority. Audiences are moved by many cues but the most satisfactory to them is probably the voice of their abdomen. There are speakers who give a sense of security to the abdomen, and they always elicit the warmest kind of applause. Mailer was not this sort of speaker; Lowell was. The hand of applause which followed this remark was fortifying. Lowell now proceeded to read some poetry.

He was not a splendid reader, merely decent to his own lines, and he read from that slouch, that personification of ivy climbing a column, he was even diffident, he looked a trifle helpless under the lights. Still, he made no effort to win the audience, seduce them, dominate them, bully them, amuse them, no, they were there for him, to please *him*, a sounding board for the plucked string of his poetic line, and so he endeared himself to them. They adored him – for his talent, his modesty, his superiority, his melancholy, his petulance, his weakness, his painful, almost stammering shyness, his noble strength – there was the string behind other strings.

> O to break loose, like the chinook
> salmon jumping and falling back,
> nosing up to the impossible

> stone and bone-crushing waterfall –
> raw-jawed, weak-fleshed there, stopped by ten
> steps of the roaring ladder, and then
> to clear the top on the last try,
> alive enough to spawn and die.

Mailer discovered he was jealous. Not of the talent. Lowell's was very large, but then Mailer was a bulldog about the value of his own talent. No, Mailer was jealous because he had worked for this audience, and Lowell without effort seemed to have stolen them: Mailer did not know if he was contemptuous of Lowell for playing *grand maître*, or admiring of his ability to do it. Mailer knew his own version of *grand maître* did not compare. Of course no one would be there to accept his version either. The pain of bad reviews was not in the sting, but in the subsequent pressure which, like water on a joint, collected over the decade. People who had not read your books in fifteen years were certain they were missing nothing of merit. A buried sorrow, not very attractive, (for bile was in it and the bitterness of unrequited literary injustice) released itself from some ducts of the heart, and Mailer felt hot anger at how Lowell was loved and he was not, a pure and surprising recognition of how much emotion, how much simple and childlike bitter sorrowing emotion had been concealed from himself for years under the manhole cover of his contempt for bad reviews.

> Pity the planet, all joy gone
> from this sweet volcanic cone;
> peace to our children when they fall
> in small war on the heels of small
> war – until the end of time
> to police the earth, a ghost
> orbiting forever lost
> in our monotonous sublime.

They gave Lowell a standing ovation, much heartiness in it, much obvious pleasure that they were there on a night in Washington when Robert Lowell had read from his work – it was nice as that – and then Lowell walked back to the wings, and Mailer walked forward. Lowell did not seem particularly triumphant. He looked still modest, still depressed, as if he had been applauded too much for too little and so the reservoir of guilt was still untapped.

Robert Lowell
by Seamus Heaney (1939-)

Oddly enough, the moment when I felt most bewildered in his presence was a moment when he was bereft of his capacity to unnerve. I went with him in January 1976 to two acupuncturists in Harley Street. He was at that time confined in a small private hospital where I had called to see him earlier in the afternoon and had been given a restorative nip from his Imperial After Shave bottle, which he had assured me contained Benedictine. Then, almost it would seem in order to atone, he carried me away in a taxi, with his ever present male nurse. And the next thing we had penetrated to the inner sanctum of two friendly and, it seemed to me, slightly quackish acupuncturists, stealthy, stooped and vaguely insinuating elders from the city of Leeds.

They called him Professor. They spoke calmingly to him and he became calm. He answered their questions about what they called his tension with an unexpected childlike candour. He allowed them to palp along the line of his neck and over his temples and down the back of his skull. He took off his shirt. He bowed a little and accepted the needles, one by one, in a delicate gleaming line, from the point of his shoulder to the back of his ear. I had a great feeling of intimacy and honour and heartbreak as I watched it all from behind, yet I could not stop myself from turning that accidental moment into an image, there and then, as it was happening. Gulliver in Lilliput, disabled, pinned down, yet essentially magnificent. The bull weakened by the pics of the picador. St Sebastian. At any rate, it remains with me as an emblem of his afflicted life, his great native strength and his sorrowful, invigilated helplessness. Richard not himself, then Richard himself again.

NORMAN MAILER (1923-)
by Evelyn Waugh (1903-66)

LETTER TO ANN FLEMING, 23 SEPTEMBER 1961

Mrs Kidd's ball was very lavish – nothing remarkable if it had been in Surrey but sensational in Somerset. Two bands, one of niggers & one of buggers, a cabaret, an oyster bar in the harness room, stables flood lit, much to discomfort of the horses. One bit an American pornographer who tried to give it vodka . . .

I had never before met Lady Jean Campbell and was fascinated. She came to us next day bringing the bitten pornographer. He might have stepped straight from your salon – a swarthy gangster just out of a mad house where he had been sent after the attempt to cut his wife's throat. It is his first visit to England. His tour is Janet Kidd, Randolph, Ian Argyll. He will be able to write a revealing pornogram of English life.

Lady Jean Campbell was married to Norman Mailer from 1962–3. In the notes to Mark Amory's edition of Waugh's letters, Mailer commented: 'The horse did bite me on the finger but I was not feeding him vodka, just patting his nose . . . I did not cut my wife's throat . . . Jean Campbell asked me what I thought of him [Waugh] and I said: "Lots of fun. Much sweeter than I expected." '

Norman Mailer
by Arthur Miller (1915–)

Mailer was famously harsh about Miller in his book about Miller's second wife, Marilyn Monroe.

We were living then [in 1947] in a converted brownstone on Pierpont Street whose normal quiet was blasted one afternoon by a yelling argument in the hallway outside. Thinking violence was about to break out, I opened the door to find a small young man in army uniform sitting on the stairs with a young and beautiful woman whom I recognized as our upstairs neighbour. They went silent on seeing me, so I figured everything was under control and went back into our apartment. Later the young soldier, by now out of uniform, approached me on the street and introduced himself as a writer. His name, he said, was Mailer. He had just seen my play. 'I could write a play like that,' he said. It was so obtusely flat an assertion that I began to laugh, but he was completely serious and indeed would make intermittent attempts to write plays in the many years that lay ahead. Since I was at a time when I was hammering out my place in the world, I made few friends then, and Mailer struck me as someone who seemed to want to make converts rather than friends, so our impulses, essentially similar, could hardly mesh. (I am at an age when it is best to be charitable.) In any event, although we lived for years in the same neighbourhood, our paths rarely crossed.

Norman Mailer
by James Baldwin (1924–87)

We were at an afternoon party, Norman was standing in the kitchen, a drink in his hand, holding forth for the benefit of a small group of people. There seemed something different about him, it was the belligerence of his stance, and the really rather pontifical tone of his voice. I had only seen him, remember, in Malaquais' living room, which Malaquais indefatigably dominates, and on various terraces and dives in Paris. I do not mean that there was anything unfriendly about him. On the contrary, he was smiling and having a ball. And yet – he was leaning against the refrigerator, rather as though he had his back to the wall, ready to take on all comers.

Norman has a trick, at least with me, of watching, somewhat ironically, as you stand on the edge of the crowd around him, waiting for his attention. I suppose this ought to be exasperating, but in fact I find it rather endearing, because it is so transparent and because he gets such a bang out of being the centre of attention. So do I, of course, at least some of the time.

We talked, bantered, a little tensely, made the usual, doomed effort to bring each other up to date on what we had been doing. I did not want to talk about my novel, which was only just beginning to seem to take shape, and, therefore, did not dare ask him if he were working on a novel. He seemed very pleased to see me, and I was pleased to see him, but I also had the feeling that he had made up his mind about me, adversely, in some way. It was as though he were saying, Okay, so now I know who you are, baby.

I was taking a boat in a few days, and I asked him to call me.

'Oh, no,' he said, grinning, and thrusting that forefinger at me, '*you* call me.'

'That's fair enough,' I said, and I left the party and went on back to Paris. While I was out of the country, Norman published *Advertisements for Myself*, which presently crossed the ocean to the apartment of James Jones. Bill Styron was also in Paris at that time, and one evening the three of us sat in Jim's living room, reading aloud, in a kind of drunken, masochistic fascination, Norman's judgment of our personalities and our work. Actually, I came off best, I suppose; there was less about me, and it was less venomous. But the condescension infuriated me; also, to tell the truth, my feelings were hurt. I felt that if that was the way Norman felt about me, he should have told me so. He had said that I was incapable of saying 'Fuck you' to the reader. My first temptation was to send him a cablegram which would disabuse him of that notion, at least insofar as one reader was concerned. But then I thought, No, I would be cool about it, and fail to react as he so clearly wanted me to. Also, I must say, his judgement of myself seemed so wide of the mark and so childish that it was hard to stay angry. I wondered what in the world was going on in his mind. Did he really suppose that he had now become the builder and destroyer of reputations?

And of *my* reputation?

We met in the Actors' Studio one afternoon, after a performance of *The Deer Park* – which I deliberately arrived too late to see, since I really did not know how I was going to react to Norman, and didn't want to betray myself by clobbering his play. When the discussion ended, I stood, again on the edge of the crowd around him, waiting. Over someone's shoulder, our eyes met, and Norman smiled.

'We've got something to talk about,' I told him.

'I figured that,' he said, smiling.

We went to a bar, and sat opposite each other. I was relieved to discover that I was not angry, not even (as far as I could tell) at the bottom of my heart. But, 'Why did you write those things about me?'

'Well, I'll tell you about that,' he said, – Norman has several accents, and I think this was his Texas one – 'I sort of figured you had it coming to you.'

'Why?'

'Well, if you think there's some truth in it.'

'Well, if you felt that way, why didn't you ever say it to – to me?'

'Well, I figured if this was going to break up our friendship, something else would come along to break it up just as fast.'

I couldn't disagree with that.

'You're the only one I kind of regret hitting so hard,' he said, with a grin. 'I think I – probably – wouldn't say it quite that way now.'

With this, I had to be content. We sat for perhaps an hour, talking of other things and, again, I was struck by his stance: leaning on the table, shoulders hunched, seeming, really, to roll like a boxer's, and his hands moving as though he were dealing with a sparring partner. And we were talking of physical courage, and the necessity of never letting another guy get the better of you.

I laughed. 'Norman, I can't go through the world the way you do because I haven't got your shoulders.'

He grinned, as though I were his pupil. 'But you're a pretty tough little mother, too,' he said, and referred to one of the grimmer of my Village misadventures, a misadventure which certainly proved that I had a dangerously sharp tongue, but which didn't really prove anything about my courage. Which, anyway, I had long ago given up trying to prove.

JACK KEROUAC (1922–69)
by Kingsley Amis (1922–95)

In 1970, eleven years after the first publication of this account, Amis commented: 'I think I was a bit urbane in my description of the late Jack Kerouac's activities. This was complacent and unimaginative of me. I did not give him sufficient credit as a pioneer of the movement, now in full career, to reduce argument to animal bawling and culture to egoistic tomfoolery.'

It must have been vanity rather than greed which induced me to appear on a kind of public panel in a playhouse in New York: the topic, *Is There a Beat Generation?* My colleagues were Mr James Wechsler, the editor of the New York Post, Mr Ashley Montagu, the anthropologist, and Mr Jack Kerouac, who as they say needs no introduction. At the preludial dinner it was explained that Mr Kerouac was very nice, perfectly charming in fact, provided he was convinced that those present were on his side, felt sympathetic to him, in short *liked him*. I said I saw what was meant. Over in the theatre we encountered Mr Kerouac, conservatively attired in giant's-chessboard shirt, black jeans and pigskin ankle-boots. With hand on hip he piped to me: 'Hallo my dear' (I did need a haircut at the time, admittedly) and said to Mr Montagu: 'I saw you on the Jack Paar show. You didn't have anything new to say.'

Having thus variously put the pair of us at our ease, he crossed to the back-stage piano without giving us the chance to tell him how much we liked him. Then, seating himself at the instrument, he began a version of the dear old Warsaw Concerto, but broke off every now and then to appear before the photographers. When he did this he weaved and bobbed rather as if about to start what we squares used to call jitterbugging. The Warsaw Concerto gave place at one stage to a boogie-woogie left hand, but was resumed after an interval when no boogie-woogie right hand was forthcoming.

Though Mr Wechsler had still not arrived, some sort of gesture towards getting started was obviously called for. We trooped on to the stage and huge high-pitched enthusiasm arose from certain sections of the audience, a salute intended not for Mr Montagu or me, I recognized sadly, but for Mr Kerouac, who responded with more weaves, bobs, and a chimpanzee shuffle or two. After some determinedly sedate remarks from the chair, Mr Kerouac arose for what we all thought was understood to be a ten-minute stint. During it, a stocky figure with overcoat thrown open entered at the back of the hall and made its way on to the stage; no beatnik anarch, as I had begun to fear, but Mr Wechsler, in pretty good shape after a three-day editorial crisis and soon disabused of the idea that I was Mr Montagu. Mr Kerouac was talking about a swinging group of new American boys intent on life, forecasting the appointment of a beat Secretary of State, and saluting Humphrey Bogart, Laurel and Hardy, and Popeye as ancestral beats. Half an hour or so later he said he would read his poem on Harpo Marx. The texture of his discourse did not change. Throughout it seemed to illustrate the theme of the symposium rather than actually expound it.

Next there was me. Then there was Mr Wechsler, who performed the considerable feat of advocating political commitment in terms that were both rational and free of cliché. Right at the start of it Mr Kerouac muttered: 'I can't stand this activist crap,' and, wearing Mr Wechsler's hat, began a somnambulistic pacing of the stage, occasionally breaking off to wave balletically at the photographers in the wings. He went on doing this while Mr Montagu's ironies flew above the beat sections of the audience.

Finally there was 'discussion'. Mr Kerouac accused Mr Wechsler, very inaccurately, of having said a lot about what he didn't believe in and nothing about what he did believe in. Mr Wechsler gamely responded with a capsule version of his positive views. Mr Kerouac leaned on the podium and said: 'Admit it, Wechsler, you came here tonight determined to hate me.' It was clear that none of us had managed to convince him that we liked him.

Disengaging myself from a 250–pound brunette who had leaped on to the stage to assure me that, contrary to my apparent belief, there was a beat generation, I followed the others out, reflecting that Mr Kerouac's performance had acted as a useful supplement to his novels in demonstrating how little spontaneity has to do with talking off the top of the head. I also wondered, and still do, just what it is that people anywhere in the world get out of attending discussions or lectures by literary persons. For the majority, I imagine, one might as well speak in Choctaw; the visual appeal is what counts. For all his evident casualness, Mr Kerouac was shrewd enough to have grasped that.

KINGSLEY AMIS (1922–95)
by Philip Larkin (1922–85)

During these first two terms [at Oxford University] our friends were mostly outside College; Norman had a group in Queen's, while I kept up with other Old Coventrians or enjoyed jazz evenings with Frank Dixon of Magdalen and Dick Kidner of Christ Church. At the beginning of the Trinity term, however, Norman, who had been idly looking over the notice-board in the lodge, hailed the mention of a newcomer, name of Amis.

'I met him at Cambridge on a schol . . . He's a hell of a good man.'

'How is he?'

'He shoots guns.'

I did not understand this until later in the afternoon when we were crossing the dusty first quadrangle a fair-haired young man came down staircase three and paused on the bottom step. Norman instantly pointed his right hand at him in the semblance of a pistol and uttered a short coughing bark to signify a shot – a shot not as in reality, but as it would sound from a worn sound-track on Saturday afternoon in the ninepennies.

The young man's reaction was immediate. Clutching his chest in a rictus of agony, he threw one arm up against the archway and began slowly crumpling downwards, fingers scoring the stonework. Just as he was about to collapse on the piled-up laundry, however (Oxford laundries were at that time operating a system described by James Agate as collecting every two weeks and delivering every three, so that the place was generally littered with bundles in transit one way or the other), he righted himself and trotted over to us. 'I've been working on this,' he said, as soon as introductions were completed. 'Listen. This is when you're firing in a ravine.'

We listened.

'And this is when you're firing in a ravine and the bullet ricochets off a rock.'

We listened again. Norman's appreciative laughter skirled freely: I stood silent. For the first time I felt myself in the presence of a talent greater than my own.

V. S. NAIPAUL (1932–)
by Shiva Naipaul (1945–85)

Sometimes, the postman arrived with blue air-mail letters, the cause of much excitement in our household. Once, a couple of books arrived for me – an illustrated history of science and (I believe) a book about the young Walter Scott. Occasionally, I would listen with a kind of dazed astonishment to this notional being – *my* brother! – reading a short story on the radio: in those days the BBC still had a Caribbean Service. But none of these stray items allowed me to construct a picture. In fact, they only aggravated my confusion. When I was about eleven, this mysterious figure suddenly arrived among us. Why he should thus manifest himself, I had no idea. Still, it was an interlude of wonder; of intense excitement for me. I would go and stand in the doorway of his bedroom and gaze curiously upon him as he lay on the bed, smoking cigarettes out of a green tin. The tableau revived my father's fading image. He too, in the warm, quiet afternoons, would lie on that same bed, reading and smoking cigarettes. We must have talked, but I can no longer remember what we talked about. One day I showed him a childish story I had written out in a copy-book. It was about a boy – an English boy – running away to sea. This narrative I had begun in the third person and, quite unconsciously, ended in the first. (I had stumbled on to one of the tricks of 'modernism' without effort.) He pointed this out to me, at the same time praising the endeavour. Then he went away again.

Abstraction only began to lessen when I myself went to England (even unto Oxford!) at the age of eighteen. Yet, the gap of twelve or thirteen years that separates us remained important. We did not, overnight, cease to be strangers to one another. He perplexed me; and I, no doubt, perplexed him. We had, after all, come out of different worlds. The Hindu Trinidad of his youth was not the Hindu Trinidad of my youth. We did not have a shared past; we did not have a shared pool of memory, ancestral or otherwise. I had vulnerabilities he did not always find easy to understand. Our natural ties of affection would have to discover new modes of expression – and, for a long time, neither of us knew what those might be; for a long time there was mutual distress. No grand solutions have ever occurred. But there have been a series of small resolutions along that difficult, treacherous road. We have come to recognise each other's autonomy, to acknowledge the existence of areas of privacy and inaccessibility. Writing has helped, not hindered, that process of slow accommodation. It has offered a means of communication.

V. S. Naipaul
by Paul Theroux (1941–)

This is an extract from Theroux's extraordinary book-length account of friendship and disenchantment, Sir Vidia's Shadow: A Friendship across Five Continents. *This is, perhaps, the turning-point in the book, the moment when Theroux stops being Naipaul's disciple and becomes – what? – his grown-up son? his equal? his rival? the Freudian son slaying the father?*

In the spring of 1973, having finished *The Black House*, I cycled to Waterloo, put my bike on the train, and went to Salisbury, cycling from there to Wilsford Manor. Vidia could see that my finances were as miserable as ever, but I told him why I had left the University of Virginia.

'You had said you'd never teach again,' Vidia said. 'You broke your own rule. If you make a rule, keep to it.'

We walked to Stonehenge, through the fields, and he explained the water meadows once more.

'You'd like Virginia,' I said. 'The countryside is beautiful – rolling hills and meadows.'

'I'm afraid that America is not for me. I don't think I could live in a rural setting.'

'In some ways it's a bit like this.'

But I was thinking: It is much more beautiful than this funny fenced-off part of Salisbury Plain, with a highway running alongside this weird ancient monument, belittling it.

'I have to stick with what I have,' Vidia said. 'It's too late for me to transfer to another country.'

We kept walking toward the big biscuit-coloured cromlech that lay on the other side of the whizzing cars on the motorway.

'So what's the plan?'

'I'm still looking for money,' he said.

'Are you serious about buying a place in London?'

'Yes. I think it's just what I need.'

'I'm sure you could get something for less than forty thousand.'

He said, 'No. I want something uncompromisingly fashionable.'

He said this while looking at the sky.

A few days after I returned to London, my editor at the Bodley Head, a cigar-smoking Scotsman and sometime poet named James Michie, invited me to lunch at Chez Victor. He said he wanted to discuss *The Black House*. He was very friendly when I met him, but it seemed ominous that we had finished the first course and most of the bottle of wine before he mentioned my book, and then he told me he did not like it at all.

'I'm afraid I can't publish it,' Michie said.

'You mean you're turning it down?' I could not believe this.

'It will hurt your reputation,' he said.

'I have no reputation.'

'I think if you reread the book you will agree with me,' he said.

'I don't have to reread the book. I wrote the book. If I thought it was no good I wouldn't have submitted it.'

My voice was shrill, and I think that surprised him. I was hurt and angry. Probably he thought he was softening the blow, because Londoners are such eager lunchers, but it seemed callous to turn lunch into an occasion for such a rejection. And why was I being rejected? The novel was good, surely?

'I let William Trevor look at it. He agreed with me.'*

Trevor was one of his authors, a talented one, I thought.

I said, 'My last novel got great reviews. You paid me two hundred and fifty pounds. I assumed you'd give me the same for this. You'd be getting it for a pittance.'

'It's the principle of the thing,' he said. He had lit a cigar and, feeling defensive, he had stopped eating. 'I don't believe in the book. I can't publish something I don't believe in.'

'You publish lots of crappy books,' I said.

---

* William Trevor is bewildered by this; he has never read *The Black House*. The book he read in typescript – and liked – was *Sinning with Annie*. [Theroux's note.]

I guessed he saw the truth of this, because he hesitated, at least looked uncertain.

I said, 'If you turn this down you'll lose me as an author. I'll go to another publisher. I'll never let you publish another book of mine. And all it's costing you is two hundred and fifty quid. This lunch is costing you thirty!'

Michie was bald but he had a hank of hair that grew from the side of his head that he arranged over his pate to give the semblance of hair. This damp, fussed-with strand had slipped down and hung by the side of his ear like a strange Hassidic sidecurl. It made him look desperate.

'If you twist my arm, I'll publish it,' he said.

'That's it, then. That's all. Forget it – I want my manuscript back.'

Feeling ill, I finished my meal and walked back to his office, wishing the whole way I could push him in the path of a car. He gave me the typescript and still seemed surprised and somewhat embarrassed by my anger.

I found another publisher, but in the meantime seriously wondered how I would ever make a living as a writer. I told Vidia. He invited me to tea at the Charing Cross Hotel.

'You should have shown the book to me. Why didn't you?' he said.

'I didn't want to bother you with my problems.'

'That's what friends are for,' Vidia said.

He could not have said anything truer or kinder. After eight years he was still on my side, still a well-wisher.

'He gave it to William Trevor to read. Apparently Trevor didn't like it either.'

'Who is William Trevor?'

That was what I needed, the old corrosive contempt.

'He is no one,' Vidia said coldly. 'Something similar happened to me when I was starting out. Deutsch told me to put the book aside. It was *Miguel Street*. He didn't know what to do with it. And one still gets the odd foolish remark about one's work.'

'Why do they do it?'

'They do it because they are common, lying, low class, and foolish. That is why they do it.'

He was so angry he could not continue the conversation. He sipped his tea, looking around at the other tables. He saw a heavily pregnant woman moving slowly across the shabby room, bracing herself by resting on chairs and with one hand pressed for balance on the small of her back.

'To me, one of the ugliest sights on earth is a pregnant woman.'

This astonished me. I did not know what to say. He turned away from the woman.

'I have an idea for a book,' I said.

'Tell me.'

'A long railway trip.'

I explained how, in Virginia, I had read Mark Twain's *Following the Equator*, an obscure and out-of-print travel book, but lovable for its geographical non sequiturs and incidental mishaps. I liked the spirited jokes and the long journey. It was about nothing but his trip. A lot of it was dialogue. Twain did not pretend to be knowledgeable about the countries he passed through – Australia, India and South Africa, among many others.

'I checked the maps,' I said. 'I can leave Victoria Station and go to Paris, to Istanbul – to the border of Afghanistan. Then there's the Khyber Pass, and trains all through India. Burma has railways, so does Thailand. Even Vietnam has trains. I would travel around Japan and come home on the Trans-Siberian, and then write about it.'

'That's a lovely idea,' Vidia said. He was seriously concentrating on it, looking for a flaw or something suspect. But it was too simple an idea to have a flaw. Taking trains from London to Japan and back: it was surprising that no one had done it before.

'I'm thinking of leaving in September,' I said. 'I would be in India in October. What's the weather like then?'

'Delicious.'

He seemed distracted; he was still thinking about my book, my trip. He saw something I did not see – I could tell from his reaction. He knew it was a good idea, but he saw something more. He saw a hugely successful book.

'Who do you think I should visit in India?'

He thought a moment. He frowned. 'You'll find your way.'

For the first time in the years I had known him, I sensed a reluctance on his part to help me. Only a few minutes before he had said, 'That's what friends are for.'

'Isn't there anyone you could introduce me to?'

He had been to India six or seven times recently and had lived there for a year. He had written about it many times. It was his obsessive subject. He knew India intimately.

'I don't know. You might see Mrs Jhabvala when you're in Delhi.'

As he was speaking, giving me the name with such reluctance, I vowed that I would not visit Ruth Prawer Jhabvala.

'You'll be all right,' he said. But this time the statement was tinged with self-pity, almost resentment, a feeling I had never detected in him before. It was as though I were abandoning him. And why? This train-riding idea I had conceived out of sheer desperation, in the urgency to have a book to write and money from a publisher.

The bill was brought. I paid it, I left the tip. Vidia had not seen it. He did not see bills even when they were brought on the most expensive china and folded like origami and presented to him. It was one of his survival skills that a bill could come and go without ever being visible. Still, he looked disgusted.

'This hotel used to be quite grand,' he said in his pained voice. Perhaps the pain was due to the idea I had just divulged. 'Having tea here was once something special. One was glamoured by it.' He made a face. 'No longer.'

I took the trip. I left London in September 19, 1973, on the train to Paris. I changed trains and went to Istanbul, changed again for Ankara, for Tehran, and for the holy city of fanatics, Meshed. And onward, through Afghanistan (by bus, no trains) and down the Khyber, up to Simla, down to Madras and Sri Lanka, on the train and on the ferry. To Burma and Thailand and Singapore, along the coast of Vietnam (heavily bombed and still smoking), up and down Japan, a boat to Nakhoda, and the Trans-Siberian home. My heart was in my mouth the whole time. Out of fear I wrote everything down; in my misery I mocked myself, and a febrile humour crept into the narrative. In January of the following year I returned to London, still feeling miserable. I had missed Christmas. Everyone howled at me, 'Where have you been?' I propped up my note-books and wrote the book, made a single narrative out of all those train trips. The title came from a road in Kanpur: The Railway Bazaar.

Sometimes miracles happen to a writer, Vidia had said. *The Great Railway Bazaar* was a small miracle. I was not prepared for it. While I was working on it, *The Black House* was published – the reviews were respectful – and I started *The Family Arsenal* after I finished the travel book. Even before publication, *The Great Railway Bazaar* was reprinted three times, to accommodate bookstore demand. It was an immediate bestseller. It was my tenth book. I had known Vidia for ten years. In that time I had published about a million words.

'An agonizing profession,' Vidia said. 'But there are rewards.'

All windfalls are relative. I did not become rich with that book, but at last I was making a living. I paid my debts. I had enough to support me in my next book. I was out from under. I never again worried about money – that freedom from worry was wealth to me. No more drudging. I was free. I was thirty-two.

And at last I understood what Vidia meant when he had had written, 'I have never had to work for hire; I made a vow at an early age never to work, never to become involved with people in that way. That has given me a freedom from people, entanglements, from rivalries, from competition. I have no enemies, no rivals, no masters; I fear no one.'

NICHOLSON BAKER (1957–)
by Martin Amis (1949–)

Writers want to disdain everything, yet they also want to have everything; and they want to have it now.

Well, everything – in the form of a capitalised success – is suddenly on offer. I arrived for our meeting in New York, and there it all was: the Hiltonic hotel room, the dilatory and much-encumbered photographer, the appalling schedule, the tuxed waiter bearing the club sandwich on his burnished tray, the soothing prospect of a public reading (that night) and a transcontinental plane ride (the next morning), and, finally, another interviewer coming through the door, with all his dreams and dreads and character flaws ... The cult author of *The Mezzanine* and *Room Temperature* has now come cruising into the commercial mainstream. Baker's third novel, *Vox*, is the season's hot book, sexually explicit, much promoted, ambivalently received; for the moment it seems to stand there, stark naked, in the primitive fever of scrutiny and demand.

Although I was of course very hurt that *Vox* was doing quite so well, it should be said – to get the B-and-Me stuff at least partly out of the way – that I entered Baker's domain with an air of some knowingness. I myself had granted many an interview, if not in this very hotel room (it was a non-smoking room on a non-smoking floor: Baker doesn't drink, either), then in this very hotel; and I was a stupefied veteran of the writer's tour that Baker now contemplated with such disquiet. He was, on the other hand, inadmissibly young (thirty-six), and never before had I inter-viewed a literary junior. This imagined hurdle turned out to be a liberation and a pleasure, but I somehow found it necessary to pre-devastate Baker with the news that one of *Vox*'s supposed coinages (a synonym for masturbation) had been casually tossed out by me two novels ago. Baker was duly devastated, and the interview began.

Those who know and therefore love his books might expect Baker to prove barely capable of sequential thought, let alone rational speech. The novels suggest a helpless egghead and meandering pedant whose mind is all tangents and parentheses. His radical concentration on the mechanics of everyday life – the escalator, the shoelace – prepares one for a crazy professor, even an *idiot savant*. One is also steeled, by his own self-mockery, for Baker's physical appearance: a balding, four-eyed, pin-headed drink of water. He is, to be sure, fabulously and pointlessly tall, tall beyond utility, and waveringly plinthed on his size 14 shoes. But these impressions soon fall away, just as the cold surface of his prose is warmed by the movement of its inner ironies, as they ceaselessly search for intricate delight. Baker, it turned out, was both droll and personable. I might even have glimpsed a quiet charisma behind his barbered beard, his messianic spectacles. Or was that just Manhattan and the dawn glow of celebrity?

Sources and Acknowledgements

William Allingham on William Barnes, Browning, Carlyle, George Eliot, Tennyson, Thackeray: *William Allingham: A Diary, 1824–1889*, Penguin, 1985.

Kingsley Amis on Kerouac and Dylan Thomas: *What Became of Jane Austen? and Other Questions*, Jonathan Cape, 1970. Copyright 1970 Kingsley Amis; reprinted by kind permission of Jonathan Clowes Ltd, London, on behalf of the literary estate of Sir Kingsley Amis.

Martin Amis on Nicholson Baker: *Visiting Mrs Nabokov and Other Excursions*, Jonathan Cape, 1993.

John Aubrey on Samuel Butler, Hobbes, Marvell, Milton: *Aubrey's Brief Lives*, edited by Oliver Lawson Dick, Secker and Warburg, 1960.

James Baldwin on Mailer and Wright: *Nobody Knows My Name*, New York: Dell, 1961. Copyright 1961 by James Baldwin; copyright renewed, reprinted by arrangement with the James Baldwin Estate.

Saul Bellow on Berryman: *It All Adds Up*, Secker and Warburg, 1994.

John Berryman on Yeats: *Writers at Work: The Paris Review Interviews, Fourth Series* edited by George Plimpton, Secker and Warburg, 1977.

James Boswell on Hume, Johnson, Rousseau, Voltaire: *The Journals of James Boswell 1761–1795*, selected by John Wain, William Heinemann, 1991.

Paul Bowles on Auden: *Without Stopping*, Peter Owen, 1972. Reprinted by permission of the publisher.

Charlotte Brontë on Thackeray: *Thackeray: Interviews and Recollections*, edited by Philip Collins, Macmillan, 1983.

George Gordon, Lord Byron on Hogg, Leigh Hunt, Matthew Lewis, Moore, Rogers, Shelley, Southey: *Byron's Letters and Journals*, edited by Leslie A. Marchand, John Murray, 1973–82.

Truman Capote on Tennessee Williams: *A Capote Reader*, Hamish Hamilton, 1987.

Thomas Carlyle on Dickens: *Dickens: Interviews and Recollections*, edited by Philip Collins, Macmillan, 1981; on Tennyson: *Tennyson: Interviews and Recollections*, edited by Norman Page, Macmillan, 1983; on Thackeray: *Thackeray: Interviews and Recollections*, edited by Philip Collins, Macmillan, 1983; on Trollope: *Trollope: Interviews and Recollections*, edited by R. C. Terry, Macmillan, 1987.

François-René de Chateaubriand on Madame de Staël: *The Memoirs of Chateaubriand*, translated by Robert Baldick, Hamish Hamilton, 1961.

Anton Chekhov on Tolstoy: *The Selected Letters of Anton Chekhov*, edited by Lillian Hellman, translated by Sidonie K. Lederer, Hamish Hamilton, 1955.

G. K. Chesterton on Hardy, Henry James: *Autobiography*, Hamish Hamilton, 1986. Reprinted by permission of A. P. Watt Ltd on behalf of the Royal Literary Fund.

Thomas De Quincey on Coleridge, Wordsworth: *Recollections of the Lakes and the Lake Poets*, edited by David Wright, Penguin, 1970.

Charles Dickens on Thackeray: *Thackeray: Interviews and Recollections*, edited by Philip Collins, Macmillan, 1983.

Charles Dodgson ('Lewis Carroll') on Tennyson: *Tennyson: Interviews and Recollections*, edited by Norman Page, Macmillan, 1983.

John Dos Passos on Cummings, Dreiser, Hemingway: *The Best Times*, André Deutsch, 1968. Copyright John Dos Passos; reprinted by permission of A. M. Heath and Co. Ltd on behalf of the Estate of the late John Dos Passos.

George Eliot on Dickens: *The George Eliot Letters*, edited by Gordon S. Haight, 1954; *Dickens: Interviews and Recollections*, edited by Philip Collins, Macmillan, 1981; on Trollope: *Trollope: Interviews and Recollections*, edited by R. C. Terry, Macmillan, 1987.

T. S. Eliot on Joyce, Katherine Mansfield: *The Letters of T. S. Eliot, Volume 1: 1898–1922*, edited by Valerie Eliot, Faber and Faber, 1989. Reprinted by permission of the publisher.

William Faulkner on Hemingway: *Selected Letters of William Faulkner*, edited by Joseph Blotner, Scolar Press, 1977.

F. Scott Fitzgerald on Hemingway: *The Letters of F. Scott Fitzgerald*, edited by Andrew Turnbull, Bodley Head, 1964. Reprinted by permission of David Higham Associates.

Gustave Flaubert on Théophile Gautier, Guy de Maupassant: *The Letters of Gustave Flaubert, Volume II: 1857–1880*, edited and translated by Francis Steegmuller, Cambridge, Mass.: The Belknap Press of Harvard University Press. Copyright 1982 by Francis Steegmuller; reprinted by permission of Harvard University Press.

Ford Madox Ford on Stephen Crane: *The Bodley Head Ford Madox Ford, Volume V*, edited by Michael Pettigrew, Bodley Head, 1971. Reprinted by permission of David Higham Associates.

John Fowles on Golding: *William Golding: The Man and His Books*, edited by John Carey, Faber and Faber, 1986. Reprinted by permission of the publisher.

John Galsworthy on Lawrence: *D. H. Lawrence: A Composite Biography*, by Edward Nehls, Madison 1957–9.

Elizabeth Gaskell on Charlotte Brontë: *The Life of Charlotte Brontë*, edited by Alan Shelston, Penguin, 1975; on Dickens: *Dickens: Interviews and Recollections*, edited by Philip Collins, Macmillan, 1981.

Edmond de Goncourt on Zola: *Pages from The Goncourt Journal*, translated by Robert Baldick, Oxford University Press, 1962.

Edmund Gosse on Tennyson: *Tennyson: Interviews and Recollections*, edited by Norman Page, Macmillan, 1983.

Robert Graves on T. S. Eliot: *The Crowning Privilege: Collected Essays on Poetry*, Penguin, 1955; on Hardy: *Goodbye to All That*, 1929. Reprinted by permission of Carcanet Press.

H. Rider Haggard on Trollope: *Trollope: Interviews and Recollections*, edited by R. C. Terry, Macmillan, 1987.

Benjamin Robert Haydon on Lamb: *Charles Lamb: Selected Prose*, edited by Adam Phillips, Penguin, 1986.

William Hazlitt on Coleridge: *Selected Writings*, edited by Jon Cook, Oxford University Press, 1991.

Seamus Heaney on Lowell: *Erato: The Harvard Book Review*, Winter and Spring, 1988.

Ernest Hemingway on Faulkner: *Hemingway: Selected Letters 1917–1961*, Panther Books, 1985; on Scott Fitzgerald, Ford Madox Ford: *A Moveable Feast*, Jonathan Cape, 1964.

Christopher Isherwood on Virginia Woolf: *Recollections of Virginia Woolf by her Contemporaries*, edited by Joan Russell Noble, Peter Owen, 1972. Reprinted by permission of the publisher.

Henry James on Rupert Brooke, George du Maurier, Robert Louis Stevenson, Trollope: *Henry James: Essays, American and English Writers*, New York: Library of America, 1984; on Flaubert, Zola: *Henry James: European Writers and the Prefaces*, New York: Library of America, 1984.

Samuel Johnson on Savage: *Samuel Johnson: Rasselas, Poems and Selected Prose*, edited by Bertrand H. Bronson, Holt, Rinehart and Winston, 1971.

Ben Jonson on Shakespeare: *The Riverside Shakespeare*, Boston: Houghton Mifflin, 1974.

John Keats on Coleridge, Shelley: *Letters of John Keats*, edited by Robert Gittings, Oxford University Press, 1970.

Charles Lamb on Coleridge, Hazlitt: *Selected Prose*, edited by Adam Phillips, Penguin, 1986.

Philip Larkin on Amis: *Required Writing: Miscellaneous Pieces 1955–1982*, Faber and Faber, 1983, Copyright 1983 by Philip Larkin; reprinted by permission of Faber and Faber Ltd and Farrar, Straus and Giroux, Inc.

D. H. Lawrence on Forster: *The Letters of D. H. Lawrence, Volume 2*, Cambridge University Press, 1981.

Wyndham Lewis on Auden: *Blasting and Bombardiering: An Autobiography 1914–1926*, John Calder, 1982. Copyright The Wyndham Lewis Memorial Trust, reprinted by permission of Omar Pound.

Robert Lowell on Berryman: *Collected Prose* by Robert Lowell, edited by Robert Giroux, Faber and Faber, 1987, copyright 1987 by Caroline Lowell; on T. S. Eliot, Ford Madox Ford, Pound: *Notebook, 1967–68* by Robert Lowell, Faber and Faber, 1970. Copyright 1967, 1968, 1969 by Robert Lowell. Copyright renewed 1998 by Harriet Lowell. Reprinted by permission of Faber and Faber and Farrar, Straus and Giroux, Inc.

Louis MacNeice on Yeats: *The Strings are False: An Unfinished Autobiography*, Faber and Faber, 1965. Reprinted by permission of David Higham Associates.

Norman Mailer on Nelson Algren: *Cannibals and Christians*, André Deutsch,

1967; on Lowell: *The Armies of the Night: History as a Novel, The Novel as History*, Weidenfeld and Nicolson, 1968.

W. Somerset Maugham on Hardy: preface to *W. Somerset Maugham: The Selected Novels, Volume 1*, Heinemann, 1953.

Arthur Miller on Bellow, Lowell, Mailer: *Timebends: A Life*, Methuen, 1987.

Marianne Moore on Wallace Stevens: *The Complete Prose of Marianne Moore*, edited by Patricia C. Willis, Faber and Faber, 1987. Reprinted by permission of the publisher.

Shiva Naipaul on V. S. Naipaul: *An Unfinished Journey*, André Deutsch, 1986. Copyright 1986 Shiva Naipaul; reprinted by permission of Gillon Aitken Associates Ltd.

George Orwell on Spender: *The Complete Works of George Orwell, Volume 11*, Secker and Warburg, 1998. Copyright George Orwell 1938; reprinted by permission of A. M. Heath & Co. Ltd on behalf of Mark Hamilton as the Literary Executor of the Estate of the late Sonia Brownell Orwell, Secker and Warburg Ltd and Harcourt Inc.

Wilfred Owen on Graves, Sassoon: *Wilfred Owen: Selected Letters*, edited by John Bell, Oxford University Press, 1985. Reprinted by permission of the publisher.

Thomas Love Peacock on Shelley: *Thomas Love Peacock: Memoirs of Shelley and other Essays and Reviews*, edited by Howard Mills, Rupert Hart-Davis, 1970.

Alexander Pope on Swift, Lady Mary Wortley Montagu: *Alexander Pope: A Critical Edition of the Major Works*, edited by Pat Rogers, Oxford University Press, 1993.

Anthony Powell on Galsworthy, Henry Green: *Messengers of the Day*, Heinemann, 1978.

Marcel Proust on Léon Daudet: *Marcel Proust: Selected Letters 1880–1903*, edited by Philip & Kolb, translated by Ralph Manheim, Oxford University Press, 1985. Reprinted by permission of HarperCollins Publishers.

Philip Roth on Malamud: 'Pictures of Malamud', *The London Review of Books*, 8 May 1986.

George Sand on Flaubert: *The Letters of Gustave Flaubert 1857–1880*, edited and translated by Francis Steegmuller, Faber and Faber, 1984.

Delmore Schwartz on Wallace Stevens: 'Wallace Stevens: An Appreciation', from *Selected Essays of Delmore Schwartz*, edited by Donald A. Dike and David H. Zucker.

Stephen Spender on Allen Tate: *Journals 1939–83*, edited by John Goldsmith, Faber and Faber, 1985. Reprinted by permission of the publisher and Ed Victor Ltd.

Stendhal on Byron: *To the Happy Few: Selected Letters of Stendhal*, translated by Norman Cameron, John Lehmann, 1952.

Wallace Stevens on Marianne Moore: *Letters of Wallace Stevens*, Faber and Faber, 1967. Reprinted by permission of the publisher.

Robert Louis Stevenson on W. E. Henley: *Selected Letters of Robert Louis Stevenson*, edited by Ernest Mehew, Yale University Press, 1997.

William Thackeray on Dickens: *Dickens: Interviews and Recollections*, edited by Philip Collins, Macmillan, 1981.

Paul Theroux on V. S. Naipaul: *Sir Vidia's Shadow: A Friendship across Five Continents*, Hamish Hamilton, 1998.

Edward John Trelawny on Byron, Shelley: *Records of Shelley, Byron and the Author*, edited by David Wright, Penguin, 1973.

Ivan Turgenev on Flaubert, Gogol: *Literary Reminiscences and Autobiographical Fragments*, translated by David Magarshack, Faber and Faber, 1959. Translation copyright 1958 by Farrar, Straus and Cudahy, Inc., translation copyright renewed 1986 by Elsie D. Magarshack; reprinted by permission of Farrar, Straus and Giroux, Inc.

Mark Twain on Kipling: *Kipling: Interviews and Recollections*, edited by Harold Orel, Macmillan, 1984.

Izaak Walton on Donne: *Lives by Izaak Walton*, Oxford University Press, 1927.

Evelyn Waugh on Hilaire Belloc: *The Diaries of Evelyn Waugh*, edited by Michael Davie, Weidenfeld and Nicolson, 1976; on Henry Green, Graham Greene, Somerset Maugham, Mailer: *The Letters of Evelyn Waugh*, edited by Mark Amory, Weidenfeld and Nicolson, 1980. Reprinted by permission of the Peters, Fraser and Dunlop Group Ltd.

Rebecca West on Virginia Woolf: *Recollections of Virginia Woolf*, edited by Joan Russell Noble, Peter Owen, 1972. Reprinted by permission of the publisher.

Edith Wharton on Henry James: *A Backward Glance*, 1934.

Edmund Wilson on Nabokov: *Upstate: Records and Recollections of Northern New York*, 24 Farrar, Straus and Giroux, 1971. Copyright 1971 by Edmund Wilson; reprinted by permission of the publisher.

Virginia Woolf on Beerbohm, Bennett, Bowen, T. S. Eliot, Henry James, Lawrence, Katherine Mansfield, Somerset Maugham: *The Diary of Virginia Woolf*, edited by Anne Olivier Bell, Hogarth Press/Chatto and Windus, 1977–1984; *The Letters of Virginia Woolf*, edited by Nigel Nicolson, Chatto and Windus, 1975–1980.

Dorothy Wordsworth on Coleridge: *The Grasmere Journals*, edited by Pamela Woof, Oxford University Press, 1993.

Lady Mary Wortley Montagu on Fielding, Pope: *The Selected Letters of Lady Mary Wortley Montagu*, edited by Robert Halsband, Penguin, 1986.

Every effort has been made to trace or contact all copyright holders. The publishers will be pleased to rectify any omissions in the above list brought to their notice at the earliest opportunity.